The Book of Churchilliana

THE BOOK OF
Churchilliana

DOUGLAS HALL

Title page picture:
Teapot by Bairstow Manor Pottery, 2001
The Yalta Tea Party
Edition limited to 750
Modelled by Ray Noble.

First published in the UK by
New Cavendish Books
3 Denbigh Road, London W11 2SJ
Tel: (44) 207 229 6765, (44) 207 792 9984
Fax: (44) 207 792 0027
www.newcavendishbooks.co.uk
E-mail: narisa@new-cav.demon.co.uk

Design by Peter Cope FCSD

ISBN 1 872727 44 1

Printed and bound in Thailand by
Amarin Printing and Publishing (Plc) Co. Ltd.

Contents

Character jug by
Wilton Pottery, Cobridge.
1941-45
Backstamped: *Churchill.*
Never was so much owed
by so many to so few.
1940. Wilton Pottery,
Cobridge, England

'It has been a labour of love.
Labour! It is a great word.
It moves the world,
it comprises the millions,
it combines many men
in many lands
in the sympathy
of a common burden.'

Winston Churchill, Glasgow, 11 October 1906

Acknowledgements

I acknowledge with grateful thanks the considerable assistance provided by many of my friends and acquaintances
in the more than ten years I have spent in the compilation of this book.
Help with provenance; information about artists, potteries, modellers and sculptors; auction sales, catalogue pricing and
general market intelligence has come from a great many sources all around the world.
In mentioning the following I sincerely apologise to those whom I may have inadvertently omitted.

Roger Bairstow, James Blewitt, David Boler, Derek Brownleader, Jack Darrah, Rhodri Davies, Alan Fitch,
Barrie Glover, Lincoln Halinen, Richard Langworth, Stephen Mullins, Peggy Nisbet,
Kevin Pearson, David Porter, Peter Rees, Francis Salmon, Vic Schuler , Ronald Smith, Mark Webber, Devoy White

Introduction

Winston Churchill was born in Blenheim Palace on 30 November 1874, the elder son of Lord and Lady Randolph Churchill and grandson of the 7th Duke of Marlborough. He had, by his own account, an unhappy childhood. He loved and worshipped his parents but found them remote and often absent. At Harrow he made little impact and it took three attempts for him to get into Sandhurst as a cavalry cadet. Lord Randolph Churchill died, leaving large debts and an estranged wife, just before Winston was gazetted as a Second Lieutenant in the 4th Hussars in 1895. It is clear that Winston never regarded his army career as anything more than a springboard into politics and he quite brazenly sought to achieve fame and as many medals as possible while earning sufficient money from his writing to support his extravagant lifestyle. In 1898, at Omdurman, Churchill took part in the last great cavalry charge by the British Army and wrote brilliant if rather upbeat accounts of his experience in *The River War* (1899) and *My Early Life* (1930). In 1899 he went to the Boer War as a war correspondent for the *Morning Post,* was taken prisoner while travelling on an armoured train but escaped and made his way to Durban where he received a hero's welcome. He was twenty-five years old, had won some medals, was world famous and ready to begin his political career.

Winston Churchill entered Parliament as MP for Oldham in 1900. With just a short break he was to remain a member of the House of Commons for sixty-four years. Initially a member of the Conservative party he switched to the Liberals in 1904 and then back to the Conservatives in 1924. He served as Under Secretary of State for the Colonies, 1906-08; President of the Board of Trade, 1908-10; Home Secretary, 1910-11; First Lord of the Admiralty, 1911-15 and 1939-40; Chancellor of the Duchy of Lancaster, 1915; Minister of Munitions, 1917; Secretary of State for War and Air, 1919-21; Secretary of State for the Colonies, 1921-22; Chancellor of the Exchequer, 1924-29; and Prime Minister, 1940-45 and 1951-55. In 1953, during his second term as Prime Minister, Queen Elizabeth II appointed him a Knight of the Most Noble Order of the Garter.

Winston Churchill earned considerable sums from his writing. Between 1897 and 1961 he published more than forty books – many of them running to four or six volumes – and, during that time, he was also a prolific contributor to magazines and newspapers. He was awarded the Nobel Prize for Literature in 1953. A talented amateur artist Churchill exhibited at the Royal Academy and was elected Honorary Academician Extraordinary in 1948. He was made an Honorary Citizen of the United States in 1963 and received the Freedom or Honorary Citizenship of many other countries and cities around the world. When he died, aged ninety, in 1965 Churchill was given a State Funeral at St Paul's Cathedral.

In his book, *Churchill: His Life in Photographs* Winston's son, Randolph, wrote: *'Sir Winston must be one of the most photogenic men who ever lived. It is the rarest thing to find a really bad photograph of him.'* I suspect that he must also have been one of the most painted, drawn, sculpted, carved, modelled, cast and moulded men who ever lived but, unfortunately, it is by no means rare to find a really bad image of him. The word *Churchilliana* has been coined to describe a collection of places and objects relating to Winston Churchill. These range from the sublime to the ridiculous and embrace a glorious assortment of the good, the bad and the ugly. Collecting Churchilliana has now entered its second century and this selection from the first one hundred years illustrates a remarkable diversity of tributes which have been paid to the Man of the Century.

"LET US GO FORWARD TOGETHER"

DON'T MIND HOW HARD I WORK FOR WINNIE

LONDON

GERM

he Nationa
pecial agre
h will appl
ontinent
y has its

as given you th
him by getting the sign endorsed o

How you can get it endorsed, and the terms of the Nation
are explained in Ministry of War Transport Notice
get at any Mercantile Marine Office, Reserve Pool

Foreword

Good fortune comes in many forms and I had the good fortune of meeting Douglas Hall some years ago. I was attending the Annual General Meeting of the International Churchill Society at the Imperial War Museum and was, at the time, just an ordinary member of the Society but Douglas was, and still is, a frequent contributor to its journal *Finest Hour* writing regular authoritative articles on Churchilliana. Having read each of his articles I was pleased to meet him in person. We have since become good friends, sharing a common interest in keeping the memory of Sir Winston Churchill green and fresh – Douglas with his fascinating collection of Churchilliana drawn from all corners of the globe and me with a complementary collection of Churchill memorabilia based at Bletchley Park in Buckinghamshire.

This thread has drawn us together and my collection has benefited from Douglas's kindness and generosity. I have been the recipient of divers related gifts and he has often alerted me to newly produced items which he felt would be worthy of inclusion in my thematic lay-out at Bletchley. I have never failed to be amazed by the thoroughness of his research and the scope of his knowledge of the subject. Douglas cannot be aware of the number of times his monographs have been consulted by students, at all educational levels, visiting the exhibition at Bletchley Park. Recently a young lady student, writing a thesis for her doctorate in history, spent several hours concentrating on Douglas's journals which she described as '... *just the information I'm looking for.*'

Douglas has often reminded me, tongue in cheek, that he served in the Royal Air Force when Winston Churchill was Prime Minister. Since then, I know he has met many members of the Churchill family – including Sir Winston's daughter, Lady Soames, and no less than three of his grandchildren. It was therefore my pleasure last year to be able to introduce Douglas to three of Churchill's great-grandchildren and two of his great-great-grandchildren when they visited Bletchley Park.

My own regret is that my wife Rita did not survive to see the publication of this book since sadly she was stricken with a cerebral haemorrhage at the end of last year. She had read the draft sample chapters and was so looking forward to seeing it in print. I feel honoured to have been asked to write this foreword and I trust all those who read the book *ab ovo usque ad mala* will enjoy the graphic descriptions, colourful photographs and excellent references put together by Douglas Hall.

Jack Darrah
Churchill Room
Bletchley Park
September 2002

A note on values

Frequently, I am asked the question: *'What is it worth?'* I cogitated over whether this book should include any reference at all to the value of items. The subject is certainly a minefield. I have seen the most common piece of Churchilliana – a little plastic resin bust, originally sold by Woolworth's in 1965 for twenty-five pence – priced at less than a pound to over a hundred pounds!

The millionaire's bauble may well be beyond the means of the ordinary collector. Data collected over more than twenty years indicates that Churchilliana in the United States will on average cost more than three times as much as in Britain. But what is the average price? That at a Sotheby's auction in New York or a chance purchase at a Texas car boot sale? That asked by a dealer operating from opulent premises in London W1 or a house clearance merchant with his stock laid out on the grass at a small UK provincial antiques fair? Well, in the same month that an example of the 1964 Thomas Goode Abbeydale vase ('the single most desirable Churchill ceramic') was being offered for $3000 in the USA another example sold for £315 at Christie's in London. At the same Christie's auction an example of the 1967 Spode Churchill Memorial vase sold for £360, just a month after a sale at $2,750 had been reported from the USA. But it is not entirely all one way. In 1996 a lucky Texan found a 1940 Charles Noke Royal Doulton Churchill loving cup at a Houston car boot sale. He paid $15 and Phillips sold it for him in London for £4,370.

The real bargains are almost certainly to be found at car boot sales and provincial antiques fairs. But don't get carried away – I have seen some remarkable examples of over-pricing at such events. And, of course, such Churchilliana bargains as there may be will be very thinly spread amongst endless piles of everything under the sun. Targeting specific items at auction or by registering your 'wants' with specialist dealers, may well be the least arduous route, but you will invariably pay the top price. Auctions, even those held at the principal international houses, can be a wonderful source of bargains, but it needs only one other determined bidder in the saleroom to send the price rocketing.

Outside the auction salerooms, where you must decide your limit and stick to it, haggling is expected. Never offer the ticketed price even in the most sumptuous London W1 showroom. On rare occasions you may be rather loftily informed that the price is not negotiable but more often than not you will secure a useful discount. At one London W1 emporium, specialising in commemorative items, discounts of 25-50% on the asking price are usually available.

The values quoted in this book are based on a wide sample of auction results, catalogue entries and dealers' quotations collected over many years. In the UK, as well as my own observations, a number of collector and dealer friends have contributed regular reports covering all regions of the country. In the USA a group of correspondents has provided similar information – chiefly from New England, New York, California, Kentucky, Illinois, Virginia and Texas.

The figures quoted should be reasonably representative but you must expect to find wide variations. The best advice is that you should decide the maximum price you can feel comfortable with and never pay more than that. *'Never give in, never give in, never, never, never...'* (WSC at Harrow School, 29 October 1941).

Where to acquire Churchilliana

Antiques fairs, markets & auctions
Antiques fairs, held all over the country, can be rich sources of Churchilliana but you might have to search through piles of everything under the sun to find it. The big fairs, held up to six times a year at places like Newark, Ardingly and Birmingham, attract dealers as well as collectors and you will have to get up very early in the morning, or pay a higher preview day admission price, to stand any chance of seeing the best material. The permanent regular antiques markets, such as Bermondsey, Covent Garden, Portobello Road and Camden Passage in London can also be recommended. Held on one or two days each week, early rising is obligatory. One of the best selections for collectors of Churchilliana can usually be found at:

Personalities & Events, 5 Georgian Village, Camden Passage, London, N1 (open Wednesday & Saturday).

Brittannia, Gray's Antique Market, Davies Street, London, W1 often has examples of the more expensive pieces.

Much of the Churchilliana sold in the United Kingdom passes through auction houses. The London fine arts auctioneers – Sotheby's, Christie's and Phillips – have periodic specialist sales at which entire collections or particular categories are on offer. Sotheby's occasional *Political Sales* are often a rich source. Most auctions issue catalogues, several weeks before a sale, but nowadays the best way of finding out what's on sale, and where, is via the Internet.

Belvoir Castle
The home of the Dukes of Rutland, across the Leicestershire border from Grantham in Lincolnshire, houses the regimental museum of the Queen's Royal Lancers. The castle souvenir shop sometimes stocks cold-cast bronze busts of Churchill by local sculptress Elizabeth Sharpe.

Blenheim Palace
The magnificent home of the Duke of Marlborough, in a 2,500 acre park near Woodstock in Oxfordshire, was the birthplace of Winston Churchill. A large souvenir shop stocks a wide selection of books and mementoes.

Bletchley Park
Home of the Code and Cypher School – an euphemism for a secret intelligence section of MI6, responsible to the Foreign Office. Known as *Station X* it was given the role of deciphering the 'unbreakable' Enigma coded signals used by the Germans. In recent years a series of museums has been developed covering the wartime role of the site including the inestimable Darrah-Harwood Collection of Churchilliana. The collection is open to the public at weekends and at other times by arrangement. A comprehensive bookshop serves the site and is complemented by a small souvenir shop in the Churchill Rooms.

Cabinet War Rooms
Situated at Clive Steps, King Charles Street, London – opposite St James's Park, the carefully restored underground suite of rooms used by the War Cabinet during World War II are now administered by the Imperial War Museum. Brings back evocative memories of those grim war days, supported by a well-stocked souvenir shop.

Chartwell
Near Westerham, Kent. Churchill's home from 1924-64. Now managed by the National Trust. A large and well-stocked souvenir shop has a wide range of gifts ranging in price from a few pence to hundreds of pounds.

Churchill College
Churchill College is situated on the west side of Cambridge and is the National and Commonwealth Memorial to Sir Winston Churchill. The Churchill Archives Centre, housing Sir Winston's papers and those of other famous people of his era, was added in 1973. As well as priceless papers, there are many unique pictures and sculptures and a small souvenir shop.

HMS Belfast
Since 1971 *HMS Belfast* has been moored on the River Thames in London, close by Tower Bridge, as a floating branch of the Imperial War Museum. Souvenirs of her exploits are plentiful in a well stocked shop.

Imperial War Museum
Founded in 1917 the Imperial War Museum on Lambeth Road, London, SE1 chronicles all aspects of the two world wars and has a large and well-stocked souvenir shop which carries a wide range of Churchilliana.

Royal Air Force Battle of Britain Memorial Flight
Located at RAF Coningsby – between Sleaford and Horncastle – in Lincolnshire the Battle of Britain Memorial Flight now comprises 5 Spitfires, 2 Hurricanes, a Lancaster and a Dakota which, between flying assignments, can be seen in their purpose-built hangar at Coningsby. A Visitor Centre houses a range of exhibits relating to the Battle of Britain and there is a souvenir shop stocking a good choice of models, books and pictures. *Good hunting.*

Admiralty, First Lord

Churchill twice held the position of First Lord of the Admiralty – the department of State which controls the Royal Navy. His first term (1911-15) was initially judged a great success. His task was to put the Navy in a state of readiness in case of war. He thoroughly modernised the service, converted ships from coal burning to oil burning, commissioned faster ships and bigger guns and recognised the future importance of air power by forming the Royal Naval Air Service.

On 2 August 1914 the fleet was ready for full mobilisation but the tragedy of the Gallipoli venture, which he had strongly supported, led to his demise. Although he argued the merits of his case, and was indeed later to be exonerated, he bore the brunt of the blame in 1915 and was forced to resign from the government.

Churchill returned to the Admiralty on the outbreak of World War II. This time his tenure was a mere eight months but his reason for leaving office was very different – he was promoted to Prime Minister in May 1940.

Three very well conceived and rather different pieces of pottery commemorated Churchill's second term as First Lord of the Admiralty.

This little dish is one of the few pieces to mark Churchill's first term at the Admiralty.

A character jug from Shorter and Son of Stoke-on-Trent. Nicely moulded but spoiled by incorrect paintwork which gave Churchill stark black hair and eyebrows.

The Shorter moulds were reused by other potteries many times for more than sixty years.

A fine character jug from Kirklands of Etruria, Stoke-on-Trent, depicting Churchill as a ship's figurehead with waves breaking around his face. A coloured version of this jug was also available.

Churchill strides like a Colossus over a warship titled *HMS Winston*. Pottery unknown,. Companion pieces were Neville Chamberlain and Lord Gort (Commander of the British Army in France).

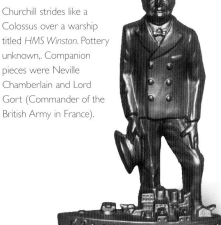

Admiralty House

On the opposite side of Horse Guards Parade to Downing Street stands Admiralty House, surely the grandest of the official ministerial residences. In its back yard, so to speak, is Admiralty Arch, the gateway from Trafalgar Square to the Mall and Buckingham Palace. The house itself is tucked in between the Admiralty offices and the Horse Guards building overlooking both Horse Guards Parade and Whitehall. Although it has now been converted into flats and offices for ministers the grander rooms have been retained for government entertaining and official banquets.

Winston Churchill first qualified for residence when he became First Lord of the Admiralty in October 1911. The grandeur of Admiralty House was awe inspiring to the twenty-six year old Clementine and she also feared that the family finances would not stand the strain of running a house needing at least a dozen domestic servants. Therefore, she prevailed upon Winston to delay the move from their own much smaller house in Eccleston Square and, with his mind fully occupied by his new job, he quietly acquiesced. They did not in fact move in until April 1913 and even then Clementine got Winston to agree that they would not use the main rooms on the ground floor and live only on the upper three floors. This would mean that they would be able to manage with only nine servants instead of twelve. Clementine enjoyed the prospect of choosing the furnishings for their private quarters, but found that her choice was restricted to the Ministry of Works official inventory She was not impressed with the selection on offer. Nevertheless she quickly established herself as lady of the house and in spite of her relative youth, soon gained a reputation as an accomplished hostess.

The Churchills' first tenure of Admiralty House came to an end in May 1915 when Winston was relieved of the office of First Lord. They were unable to move back to their Eccleston Square house since it had been let to Sir Edward Grey and stayed temporarily with Winston's cousin, Ivor Guest, before moving to share his brother Jack's house at 41 Cromwell Road.

Winston and Clementine Churchill moved more quickly into Admiralty House when he became First Lord of the Admiralty for the second time in September 1939. Twenty-six years earlier Clementine's financial caution had limited their domestic quarters to the three upper floors. This time wartime constraints prevailed and they confined themselves to just the top two floors. Their tenure was to be very much shorter.

After his appointment as Prime Minister on 10 May 1940 Churchill stayed on in Admiralty House for five more weeks. Although he was personally keen to consummate his life-long ambition and move into 10 Downing Street he was anxious not to put pressure on the sick and dying Neville Chamberlain to make the traditional peremptory departure.

Thus it was that Winston Churchill, who had written his first great speeches of World War I at Admiralty House, also wrote his first great speeches of World War II at the same address, including possibly the greatest.

In a speech in the House of Commons on 4 June 1940 Churchill said: *'We shall not flag or fail. We shall go on to the end ... We shall defend our island ... We shall fight on the beaches, we shall fight on the landing grounds, we shall never surrender.'*

Advertisements

Winston Churchill featured prominently in advertisements of cigar manufacturers. Businesses which happen to bear his name – insurance companies, manufacturers of stair lifts and adjustable chairs, mortgage brokers and gift shops – benefit by adding his image to their name, while others who featured him in their advertising include Dollar Rent-a-Car; the Hotel Queen Mary, Long Beach, California; Brooke Bond Tea; Sharp's Toffee; Aston Martin and Domecq Sherry.

In some cases the connection seems tenuous, but what are we to make of this advertisement from the nineteen-eighties by Van Heusen?

Airman extraordinary

Winston Churchill enjoyed a distinguished Army career during the closing years of the 19th century. He returned briefly, if controversially, to the colours on the Western Front during World War I. From his first appointment as First Lord of the Admiralty in 1911 he was to find lifelong satisfaction in considering himself a sailor. He delighted in wearing the full-dress uniform of an Elder Brother of Trinity House and, later, the even more flamboyant full-dress uniform of the Lord Warden of the Cinque Ports. During World War II his favoured workaday dress when aboard one of HM ships, or visiting a naval shore establishment, was his own unique 'naval' concoction of Royal Yacht Squadron cap and navy blue blazer.

However, for all his military and naval leanings, Churchill was at heart an aviator. Fascinated by the achievements of the Wright Brothers he was among the first to foresee the importance of aircraft in any future war. He formed the Royal Naval Air Service in 1911. At that time the Army were contemplating that an air service would have only a reconnaissance role but Churchill was convinced that the Navy should plan to use its aircraft more aggressively, and bombing and machine-gunnery were included in the RNAS training schedules. To the alarm of his Cabinet colleagues, and his wife, Churchill took up flying lessons. He was exhorted to desist from all sides but was not persuaded to do so until his instructor was killed in June 1914 when his plane, the one in which Churchill had been receiving instruction, crashed into the sea. He served as Secretary of State for War and Air, 1919-21, when he ensured that the Royal Air Force would retain its independence and founded the Royal Air Force College at Cranwell.

One of the most cherished of Churchill's many awards was being appointed Honorary Air Commodore of No 615 (County of Surrey) Squadron, Royal Auxiliary Air Force, in April 1939. It brought the great delight of yet another new uniform to wear – the actual uniform is on display at Chartwell – and he wore it proudly on every appropriate occasion. Photos of Churchill wearing his Air Commodore's uniform caused some debate in RAF messes. In place above five rows of medal ribbons was the badge of a qualified RAF pilot – the wings. Was Churchill entitled to wear the wings? He was certainly not qualified to do so under normal regulations. Did his honorary appointment give him the right? It hadn't in certain other comparable cases. The debate flickered on for a while but faded away as Churchill's exploits brought him into the highest esteem throughout the Royal Air Force. And of course even if he had been guilty of being improperly dressed who was going to tell him? The matter was rectified in March 1943 when the Air Council, with the King's approval, awarded Churchill his honorary wings.

After the fall of France in 1940 Churchill was effectively grounded. He was dissuaded from making internal flights over the southeast of England for fear of unwelcome attention from the Luftwaffe. At the time there was no passenger aircraft available with the range to take him to such international destinations as he needed, or thought he needed, to visit and he was delighted when, in 1943, he was allocated his own personal aircraft. It was a specially adapted Avro York, named *Ascalon*, which had been adapted from the Lancaster bomber. Equipped with four Rolls Royce Merlin 20 engines, *Ascalon* was fitted out like a yacht. It had a forward cabin, dining saloon, state room and galley with not less than three Elsan-type toilets. The one for the PM's personal use had an intricate self-circulating pump action.

Churchill was delighted with his new toy and during his first flight sat with his nose squashed against the cabin window vigorously returning the V-signs of the escorting Spitfire pilots. Before long he made the first of what were to be his frequent visits to the flight deck. He asked to have a go at flying the aircraft and, lowering himself into the swiftly vacated co-pilot's seat, he parried the Captain's attempt to switch on the automatic pilot with a terse *'Leave that damn thing alone.'* *Ascalon* swerved gracefully to starboard scattering the fighter escort like a flock of

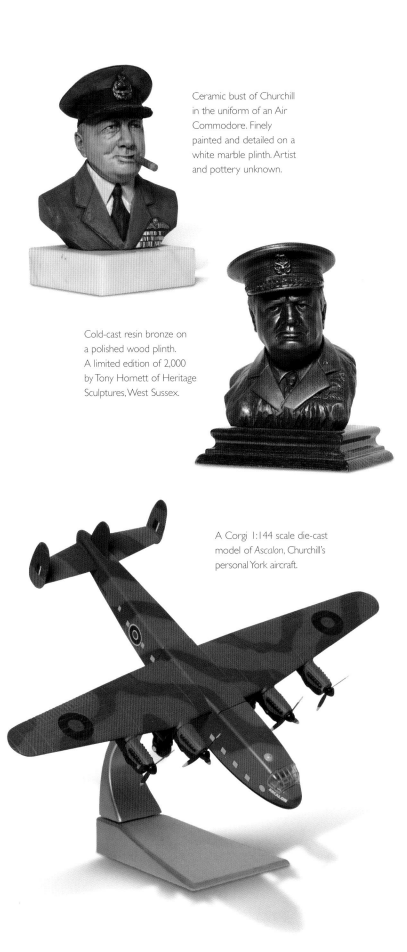

Ceramic bust of Churchill in the uniform of an Air Commodore. Finely painted and detailed on a white marble plinth. Artist and pottery unknown.

Cold-cast resin bronze on a polished wood plinth. A limited edition of 2,000 by Tony Hornett of Heritage Sculptures, West Sussex.

A Corgi 1:144 scale die-cast model of *Ascalon*, Churchill's personal York aircraft.

alarmed seagulls. The Captain put *Ascalon* back on course, the escorting aircraft retired to a safe distance and Churchill enjoyed himself hugely.

In 1945 *Ascalon* was mothballed and in October 1951 was reactivated and assigned to the Far East Communications Squadron until April 1954. It was then flown to RAF Langar, Nottinghamshire to be broken up. All reusable parts were salvaged to be used as spares for the RAF's Airborne Early Warning fleet of Avro Shackletons, also derived from the Lancaster, which flew well into the 1970s. Churchill would have loved that!

Ascalon was later replaced by a longer-ranged American Douglas C54 Skymaster similar to President Roosevelt's personal aircraft. Churchill was impressed by its superior capability, but less enthusiastic over its creature comforts. The Skymaster's shiny chromium interior contrasted sharply with *Ascalon's* plush velvet, braid and tassels. Above all, its in-flight catering of plastic-wrapped sandwiches and coffee from a Thermos could not compare with haute cuisine and accompanying cellar, conjured up from the imaginatively crewed galley of the York. Churchill first flew on the Skymaster to Athens on Christmas Eve 1944. He did not venture to the flight deck. Aged seventy, it was the end of an era.

In 1948 Churchill was appointed an Honorary Academician Extraordinary by the Royal Academy, in recognition of his achievements as an artist. A decade earlier the Royal Air Force had seen fit to consider him an Honorary Airman Extraordinary.

Ashtrays

In Churchill's day smoking was a majority pursuit. It was socially acceptable – indeed socially encouraged. Churchill told the King, who was also a smoker, that he never smoked before breakfast but the King knew perfectly well that Churchill habitually breakfasted in bed! Later Churchill declared that: *'Tobacco is bad for love; but old age is worse.'* It is little wonder that so much Churchilliana should be in the form of smokers' requisites.

Stone ashtray from House of Commons, damaged in air raid. Portrait medallion of Churchill made of lead from damaged roof.

Embossed with portraits of Churchill, Roosevelt and Stalin insc.: *'Cast with metal from German aircraft shot down over Britain 1939-45 – RAF Benevolent Fund.'*

A post-war piece, in china. The little bust turned up on various pieces of cheap and cheerful Churchilliana.

Burleighware by Burgess & Leigh, a high-relief portrait of Churchill and three-dimensional cigar.

Pressed brass – a 1950s issue after brass was released from wartime restrictions.

Grimwades (Royal Winton) decorated with UK and US flags.

Made by workers at de Havilland, reputedly using surplus aluminium from the *Wooden Wonder* Mosquito fighter/bomber.

'Utility' ashtray by Royal Doulton.

An ashtray designed for a cigar smoker decorated with a cartoon by David Low.

'Utility' ashtray by Wellington China.

Royal Winton from Grimwades, Stoke-on-Trent.

'Utility' ashtray by Elijah Cotton/BCM Nelsonware.

Atlantic Charter

On 20 January 1941 President Roosevelt wrote to Churchill from the White House quoting five lines from the poem *Building of the Ship* by the American poet, Henry Wadsworth Longfellow. Churchill replied that he was deeply moved by the verse and would: *'...have it framed as a souvenir of these tremendous days.'* Later he quoted Roosevelt's letter in full in volume 3, page 24, of *The Second World War*. In August 1941 Churchill crossed the Atlantic on *HMS Prince of Wales* to meet Roosevelt at Placentia Bay, Newfoundland for what was to become known as the Atlantic Charter meeting. He took with him a small number of illuminated copies of the verse which he and Roosevelt signed and they both kept a copy before distributing the remainder to members of their respective entourages. This facsimile of the document signed by the President and the Prime Minister is of inestimable value – an original would probably be priceless.

Autographs

Unless you have a significant disposable income *and* the advice of an expert this is an area of Churchilliana that must be approached with very great caution. Genuine documents bearing Churchill's signature command very great prices. At Christie's, London, in 1995 an autograph album which had belonged to Churchill's Chief Steward made £20,250 and an inscribed seating plan for a dinner at the Potsdam Conference in 1945 made

A signed postcard handed out by Churchill when he stood as a candidate at Oldham in the general election of 1900. This signature is a facsimile. A postcard, framed and glazed, with an attributed signature made £1,495 in 1999 at Sotheby's, London.

Menu of the El Alamein Reunion Dinner held at Claridge's Hotel, London on 23 October 1945. Churchill declared: *'...up till Alamein we survived. After Alamein we conquered. Monty, as I have for some time been allowed to call him, is one of the greatest living masters of the art of war.'* The menu was signed by Churchill, Montgomery and General Freyberg, the

Commander of the New Zealand Division at the Battle of El Alamein. A similarly inscribed menu, and a volume of *Poems from the Desert* by members of the Eighth Army, was sold at Sotheby's London in December 1996 for £3,450.

A 'handwritten' letter sent from 10 Downing Street to members of the public who had subscribed to Churchill's 80th birthday present in 1954. Over 400,000 did so and the facsimile machine must have worked overtime. The letters were uniquely addressed to recipients in official Downing Street envelopes and whilst of no great commercial value were usually considered to be worth framing.

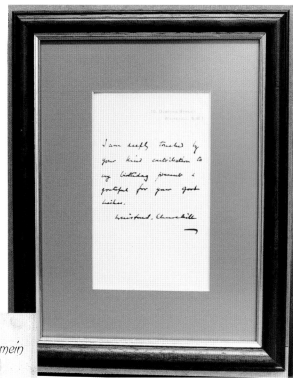

A letter to a Manchester constituent by Churchill in 1908, when he was Under-Secretary for the Colonies, airing his views on free trade and his opposition to the levying of unjust duties. He had just been offered the presidency of the Board of Trade and was to lose his Manchester seat in the obligatory by-election. The original of this letter was sold for £4,370 in July 1998 at Sotheby's, London.

£21,375. Churchill's signature was the attraction. There were other autographs but few of them would have made as much as £1,000 by themselves. At Sotheby's, London, in the following year, a letter written by Churchill in 1906 to his former mathematics teacher at Harrow made £6,900. In 1997 Christie's sold Churchill's 1926 letter of application to join the Amalgamated Union of Building Trade Workers for £4,500. Occasionally a genuine Churchill signature may be had for under £1,000 – for example a $5^1/_2$ x $3^1/_2$ inch photograph with 'some creasing' made £600 and a dinner menu signed in pencil was sold for £795. You must beware of facsimiles (Churchill's secretarial staff made extensive use of a sophisticated facsimile machine) and forgeries. About half the 'Churchill's' submitted to the two main London auction houses by hopeful vendors are found to be either facsimiles or fakes. A highly respected London dealer commented: *'There is a well-known forger operating in the Midlands. I can spot his work but it is being passed off to the unsuspecting at provincial fairs and small auctions.'* Caveat emptor.

Belvoir Castle

Belvoir Castle (pronounced Beaver), the home of the Dukes of Rutland, lies just across the Leicestershire border from Grantham in Lincolnshire. The regimental museum of the 17th/21st Lancers was established at Belvoir Castle in 1964 – the great-great-great-great-great-grandfather of the present Duke of Rutland had raised the 21st Dragoons, later the 21st Lancers (Empress of India's), in 1760. Since it first opened, the museum has been enlarged to incorporate the muniments of the 16th Lancers (The Queen's) and the 5th Lancers (Royal Irish). Now, as the Queen's Royal Lancers Museum, it houses the combined relics of all those famous old regiments.

In 1898 Winston Churchill was attached to the 21st Lancers as a supernumerary Lieutenant for the purpose of reporting the Sudan campaign for the *Morning Post*. His letter of appointment from the War Office read: *'It is understood that you will proceed at your own expense and that in*

Belvoir Castle.
The West Front.

The Battle of Omdurman, a painting by Bud Bradshaw c.1990, depicting Churchill charging on his grey Arab pony.

Winston Churchill (Sir Winston's grandson) and the Duke of Rutland in 1998 at the opening of the exhibition to celebrate the centenary of the Battle of Omdurman.

the event of your being killed or wounded ... no charge of any kind will fall on British Army funds'. Officially present as a newspaper correspondent rather than a full-time soldier Churchill nevertheless rode as one of 440 Lancers in the cavalry charge at the Battle of Omdurman. *'Nothing like the Battle of Omdurman will ever be seen again'*, he wrote later in two breathtaking chapters in *My Early Life*.

A special exhibition at Belvoir Castle in 1998 marked the centenary of the battle.

Churchill's telegram to his mother after the battle. He was being paid by the word for his newspaper columns but displays great economy here!

Biscuit tins

A Dutch tin from 1945 with portraits of Chiang Kai Shek, Stalin, Roosevelt and Churchill.

A smaller version of the United Biscuits 1965 tin.

United Biscuits 1965.

Huntley & Palmers 1965.

Blenheim Palace

Winston Churchill was born at Blenheim on 30 November 1874, heir presumptive to the Dukedom of Marlborough for twenty three years until his cousin 'Bert' was born in 1897. Churchill was later to express relief that the 9th Duke's first and only child had been a boy otherwise he would have inherited the title in 1934 and been in 'Another Place', and on equal terms with Lord Halifax, when Chamberlain resigned in 1940. Churchill declared: *'At Blenheim, I took two very important decisions: to be born and to marry. I am happily content with the decisions I took on both those occasions.'* It was in the *Temple of Diana* at Blenheim that he proposed to Clementine Hozier, in August 1908. A plaque to commemorate the event is mounted on a wall of the temple.

Blenheim Palace, Woodstock, Oxfordshire, was built between 1705 and 1722 by Sir John Vanburgh, a pupil of Sir Christopher Wren. It was a gift from Queen Anne to John Churchill, 1st Duke of Marlborough, as a reward for his services to the nation. The project was bedevilled by difficulties and clashes of personality between Sarah, the first Duchess, and the Queen. As a result Treasury payments for the building dried up, leaving the Duke having to finish the Palace at his own expense.

Winston Churchill was born, prematurely, in a small room on the ground floor to the west of the Great Hall, the son of Lord Randolph Churchill and the American beauty, Jennie Jerome. In the Birth Room is preserved a lock of Churchill's red curly hair taken when he was five years old and various other artefacts including cartoons, a maroon velvet siren suit worn by him during World War II and a pair of his monogrammed slippers. The Churchill Exhibition in a nearby room was opened by Clementine Churchill in 1974 to celebrate the Centenary of her husband's birth. It includes an audio-visual show of Churchill's life, his oil-painting of the Great Hall at Blenheim, various letters and documents and a maquette of Oscar Nemon's full-size double statue of Sir Winston and Lady Churchill which stands by the lake at Chartwell.

An aerial view of Blenheim Palace from the southeast.

Churchill's Birth Room.

Poster advertising *Churchill Centenary Year* celebrations at Blenheim Palace.

Lady Randolph Churchill wrote on her first visit to Blenheim: *'As we passed through the entrance archway and the lovely scenery burst upon me, Randolph said with pardonable pride, "This is the finest view in England." Looking at the lake, the bridge, the miles of magnificent park studded with old oaks...and the huge and stately palace, I confess I felt awed. But my American pride forbade the admission.'*

To the west of the Great Hall in a suite of apartments originally alloted to Dean Jones, the 1st Duke of Marlborough's domestic chaplain, is the modest room in which Winston Churchill was born in 1874. It is unlikely that any of the furniture now in the room was there at Churchill's birth. The items of Churchilliana on display are changed from time to time.

Bletchley Park
Churchill Rooms

In 1883 a wealthy stockbroker and close friend of Lloyd George, Sir Herbert Leon, purchased a small house standing in the 55 acre Bletchley Park. Over the next 40 years Leon greatly extended the house so that at his death in 1926 it was a huge mansion, much of which is still standing today. Something of a hotch-potch of architectural

Top: A plaque in the entrance hall of the mansion at Bletchley Park recording the Park's codebreaking role in World War II.

Above: A paperweight in resin bronze, on a polished wood base – a souvenir on sale at Bletchley Park.

styles, the mansion had many grand and opulent rooms with large ornate fireplaces, lavishly decorated ceilings and a wealth of carved wood panelling. When Leon's widow, Lady Fanny, died in 1937, Bletchley Park was acquired by a local consortium of property developers who prepared plans to demolish the mansion and build an estate of houses. However site clearance had only affected part of the stable block when agents for the Government Property Agency arrived. They were looking for a quiet country location for the Government Code & Cypher School. GC & CS was in fact an euphemism for a secret intelligence section of the Military Intelligence service, MI6, responsible to the Foreign Office. The Government initially took a three month's lease on Bletchley Park and when that lease expired, acquired the property by compulsory purchase. GC & CS was established at Bletchley Park by the summer of 1938. It was presided over by a gentleman referred to only as 'C' – and not publicly identified until after the war was over as Major General Sir Stewart Menzies (1890-1968) – and known as *Station X*.

The accommodation provided in the mansion and its existing outbuildings was expanded by the erection of an unlovely collection of wooden army huts and other temporary buildings needed for the growing team of scientists and cryptographers being recruited. This was the team that were to break the 'unbreakable' Enigma coded signals used by the Germans. The information so gained was of absolutely vital importance to the British and (later) American authorities in the strategic planning of the war and it was equally vital that the Germans should not discover that their signals were being intercepted and successfully decrypted. To maintain that secrecy Churchill ordered that those receiving the information should be kept to an absolute minimum and he appointed Group Captain Fred Winterbotham as his personal liaison officer at Bletchley Park. Winterbotham's brief was to select daily the more important messages which had been deciphered and send them to MI6 headquarters at Broadway – only five minutes from Downing Street. There a further scrutiny would be made and

Above: Bletchley Park Mansion requisitioned in 1938 to become the Government Code & Cypher School – an euphemism for the Department of Secret Military Intelligence, responsible for breaking the signal codes used by potential enemies.

Below: One of many showcases exhibiting the extensive Darrah-Harwood Churchilliana Collection at Bletchley Park. The display is currently open every weekend and during the week by arrangement.

The Winston Churchill Quilt made by Mrs Mary Mayne in 1987. A prize-winning entry in the Great British Quilt Festival held at Harrogate, in a class to design a quilt for a bedroom in a Stately Home. The quilt was designated to furnish Churchill's Birth Room at Blenheim Palace.

interpretations added before they were locked in a distinctive box and taken by special messenger to 10 Downing Street. Churchill alone had the key to the box.

It is perhaps remarkable that the secrecy of the operations at Bletchley Park was so well maintained for the duration of the war. Post-war research established that the Germans had no inkling that their signals traffic was being successfully decoded. Almost 9,000 personnel were employed at Bletchley Park by 1944 and they were a very disparate crowd, many of whom were eccentric or self-important academics whose personal ambitions, jealousies and tantrums frequently led to quarrelling and intrigue among themselves! The primitive and crowded nature of the accommodation did not help matters. Sir Stewart Menzies' biographer describes how discontentment amongst the staff became a serious issue in the late summer of 1941.

Churchill was made aware of the problem and he paid a visit to Bletchley Park on 6 September 1941. This is his only recorded visit to *Station X*, although Menzies, Jones and Winterbotham were frequently called to Downing Street.

Later, Churchill referrred to the Bletchley staff as: *'My geese that laid the golden eggs and never cackled,'* and in his messages to President Roosevelt he quoted his source as *Boniface* – a spurious identity for a non-existent British spy. Bletchley's role in breaking the German, Italian and Japanese signals codes is held by many historians to have been the paramount factor in the Allied victory of 1945. Some have argued that the valuable intelligence garnered by the Ultra team probably shortened the war by at least two years, thus saving thousands of lives on both sides.

After the war, Bletchley Park remained in government ownership and was used by the Post Office telecommunications division. When PO telecommunications were privatised, British Telecom remained as the principal tenant and used the mansion as a management training school. During the Post Office / British Telecom years, many of the wartime buildings were demolished but, 60 years on, it is perhaps remarkable that many more remain well preserved. Meantime the small town of Bletchley had become absorbed into the post-war new town of Milton Keynes and the local authority, mindful of British Telecom's gradual rundown of activities and declared intention of vacating Bletchley Park, drew up a redevelopment plan which envisaged building over 200 houses and a business park. The Bletchley Park Trust was formed to preserve the site as a National Heritage. It has now been declared a conservation area and is being developed into a series of museums to cover the top-secret wartime role of the site, the history of computers and development of radar and telecommunications.

Originally housed in two rooms in the mansion and one of the first of the new exhibitions to open to the public, the Darrah-Harwood Collection of Winston Churchill memorabilia soon outgrew its accommodation and was moved into a large room in 'A' block which had been built in 1941 to house wall-mounted charts of the Atlantic on which the movement of German U-boats were plotted. Now four ranks of showcases house a magnificent collection of Churchilliana and the walls are hung with an inestimable assembly of prints, some of Churchill's own paintings, photographs, drawings and tapestries. An eye-catching display on one wall is the Winston Churchill Quilt made in 1987 by Mrs Mary Mayne. Originally, it was a prize-winning entry in the Great British Quilt Festival at Harrogate where it represented the Birth Room at Blenheim Palace in a competition to design a quilt for a bedroom in a Stately House. Measuring 7 x 5 feet, appliquéd and hand-quilted, it took nine months to make. A notice alongside recounts that when making the quilt Mrs Mayne had difficulty in finding a piece of fabric suitable for Churchill's overcoat. In desperation she raided her husband's wardrobe and cut off a large part of the leg from a pair of his trousers! So the cost of the quilt included a new pair of trousers for Mr Mayne!

The major part of the collection was built up over many years by Ulsterman Jack Darrah. Since the exhibition first opened in June 1994 the Churchilliana Collection has been boosted by donations from visitors offering all manner of Churchill-related material. Much of it is unique with most interesting historical significance.

Bookends

Bookends of stone from the bomb-damaged House of Commons in 1941. Medallions depicting Roosevelt and Churchill were cast in lead from the roof.

Cold-cast bronze busts incorporating bookends by Jon Douglas, made in 1955 to commemorate Churchill's retirement as Prime Minister.

Bookmarks

Left: In woven silk from Spain. 'The Right Honourable Winston Churchill, Prime Minister of Great Britain, Bastion of Democracy, Justice and Peace'.

Centre: A leather bookmark from 1990 commemorating the 50th anniversary of the Battle of Britain with a quotation from Churchill's speech of 20 August 1940 – *'Never in the field of human conflict was so much owed by so many to so few'.*

Right: A silver-plated profile of Churchill in a typical oratorical posture. Clips over the top of your page and does the job in style.

Books

Winston Churchill wrote more than fifty books ranging from 6-volume blockbusters covering each of the two World Wars to a potboiler first (and only) novel, *Savrola* (1899), and a charming essay about his abiding hobby, *Painting as a Pastime* (1948). He was awarded the Nobel Prize for Literature in 1953 for his four-volume *History of the English-Speaking Peoples.*

What is remarkable is that Churchill's accomplishments as a writer were achieved on a part-time basis within a sixty-year political career which would alone have fully extended most men. Churchill's books have been the subject of several substantial volumes of critique in their own right and there is no place, or space, here for more than this brief mention. For further reading I would recommend: *A Bibliography of the Works of Sir Winston Churchill* by Frederick Woods (St Paul's Bibliographies, 1979); *Artillery of Words – The Writings of Sir Winston Churchill,* also by Frederick Woods, (Leo Cooper, 1992) and *A Connoisseur's Guide to the Books of Sir Winston Churchill* by Richard Langworth (Brassey's, 1998).

Churchill's early books are keenly sought after by collectors. A first edition of the 2-volume *The River War* (1899) without dust jackets made £5,640 at Sotheby's, London in July 2000 and Richard Langworth suggests that a genuinely fine first edition set with original dust jackets would command over $10,000 in the USA. A set of 5 volumes in 6 books of *The World Crisis* (1923-31) inscribed by Churchill to his secretary Eddie Marsh – four volumes with slightly darkened and stained dust jackets – made £22,100 at Sotheby's, London in July 2000.

The Second World War belongs to the first rank of Churchill's books. It is necessary

reading for anyone seeking understanding of what Britain was fighting for. Asked that question in March 1940 Churchill replied: *'If we left off fighting you would soon find out!'* The first English edition of *The Second World War* was published, in six volumes, by Cassell between 1948 and 1954 with the first impression of each volume running between 200,000 and 300,000 copies. The first American edition was published by Houghton Mifflin between 1948 and 1953 and there were editions in Canada and Australia as well as translations into seventeen languages – Arabic, Danish, Dutch, French, German, Greek, Hebrew, Italian, Japanese, Korean, Norwegian, Polish, Portuguese, Russian, Spanish, Swedish and Turkish. A number of de luxe and illustrated editions were published.

Churchill's third book, and first and only novel, was *Savrola*, published in 1899. Its theme was a revolt in an imaginary Balkans or South American republic and traced the fortunes of a (thinly disguised) liberal leader who overthrew the government only to be swallowed up by a socialist revolution. An impecunious junior army officer at the time, Churchill wrote the book in about two months as an unashamed potboiler (the shame came later when he constantly urged his friends *'to abstain from reading it.'*) The first edition, by Longmans, Green & Co was of 1,500 copies priced at six shillings, so his royalties would not have much improved

Showcard for *The Second World War* from Heron Books, a twelve-volume leather-bound edition published to mark the Churchill Centenary, 1974.

Far left: Sir Winston S Churchill Honorary Citizenship of the United States, 1965.

Savrola, first published in 1899. This paperback edition published by Beacon Books, 1957.

The Sir Winston Churchill Birthday Book, published by Castell Brothers, 1958.

his then current life style. In *My Early Life*, written in 1930, Churchill claimed that *Savrola* yielded in all about £700 over several years. But there were several more editions to follow, including a splendid and colourfully jacketed Beacon Books paperback edition of 1957.

Sir Winston S Churchill Honorary Citizenship of the United States, was published in a limited edition of 1,000 to mark this momentous occasion. This little book, measuring just $2^{1}/_{2}$ x $1^{1}/_{2}$ inches with 30 pages, represents a triumphantly small step for mankind! Leather bound with gilt page edges and printed on linen paper it was produced in 1965 in the USA.

The Sir Winston Churchill Birthday Book. This smart little leather-bound book, 5 x $3^{1}/_{2}$ inches was published in 1958 by Castell Brothers, London, as *'a small tribute to ... that giant historical figure by whom, under God, England was not only delivered in the hour of her greatest peril but inspired to live or die by his words of wisdom...'* A Churchillian quotation, aphorism or maxim for each of 366 days with space in which to enter your own *Thought for the Day.*

'Books in all their variety are often the means by which civilization may be carried triumphantly forward.' (Winston Churchill introducing a Ministry of Information film, 1941.)

Photo courtesy Richard Langworth

Bottle openers

These devices for removing the seals from crown capped bottles were an essential household implement throughout the first half of the 20th century. Usually they carried advertisements for brewers or soft drinks manufacturers.

During World War II bottle openers soon began to carry the profile of the Prime Minister. Around 1990 one was listed in an American dealer's catalogue: *'The only one we've ever seen – $120'*. I went to an antiques fair and bought up twenty at £4-£5 each, advertised them in *Finest Hour* at £20 and made a handsome profit for the International Churchill Society!

Bottle pourers

During Churchill's second term as Prime Minister (1951-55), a number of bottle pourers modelled in his image were marketed as souvenirs. Fitted to a cork and designed to push into the neck of a bottle of spirits they generally poured the drink through an ubiquitous hollow cigar. Most were rather cheap and cheerful, produced in lightweight plastic and crudely painted but the one illustrated is a rare exception. Skilfully modelled in porcelain and nicely decorated this one poured the drink through the back of Churchill's head. When not in use the pourer could be parked in its own miniature barrel.

Bottle opener c.1945   Bottle pourer c.1951

Brassware

Under wartime regulations the use of brass for non-essential purposes was forbidden and thus decorative items made from brass during World War II are virtually non-existent. A small amount of low-grade or scrap brass was used for such things as ashtrays and crown cork bottle openers (they were perhaps considered to be essential items!) On this rather crude little sand-cast dish the portrait of Churchill is identical to that on many crown cork bottle openers but I doubt whether it was made for commercial sale. Probably either a trial casting or a piece of individual enterprise by a foundry worker.

Bulldog Churchill

Less than a month after Churchill became Prime Minister in 1940 the *Daily Express* published a cartoon by Sidney Strube. Standing pugnaciously astride a map of the British Isles was a bulldog wearing a collar with a number 10 tag and a steel helmet captioned *'Go To It'*. Well, not quite a bulldog because grafted onto the sturdy canine body were the unmistakable heavily bejowled features of Winston Churchill. Strube's association of the Prime Minister with that broad-headed, muscular breed of dog was to become a latter-day personification of John Bull – the 17th century literary character deemed to be representative of the British people – and would be picked up by many other artists throughout World War II and beyond.

In August 1942 Churchill flew from Cairo to Moscow to visit Stalin and an Illingworth

The Bulldog has Wings. Illingworth's cartoon in *Punch* on 26 August 1942, alluded to Churchill's flight to Moscow to visit Stalin.

cartoon in *Punch* added a large pair of wings to the man / dog hybrid and gave it the caption, *The Bulldog has Wings*. Vicky (Victor Weisz) was of Hungarian parentage, born in Berlin. Vicky came to England in 1935 and worked as a freelance illustrator. His cartoon for *Time and Tide* on 10 July 1943 used the Churchill's head/bulldog's body to comment upon the increased bombing attacks by the RAF on German targets above the caption: *'Never was there such a case of the biter bitten, Mr Churchill.'*

Go To It. Sidney Strube's cartoon for the *Daily Express* – 8 June 1940. The first known association of Churchill with the bulldog.

Sculptors and potters also picked up the theme. A bronze-effect china cigar-smoking bulldog with Churchill's features wore a yachting cap at a jaunty angle. A solid bronze figure had Churchill and a bulldog side-by-side in equally aggressive stances.

Burgess & Leigh had Churchill standing astride a bulldog for their 1941 toby jug titled *'Bulldogs'* and Wilkinson's superb toby jug in the same year had Churchill seated on a bulldog. Various ashtrays depicted the duo with captions like *'The Star Turns'* and *'Who Said Hitler?'*

Royal Doulton and Crown Devon produced bulldog figures which, although having a dog's features, sported a yachting cap and a cigar to make the allusion quite clear.

As late as the 1990s Kevin Francis Ceramics reissued the Churchill/bulldog combination for several commemorative toby jugs, while Manor Collectables' cigar-smoking bulldog wearing a yachting cap left no illusions as to its allusion.

A 10-inch long painted plywood bulldog with an unmistakably Churchillian canine expression. Signed (indecipherable) and dated 1943 on the back.

Carved and painted wooden bulldog with Churchill's features, dressed in a Union Jack coat and RAF cap. Modern; made to order for customers of *Personalities and Events*, Camden Passage, London.

Burgess & Leigh's 1941 *Bulldogs* toby jug (left) modelled by Ernest Bailey. This must surely have been the inspiration for Douglas Tootle's 1990 toby jug (right) for Peggy Davies/Kevin Francis Ceramics.

Winston is the most popular name for a bulldog. Potteries make the association with Churchill quite plain. Left: Blythe Collectibles. Right: Robert Harrop.

Royal Doulton's *Character Jug of the Year* for 1992 by Stanley James Taylor. Each year Doulton produce a special edition character jug. Sales are 'limited' to the year of issue. At the end of the year the moulds are destroyed. The RRP was £75 but the jug was often discounted by 10-20%.

A much reproduced china bulldog in a steel helmet titled *Hitler's Terror*. There was only an indirect allusion to Churchill but it was clear who it represented.

Pottery unknown, c1941. The only known piece of pottery which combines Churchill's head and a bulldog's body. Very scarce.

Yes it is called Winston! Backstamp reads: 'Kevin Francis / Winston / Modelled by Andy Moss / Limited edition of 500 worldwide / This is number 44 / Hand made and hand painted in Staffordshire England / Produced by Peggy Davies Ceramics'. On sale during 2000 at around £40.

Busts

1. Parianware bust. 1914

Parianware bust, Robinson & Leadbeater, Stoke-on-Trent. First known portrait bust depicting Churchill. 6½ inches high, signed and dated, *'WC Lawton, Sculptor, Copyright, September 1914.'* Churchill is wearing First Lord of the Admiralty uniform. Some have patriotic transfer or town crest on the plinth. Value around £160. A contemporary Parianware bust marked *'Shelley late Foley'* can also be found. Both are scarce.

2. Plaster bust. c1924

Thought to be from Churchill's Chancellor of the Exchequer period, 1924-29. The mystery is that this bust, in varnished plaster, is signed behind left shoulder – *'M Lindman'.* A colleague has an identical bust signed *'JH Bird'.*

3. The Epstein Bust. 1946

This bust was commissioned by the British government from sculptor Jacob Epstein. The arrangement seemed convenient since Epstein lived close to Churchill in Hyde Park Gate. American born, Epstein had lived and worked in London for forty years but his work had often aroused violent criticism and derision. After a number of sittings Churchill became uneasy about the very rugged form the bust was taking and walked out of Epstein's studio. The latter finished the sculpture using photographs but because of Churchill's aversion it was not put on display until after his death. There are seven examples of the bust on semi-public display in England and at least three more in private collections in the USA. One of the latter was sold for $25,500 in 1991.

4. The Pikering Bust. 1949

This little bust, 5½ inches high in solid bronze on a marble plinth, is generally regarded as one of the most commanding likenesses of Churchill. It has become one of the the most replicated pieces of Churchilliana. Mr Pikering's registered design licence expired in 1964 just before Churchill died, and Woolworth's reproduced the bust in lightweight plastic resin as a memorial piece. They sold tens of thousands at five shillings each, in either white simulated marble or a bronze effect

finish. Within a few years all the bronze busts had oxidised to black! The original bust has also been copied in cold-cast resin bronze, marble dust/resin, brass and even wood. Secondary market prices range from £150+ for an original bronze down to a pound or two for a Woolworth's copy but be careful, some of the cold-cast bronze replicas are faithfully reproduced – even down to the date and Mr Pikering's signature.

5. The Jon Douglas Bust. 1955

Churchill's retirement as Prime Minister in 1955 was marked by a fine pair of busts by Jon Douglas. Available individually the two busts, each 7 inches tall, came in either varnished plaster or cold cast resin bronze. One portrayed Churchill looking slightly left and grasping his lapels and the other had him looking slightly right, clutching a cigar and feeling for a match in his waistcoat pocket. The pair were also sold mounted as bookends. Individual varnished plaster busts now cost £50-100 each on the secondary market (£200 a pair) and at least twice as much in resin bronze.

6. Spode/Nemon Bust. 1965

A 1965 advertisement read: *'This bust of Sir Winston Churchill, sculpted by Oscar Nemon, has been reproduced in miniature in Spode china. Seven inches high, it is polished instead of glazed, to retain the detail of the original. The first edition is limited to 1,000 copies. 12 guineas (£12.60).'* An example sold for £225 at auction in London in 1995.

7. The Royal Doulton Churchill Centenary Bust. 1974

Designed by EJ Griffiths this black basalt bust is 11½ inches high atop an 8 x 6½ x 2½ inch polished wood plinth. Black basalt is a rare medium for Doulton, it is more closely associated with Wedgwood, and to my knowledge they have used it on only three other occasions – busts of HM the Queen, HRH the Duke of Edinburgh and HRH the Princess Royal. *The Churchill Centenary Bust* was produced in a limited edition of 750, in a black leatherette, satin-lined, brass-bound case. Although it was produced in a reasonably large edition the bust is rarely seen on the secondary market. The 1994 *Lyle Doulton Price Guide* listed

1. Parianware bust. 1914

4. The Pikering Bust. 1949

2. Plaster bust. c1924

5. The Jon Douglas Bust. 1955

3. The Epstein Bust. 1946

6. Spode/Nemon Bust. 1965

7. The Royal Doulton Churchill
Centenary Bust. 1974

10. Cooper Knight, Northants. 1975

8. The Burgess Bust. 1976

11. The Sylvac Bust. 1974

9. Jessica Borthwick. 1940

12. Sculptor unknown. c1940

a value of £250 (USA $375) but I have since noted a UK auction price of £295 and an American dealer's catalogue quoting a remarkable $1,500.

8. The Burgess Bust. 1976

A very finely modelled and detailed bust in dark brown pottery. Signed *'W H Burgess'* and dated June '76 with an embossed mark *'WHB'* and the inscription *'No 9'*. I have never seen another example of this bust which probably indicates that only a small number were produced at a time when the Churchilliana market was still suffering the overhang of the centenary year. Judging from the reaction of my friends this representation of Churchill comes very much into the 'love it or hate it' category!

9. Jessica Borthwick. 1940

Ms Borthwick's inscription uses a style which had long since been abandoned by Churchill himself. The photograph in fact flatters this parian china bust which is among those regularly classified with the ugly mugs!

10. Cooper Knight, Northants. 1975

A silver bust mounted on a column of black marble. A limited edition of 250. Unique in that it depicts Churchill wearing spectacles – the half-moon reading glasses are fashioned from gold wire. Rare. Has been seen in a Bond Street gallery priced at £250.

11. The SylvaC Bust. 1974

Modelled by George Cooper for Shaw & Copestake (SylvaC) of Longton for the Churchill Centenary. White glazed china. A much liked representation of Churchill which was, perhaps undeservedly, overshadowed by the Centenary commemoratives from Coalport, Royal Doulton, Wedgwood et al. Rarely seen on the secondary market.

12. Sculptor unknown. c1940

This example is in grey painted plaster but the bust has also been seen in bronze. The inscription on the plinth is the peroration from Churchill's first speech in the House of Commons as Prime Minister on 13 May 1940. Marked at the back simply: *'Copyright. Made in England'.*

13. Sculptor unknown. c1946

We can date this excessively bull-necked representation of Churchill to some time after 1 January 1946, for that was when he was awarded the Order of Merit, the badge of which he wears on a neck riband.

14. Sculptor unknown, c1946

A more appealing bust, of similar date, made from marble dust mixed with resin. When originally issued, many such busts had been dipped in wax to give the appearance of polished marble. However, when the wax became grubby many owners washed their bust thus removing the wax coating and leaving a rather grainy finish. Both pieces under £20 in the UK but up to $150 in the USA.

15. Lawton China, date unknown

A well modelled and painted ceramic bust with its plinth inscribed with a quotation from one of Churchill's best known World War II speeches.

16. Sculptor unknown. c1920

Believed to date from around 1920 when Churchill was MP for Dundee. Black painted plaster.

17. Woolworth's Bust

When Churchill died in 1965, Woolworth's copied the 1949 Pikering bust as their memorial piece. The Woolworth's busts were produced in lightweight plastic resin, simulating either bronze or marble, and sold in their tens of thousands at five shillings (25 pence) each. Perhaps twenty years later this variation caught my eye at a car boot sale. Somebody had quite expertly coloured one of the Woolworth's simulated marble busts. At £2 I reckoned I had got a bargain. The bust makes a neat counterpoint to the original bronze and helps to demonstrate why Pikering's original sculpture was one of the best and most enduring images of Churchill.

18. Paragon China. c1942

Paragon China of Longton, Stoke-on-Trent, have long held warrants of appointment to successive Kings and Queens of England. Over almost as long they have built up a strong export trade, notably to the United States. This fine bone china bust was produced during World War II primarily for the American market. It is rarely seen in the UK but has a value of $300+ in the USA. Backstamped: *'The Rt Hon Winston Churchill, Prime Minister of Great Britain'* together with the sculptor's signature, *'R Johnson'.*

19. Noble Ceramics. 1998

Ray Noble is a talented modeller who, in addition to designing ceramic sculptures for his own Hampshire studio, Noble Ceramics, carries out commissions for the Stoke-on-Trent potteries. He is one of the finest present-day modellers of Winston Churchill. A 1998 bust, 5¹/₂ inches high, available in a variety of colourways as well as plain white glaze.

20. Noble Ceramics. 1999

A 1999 version of the bust for Bairstow Manor Pottery, also released as a character jug with a Viscount Montgomery and Union Jack handle. Both pieces about £35 direct from the potteries or £70 from high street retailers.

21. John Bromley. 1965

Signed, dated and numbered by the sculptor. 7 inches high. Issued in a limited edition of 500 in either black basalt or white bisque china. Some versions, like that illustrated, terminated just below Churchill's bow tie but others were slightly deeper finishing in mid chest. In addition, various designs of polished wood plinth, either separate or fixed, have been noted. Fairly rare in the UK at up to £150; USA price $400-$500.

22. Joseph Williams. 1978

Signed and dated by the sculptor. Cold-cast resin bronze. Eleven inches high. As good a representation of the 'scowling determined Churchill' as they come – you can almost hear the bust intoning: *'We shall go on to the end ...we shall fight on the beaches ... we shall fight in the fields and in the streets ...we shall never surrender.'* In 1998 I noted an example on sale for £225 in the UK and, in the same week, was advised that another was on offer in the USA at $475.

23.The Churchill Millennium Bust

A bust from Kevin Francis/Peggy Davies Ceramics was second in the series, after William Shakespeare, celebrating the greatest men and women of the past 1,000 years. Modelled by Ray Noble the 10¹/₂ inches high x 8¹/₂ inches wide bust is finished in 'honey glaze' to resemble creamware. A limited edition of 100. £66-£80 in the UK.

24. Sculptor unknown

Appears to be another manifestation of the 1949 Pikering bust, the 1965 Woolworth's busts and all those other resin/marble and resin/bronze copies which have appeared over the years. This one, 14 inches high, is as good as they come in hollow spelter/bronze on a polished marble socle. Also seen in solid resin/marble.

25. Heritage Sculptures

Churchill in the uniform of Air Commodore of the Royal Auxiliary Air Force. Modelled by Tony Hornett in cold-cast resin bronze for Heritage Sculptures of Horsham, West Sussex. A limited edition of 2,000. Sold to raise funds for the Churchill Rooms at Bletchley Park. £50.

26. Michael Sutty

Large-scale porcelain portrait bust by the renowned Stoke-on-Trent military modeller Michael Sutty. This one portraying Churchill in the ceremonial uniform of Lord Warden of the Cinque Ports is not a good likeness. The lavishly decorated and gilded bust was heralded in a numbered and limited edition of 250 but less than eighty had been issued by the end of 2001. UK dealers quoted £350-£400 for early numbered examples.

27. Heritage Sculptures

Churchill in his workaday naval uniform of Royal Yacht Squadron cap and navy blue reefer jacket. He habitually wore this very personal and entirely unofficial concoction when going aboard HM ships or visiting RN shore establishments during World War II. This bust, modelled by Anthony Leonard for Heritage Sculptures, in simulated ebony is in an edition of 1,000 to raise funds for the Havengore Trust. 6¹/₂ inches high. The wooden plinth is of oak removed from *Havengore,* during her restoration. £50. *Havengore,* the former PLA launch, that carried Churchill's coffin down the Thames after his State funeral in 1965, is moored at Chatham Historic Dockyard and open to visitors by appointment.

13. Sculptor unknown. c1946

16. Sculptor unknown. c1920

14. Sculptor unknown. c1946

17. Woolworth's Bust

15. Lawton China. Date unknown

18. Paragon China. c1942

19. Noble Ceramics. 1998

22. Joseph Williams. 1978

25. Heritage Sculptures

20. Noble Ceramics. 1999

23. The Winston Churchill Millennium Bust

26. Michael Sutty

21. John Bromley. 1965

24. Sculptor unknown

27. Heritage Sculptures

Cabinet War Rooms

In 1936 the Government began to consider the protection that would be needed from aerial bombing in the event of a future war. An ideal site was found in 1938, in the basement of the New Public Offices, a steel-framed building conveniently close to Downing Street and all the principal ministries.

The area selected was ten feet below ground level on the western side of the building opposite St James's Park. Work started immediately and the first rooms were ready by that summer. Enlargement continued during 1938 and 1939. The War Cabinet, with Churchill as First Lord of the Admiralty, met in one of the rooms on 21 October 1939, mainly to test the facilities.

By spring 1940, the Cabinet War Rooms comprised sixteen rooms and provided working and sleeping accommodation for sixty people. The Map Room was fully operational but the Cabinet Room was seldom used. Shortly after Churchill became Prime Minister in May 1940 he was allocated a room for his personal use, a combined office and bedroom, available as his emergency accommodation until the end of the war.

In September 1940 Churchill and his wife and their personal staff moved out of 10 Downing Street into the ground and first floors above the emergency basement. The basement was further reinforced with rolled steel joists and a three feet thick concrete slab.

The Transatlantic Telephone Room provided Churchill with a direct line to President Roosevelt in the White House. Telecommunications technology in 1940 was such that the security scrambler for this telephone link was too big to get into the Cabinet War Rooms and had to be installed a mile away in the basement of Selfridges store in Oxford Street!

Churchill was not a man who shirked risks. Although the room allocated to him in the reinforced basement boasted comforts of a higher standard than elsewhere in the complex he preferred not to sleep there.

Given the choice he would take up a position on the roof at George Street to get a better view of air raids! He insisted on having close access to the Map Room and his combined office and bedroom was sited adjacent to it, with a communicating door. Even so, his personal map-keeper, Captain Richard Pim RNVR, was required to keep a smaller map up-to-date on the wall behind his bed. Churchill's desk, in the other half of the room, was equipped with microphones supplied by the BBC to enable him to make regular broadcasts.

The Cabinet War Rooms, preserved in their 1940-45 format, are open to the public and are a branch of the Imperial War Museum.

Churchill insisted on remaining in his second-floor flat in 10 Downing Street until 20 October 1940, in spite of extensive air-raid damage to the kitchens, dining and drawing rooms. He disliked the cramped accommodation provided in the Cabinet War Rooms.

Churchill's desk in his combined study and bedroom in the underground complex.

Calendars

Churchill's image was kept permanently in the public eye through his appearance on calendars – a clever marketing ploy, as every home and office had at least one.

Car ferry

MS Winston Churchill operated by the Danish shipping company Det Forenede Dan Skibs-Selskab A/S (DFDS) – The United Steamship Company of Copenhagen – on the Esbjerg to Harwich or Esbjerg to Newcastle routes during the 1960s and

Churchill's image was kept permanently in the public eye through appearances on calendars.

1970s. The Danes are ardent supporters of Churchill, dating from World War I when he argued that Britain should go to the aid of Denmark should her neutrality be violated by Germany. In 1950 Churchill was awarded an honorary degree from the University of Copenhagen and the city created Churchill Park in his honour containing the museum of the Danish Resistance Movement and a larger-than-life bust of Churchill by Oscar Nemon.

Cartoons

Like all prominent politicians, Churchill featured in numerous political cartoons. His actions were eagerly seized upon by every cartoonist in the land. Here are two examples highlighting activities at home and abroad. (See also *Punch Cartoons).*

Winston Churchill with his taxophone, by Blam. *The Bystander,* 14 April 1926.

Artist unknown. Roosevelt, Churchill and Stalin overcoming Hitler, Mussolini and Hirohito at dominoes, (c.1944).

Carved wood caricatures

Personalities and Events, an Aladdin's cave for royal, political and military memorabilia collectors in London's Camden Passage, commissions some captivating carved wood caricature figures of Churchill in various amusing poses. Expertly and individually hand carved and painted, some are mechanical. The figures range from RAF Churchill standing astride a Spitfire, Naval Churchill posed behind a warship to this 'Victory' Churchill dated 1874, 1965 and 1945. Prices for each piece, carved to order, are around £400.

'Victory' Churchill mechanical model.

Ceramic tiles

If you are so inclined you can clad your kitchen or bathroom wall with images of Churchill. I have never seen a room done out in wall-to-wall Winston but the material is available.

Left: A Spanish tile for the American market depicts Churchill peering over St Mary Aldermanbury – now the Churchill Memorial at Westminster College, Fulton, Missouri.

Right: This tile was sold in the UK in 1965, often mounted on a felt pad or recessed into a block of wood to act as a teapot stand.

Character jugs

Character jugs (sometimes called face jugs) can be traced back through the annals of history. The British Museum holds some impressive specimens discovered in ancient sites in Greece and Italy. Further examples provide an insight to the skills of the Inca potters of Peru. In medieval England potters produced some fairly primitive vessels which appear to have been quite vicious caricatures of their contemporaries, on a par with the satirical *Spitting Images* designs of the late 20th century.

In the Staffordshire potteries in the mid-18th century the art of producing figurative jugs reached a watershed. Ralph Wood pioneered a jug portraying a full-length seated or standing, human figure. The first, Toby Fillpot, became the archetype for the genre now known by the generic title of toby jugs. Improved techniques and materials allowed other potteries to produce character jugs portraying either a faithful and benevolent portrait of the subject or a cruelly distorted parody. Both forms have been continuously developed and are an important part of the output of modern potteries.

John Doulton opened his first pottery, at Lambeth, in 1815. Amongst the earliest products were brown stoneware salt-glazed character jugs of famous personalities. Admiral Lord Nelson, potted in 1821, is now considered to be the forerunner of the modern caricature jug. Napoleon was another early subject. John Doulton's son, Henry, purchased a second pottery in Burslem, Stoke-on-Trent, in 1877. The Burslem pottery, greatly extended, is now the headquarters of Royal Doulton, Lambeth having closed in 1956.

The event which was to lead to Royal Doulton becoming the world's leading and most renowned producer of character jugs occurred when Charles Noke joined the company as a modeller in 1889. Noke was eventually to become Art Director and serve Doulton for over fifty years. His designs were innovative and inspirational and were to propel Doulton into the pre-eminent position that other potteries could only aspire to. In many respects it is sad that Charles Noke's career should have ended on such an unhappy note when, at eighty-two years of age and a year before he died, he produced the ill-fated design for his Churchill loving cup.

Around 1901 one of the early successful character jugs was produced during Charles Noke's long tenure, although actually designed by Leslie Harradine, another celebrated Doulton modeller, was that of Theodore Roosevelt, the 26th President of the United States. Doulton had begun to build up an export trade to the United States which was given a great drive forward by their participation in the Philadelphia Centennial Exhibition of 1876. This created a great interest amongst the American public which was intensified at the Chicago International Exhibition of 1893. The Theodore Roosevelt character jug was to provide the ultimate catalyst; the great American cult for Doulton began which continues to this day.

Where Doulton led, other potteries followed. When, in 1939, Winston Churchill emerged from his 'wilderness years', every pottery in the land was eager to produce a Churchill character jug.

Royal Doulton. 1989
On the 50th anniversary of the outbreak of World War II Doulton launched *The Heroic Leaders*, a set of 3 numbered jugs – Churchill, Montgomery and Mountbatten, in a limited edition of 9,500. The jugs were only available as the set of three at £139. Modelled and signed by Stanley James Taylor the jug owed more than a little to the wartime Thorley Pottery jug. I fear that had Churchill still been alive this jug might have suffered the same fate as Charles Noke's Doulton 1940 Loving Cup!

Royal Doulton No D6170, Mark 1
In plain cream with black handles the 6½ inch vessel was inscribed on the base: *'Winston Spencer Churchill/Prime Minister of Britain/1940/ This loving cup was made during the Battle of Britain as a tribute to a great leader/Modelled by Noke.'*

Technically this is a loving cup, as it has two handles, but it is more commonly described as a character jug. Charles Noke's 1940 design for Royal Doulton has become a legend. Noke had trained as a modeller at the Worcester pottery before joining Royal Doulton. He had a long and distinguished career with Doulton, rising to Artistic Director, during which time he oversaw many highly successful designs and technical innovations.

In 1940, aged eighty-two, Noke started work on the design of a loving cup intended as a 'tribute to a great leader', following Churchill's appointment as Prime Minister. A jug was sent to 10 Downing Street for presentation to Churchill but, to Noke's dismay, the Prime Minister did not like it. He thought that the likeness was most unflattering, so Doulton swiftly withdrew the piece. Fewer than one hundred items were sold, at fifteen shillings each, before the recall, following which all remaining stock was destroyed. Those who bought one of the few that got away found they had acquired an appreciating asset.

In three London auctions during the 1990s examples of Chales Noke's character jug have made between £4,400 and £6,000. In one case the vendor had bought his prize at a Texas car boot sale for $15.

Royal Doulton No. D6170, Mark 2
Charles Noke went back to the drawing board and dispiritedly carried out some remodelling and colouring trials on his original design. By some means or other at least three different versions of his trial pieces 'escaped' from Burslem. One has since been heavily restored, none of them carry an inscription. They differ slightly in colouring shades but have dark blue shoulders, spotted bow ties, sandy hair and pale complexions. One has grey handles and another has dark brown handles. A combination of remodelling and colouring made Churchill look younger than he did on the original version. One of the three known jugs was auctioned at Sotheby's, Chester in 1989 making £16,500.

Charles Noke never completed the task. It is said that he never fully recovered from the shock of Churchill's disapproval and he died the following year, aged eighty-three.

Following Churchill's reaction to Noke's loving cup, Doulton immediately put Harry Fenton to work on modelling the toby jug which became an all-time success and remained in production for over fifty years.

1. Kirklands, Etruria Stoke-on-Trent. 1939
If not the first, certainly the best of the jugs commemorating Churchill's return to office as First Lord of the Admiralty at the outbreak of World War II. Superbly modelled in plain creamy-white china, the jug portrays Churchill as a ship's figurehead with his face swathed in bow waves. A very small number of an unattractive coloured edition of this jug are in circulation, possibly trial pieces. UK value £200+; USA up to $400.

2. Shorter & Son Stoke-on-Trent. 1939
Painting lets this jug down – Churchill is given stark black hair and eyebrows. S Fielding & Co (Crown Devon), another Shorter family company, used the same moulds and produced a more correctly decorated jug – some of which included a musical movement in the base which played a tune when the jug was lifted. Current UK value £150 – more with the musical movement; USA $250+. But beware: modern replicas have been made using the original Shorter moulds.

3. Minton, Stoke-on-Trent. 1941
In 1941 Churchill took to wearing the cap of the Royal Yacht Squadron and a double-breasted brass-buttoned coat whenever he visited naval establishments or sailed on one of HM ships. His 'naval' uniform was immortalised by photographers, cartoonists and pottery modellers. This fine jug in pale blue-grey earthenware was modelled and signed by Eric Owen. Over £400 has been paid at auction in the UK and up to $800 in the USA.

4. J&G Meakin. 1941
Modelled, signed and dated by Frank Potts. Creamy-white earthenware. Now around £120-£140 on the UK secondary market and up to $450 in the USA.

5. Avon Ware c1941
Embossed *'England'* on the base. A minimum of facial colouring on an ochre earthenware body and a king-sized cigar. The modeller has given Churchill a gold-braided and splendidly badged cap of an admiral of the Royal Navy. The handle simulates a rope. UK £30-£50; US $60-$80.

6. Burgess & Leigh (Burleighware) 1941. (Reissued 1965)
Modelled by Ernest Bailey, who also designed two Churchill toby jugs for Burgess & Leigh in 1941. 5½ inches high. Embossed underneath: *'We shall defend every village, every town and every city – Churchill, 1940'*. Also issued in plain white and two smaller sizes (3 inches high and 2 inches high). The wartime coloured versions had a green handle; the 1965 reissue had a brown handle and the additional date embossed. The larger size, both issues, has made up to £200 at auction in the UK, $275 in the US. The miniature version of the wartime issue is very scarce and often sells for as much as the largest jug.

7. Wilton Pottery, Cobridge Stoke-on-Trent. 1941
A nicely modelled and painted jug from one of the smaller potteries. Backstamped, *'We shall not flag nor fall. We shall go on to the end. 1940. The Rt Hon Winston Churchill MP. Prime Minister'*. Value UK £150-£200; US $300. Sometimes more for uncoloured version, (see below).

8. Wilton Pottery, Cobridge Stoke-on-Trent. 1941
The uncoloured version of Wilton Pottery's jug. This one is backstamped, *'Churchill. Never was so much owed by so many to so few. 1940'*.

9. Grimwades (Royal Winton) Stoke-on-Trent. 1941
Made in up to five sizes – from 7 inches high down to a 2¾ inches high miniature – and at least two different colourways. Nicely modelled and painted. Backstamped *'Rt Hon Winston Churchill, Premier of Great Britain, The man of the year'*. The largest jug has a value of £200+ in the UK ($400 in the USA) but the miniature size can be found for less than £50 ($80).

10. Barry Potter. Date unknown
Indistinctly embossed underneath *'Barry Potter (?) R34 RWS F25'*. Crude modelling, roughly potted and amateurishly painted. May be by a pottery apprentice or student who used the Grimwades jug as a reference.

Royal Doulton D6170 (Mark 1) character jug by Charles Noke. 1940.

Royal Doulton D6170 (Mark 2) revised character jug by Charles Noke. 1941.

1. Kirklands, Etruria, Stoke-on-Trent. 1939

4. J&G Meakin. 1941

7. Wilton Pottery, Cobridge
Stoke-on-Trent. 1941

10. Barry Potter. Date unknown

2. Shorter & Son, Stoke-on-Trent. 1939

5. Avon Ware. c1941

8. Wilton Pottery, Cobridge
Stoke-on-Trent. 1941

11. Pottery unknown. Date unknown

3. Minton, Stoke-on-Trent. 1941

6. Burgess & Leigh (Burleighware). 1941
(Reissued 1965)

9. Grimwades (Royal Winton)
Stoke-on-Trent. 1941

12. Pottery unknown. 1941-45

11. Pottery unknown
Date unknown
An infrequently seen yachting cap design. This has a simple anchor badge. Unmarked. A love it or hate it representation of Churchill with a rubicund expression.

12. Pottery unknown. 1941-45
This design came in at least three sizes and several different finishes. All are unglazed and the standard of paintwork, usually no more than four colours, is very variable. I suspect that the jugs may well have been potted by a single pottery and sent out in blank white form to various independent decorators. Traditionally, many potteries have used out-worker painters, often ladies working part-time at home, and some potteries specialise in producing only blank whiteware which is despatched around the world for others to decorate. This particular jug is 7 inches high and has an all-over gold finish – one of the nicest. Perhaps £20-£30 in the UK but, I am told, may fetch up to $300 in the USA.

13. Pottery unknown. 1941-45
Another very common wartime design. All the jugs of this size to this pattern are embossed *'126/3 British made'* but have no other backstamp. Again there are at least three size variations and an infinite number of paintwork qualities. The best were glazed after painting. Depending upon quality, these jugs will now cost up to £50 in the UK ($200-$300 in the USA).

14. Thorley China. 1941
A side-mounted handle in the shape of a flagpole flying the Union Flag was the unusual design feature of this otherwise undistinguished little jug. Interestingly the design was closely replicated in 1989 by Royal Doulton for its *'Heroic Leaders'* jug. Usually under £40 in the UK, but up to $125 in the USA.

15. Pottery and date unknown
Embossed *'No. 78'* and signed with the decorator's initials *'DA'*. A diminutive and unremarkable jug that has a hole drilled in the corner of Churchill's mouth; came with a supply of cigars which could be inserted in the hole and lit to produce a glow and a curl of smoke.

16. Grimwades (Royal Winton), Stoke-on-Trent. 1941
The largest of the five 'Royal Winton' Churchill character jugs of the same design, this one 7 inches high. Backstamped *'Rt Hon Winston Churchill, Premier of Great Britain, The man of the year'.* Probably designed by Billy Grindy who later went on to model jugs for Thomas Wild (Royal Albert) and Shaw & Copestake (SylvaC). Grimwade's, established in 1886, better known for tablewares, formed a design studio during World War II dedicated to creating character jugs to enhance their export sales – a Canadian Mountie, Roosevelt, General MacArthur, an Indian Chief, Smuts, King George VI and Uncle Sam, along with the Winston Churchill range, were among the more successful.

17. Thorley China. 1941
The Thorley Pottery issued two character jugs and a toby jug in 1941 although some collectors dispute that the toby, titled *'The Captain'*, was meant to represent Winston Churchill. Thorley Pottery's 3½ inch high decorated Churchill character jug was not a convincing piece and the undecorated miniature version illustrated here, just 1½ inches high, is probably their best. The crisp modelling is, if anything, enhanced by the overall plain pale green body colour. This jug is seldom found around the secondary market but should cost no more than about £20. No sightings have been reported in the USA. The same mould was used to produce a decorated jug with the *'Snel Ware'* backstamp.

18. Wilton Pottery, Cobridge Stoke-on-Trent. 1941
A variant of the Wilton Pottery jug. This one has Churchill smoking a cigar and the backstamp reads *'Never was so much owed by so many to so few'* instead of *'We shall not flag nor fail. We shall go on to the end'.* Value as per the coloured and uncoloured versions without the cigar.

19. Pottery unknown
World War II
Weak moulding and poor paintwork. This example has a large hole in the left-hand end of Churchill's mouth which once contained a large cigar. Another variation of the badging on the cap – this one is a 'V'.

13. Pottery unknown. 1941-45

16. Grimwades (Royal Winton) Stoke-on-Trent. 1941

14. Thorley China. 1941

17. Thorley China. 1941

15. Pottery and date unknown.

18. Wilton Pottery, Cobridge Stoke-on-Trent. 1941

19. Pottery unknown.
World War II

20. Lancaster's, Hanley.
World War II

21. Cooper Clayton, Staffordshire
World War II

22. Arthur Bowker
Fenton. 1951-55

23. Shorter & Son.
World War II

24. Staffordshire Fine Ceramics
Tunstall, Stoke-on-Trent. 1980s

20. Lancaster's
Hanley. World War II

Embossed beneath *'Regd'* but also back-stamped *'Registration applied for'* – an odd contradiction of terms! Unusual handle consisting of a cigar and a twisted rope. Quite nicely painted. £10-£25 on the UK secondary market, $50 in the USA.

21. Cooper Clayton, Staffordshire
World War II

Not a good likeness of Churchill. The jug is embossed *'Churchill'* across the back of the shoulders, thus removing any doubt as to the modeller's intentions. Offered in two sizes with a walking stick handle. UK secondary market; Large £14-£20, Small £5-£10.

22. Arthur Bowker
Fenton. 1951-55

Arthur Bowker's pottery in King Street, Fenton produced bone china wares for just ten years – from 1948 to 1958. During its decade in operation Arthur Bowker made only five character jugs, but he had the distinction of making the only known Clementine Churchill jug, as well as this Winston Churchill jug.

Unfortunately, both jugs were very poor likenesses and largely scorned by collectors. The Churchill jug was first issued in 1951 to mark Churchill's second premiership, but the unlikely combination of black 'naval' cap and astrakhan-collared coat, together with inexpert facial modelling resulted in a low level of sales at a time when the market was saturated with Churchilliana. Rarely seen on the UK secondary market where it may be priced at up to £45. Has been spotted in a US catalogue at $100.

23. Shorter & Son
World War II

This oddly hand-painted jug gives Churchill a green jacket, a brown shirt and a yellow bow tie. Shorter backstamp and embossed mark *'Churchill SS'*.

24. Staffordshire Fine Ceramics
Tunstall, Stoke-on-Trent. 1980s

Staffordshire Fine Ceramics produce a wide range of character jugs, toby jugs and collectors' teapots mostly for export – predominantly to the USA. As well as its own in-house designs SFC regularly re-uses moulds acquired from other potteries. They reused the original Shorter mould to recreate *'Sir Winston Churchill'* for its 'London Series' of six jugs (the others were John Bull, Henry VIII, a Beefeater, a Guardsman and a Chelsea Pensioner). A few of these jugs sold in the UK at £13-£14. The paintwork is altogether superior to the Shorter original.

25. Snel Ware
Probably World War II

Backstamped *'Snel Ware, Made in England, Winston Churchill'* and also embossed *'Winston Churchill'*. From the front it looks as if Churchill is wearing a beret but at the back, the rim of a much truncated homburg hat can be seen. The arrangement provides a pouring lip opposite the handle and greater functional capability than many character jugs. UK price £10-£15.

26. Morlor, Staffordshire
Probably World War II

In this case a functional pouring lip is provided by giving Churchill a somewhat peaky forehead. Better than average paintwork. UK secondary market price £10-£12.

27. Old Ellgreave Pottery
Burslem. Early 1980s

Wood & Sons of Burslem, founded by the famous 18th century potter Ralph Wood, went into liquidation in 1981. Tony Wood started a new company at Fenton – the Tony Wood Family Pottery – but went out of business in 1984 following a fire. Mark Bolton then bought the name and restarted the business as Wood Potters of Burslem. This jug was issued in the first half of the decade somewhere between the first liquidation and the second restart. It has a Wood impressed pattern number.

28. Wood Potters of Burslem
Since c1985

From the same mould and has the same pattern number as the *'Old Elgreave'* version. One of three colourways available and this, in a simulation of traditional brown and ochre salt-glazed stoneware, is easily the most successful. Around £15 in UK high street china shops.

Noble Ceramics Hampshire. 1995
One of the best 50th anniversary of VE Day commemoratives. A large jug – 8 inches tall x 9½ inches wide. Limited edition of 1,000. The handle incorporates cameo portraits of Eisenhower, Montgomery, Stalin and Roosevelt and there is a diorama of battle scenes on the back. Price in the UK £199.

25. Snel Ware.
Probably World War II

28. Wood Potters of Burslem
Since c1985

31. Artone, England
Early 1980s

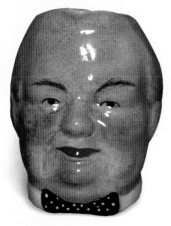

26. Morlor, Staffordshire
Probably World War II

29. Staffordshire Fine Ceramics
Tunstall. 1980s

32. Wood & Sons
England. 1980

27. Old Ellgreave Pottery
Burslem. Early 1980s

30. Shaw & Copestake, Longton
(SylvaC). 1970s

33. A Portuguese pottery
c1990

29. Staffordshire Fine Ceramics Tunstall. 1980s

A reissue of a jug originally made some years earlier by Shaw & Copestake (SylvaC) – it carries the same mould number. This one was principally made for export to the USA but was sold in a small number of UK outlets, mainly in tourist centres and at Heathrow Airport, at around £20-£25.

30. Shaw & Copestake, Longton (SylvaC). 1970s

The Sylvan Pottery closed in 1982 and this jug was almost certainly made during its final decade. A coloured version was also made – the forerunner of the Staffordshire Fine Ceramics jug. About £20 now on the UK secondary market, more for the coloured version.

31. Artone, England. Early 1980s

Very similar to a Wood & Sons design but less crisply moulded. Not so well painted.

32. Wood & Sons, England. 1980

The *'Pride of Britain'* series was one of the last from this 200 year old company before it went into liquidation. The moulds were reused by the Tony Wood Family Pottery, before it too went out of business in 1984, but the later jugs have colouring differences. The *'Pride of Britain'* jug originally sold in UK high street china shops for around £30 but it was not long before bankrupt stock was seen on the secondary market at £10.

33. A Portuguese pottery. c1990

Completely unmarked. Was being sold from market stalls in the UK for £10-£15, in the early 1990s, packed in a flimsy cardboard box labelled simply *'Churchill'* and *'Portugal'*. Those are the only clues to the subject and the provenance! A large, but very poorly painted jug.

34. Royce Wood, Derby. 1980s

Freelance modeller Royce Wood briefly ran her own studio pottery in the 1980s producing a series of jugs entitled *'The Pageantry and History of England'*. Her Winston Churchill jug, crisply modelled but garishly painted, is not a good likeness, but sports the 'props' – a homburg hat, a bow tie, a cigar and a 'V' on the handle.

34. Royce Wood, Derby. 1980s

36. Royal Doulton. 1991

38. Royal Doulton. 1992

40. Staffordshire Fine Ceramics. 1980s

35. Prestige Jugs
(Peggy Davies Ceramics). 1989

37. Kelsboro Ware, England
Date unknown

39. Kevin Francis Ceramics. 1993

41. Bairstow Manor Pottery
Hanley. 1999

35. Prestige Jugs (Peggy Davies Ceramics). 1989
The first of of a rich collection of Churchilliana from Peggy Davies. Various colourways. £20 in the UK; $125 in USA.

36. Royal Doulton. 1991
A slightly premature commemoration of the 50th anniversary of VE-Day – stealing a march on rival potteries. The handle is a replica of the front page of the *News Chronicle* of 8 May 1945. Modelled by Stanley James Taylor and an improvement on his *Heroic Leaders* design. Around £25 in UK china shops but $125 in the USA.

37. Kelsboro Ware, England Date unknown
On this jug a cigar forms the handle at the back. Nicely painted. Scarce.

38. Royal Doulton. 1992
'The Character Jug of the Year', modelled by Stanley James Taylor – his third and most successful Churchill jug. Doulton's RRP was £75 but many china shops were offering 10%, or more, discount. Every year Doulton issue a Jug of the Year, only to be sold during that year; then moulds are destroyed on 31 December. Thus the edition is 'limited' to whatever sales are achieved by a 12 months' promotional budget (bearing in mind that some of Doulton's designs are in production for over fifty years).

39. Kevin Francis Ceramics. 1993
A limited edition of 750. Modelled by Ray Noble. Described as a *'Character Bust – highly innovative it looks like a bust from the front but has a handle and a pouring hole at the back'*. Well, the pouring performance of many character jugs is limited. For this one it is negligible! Nevertheless a nicely modelled and painted jug with a bulldog medallion in the handle. UK price £65; USA $160.

40. Staffordshire Fine Ceramics 1980s
A diminutive little jug in the SFC's 'War Heroes' series – a set of eight including Churchill, Montgomery, Mountbatten, MacArthur, Eisenhower, De Gaulle, Smuts and Rommel. Sold in the UK at £61.60 for the set or £7.70 for any individual jug. SFC told me that 70-80% of this series was exported, substantially to the USA.

41. Bairstow Manor Pottery Hanley. 1999
In 1999 Bairstow Manor Pottery of Hanley produced a range of caricature character jugs portraying all the British Prime Ministers since 1940. Each subject was to be produced in a limited edition of 1500. Only Margaret Thatcher was instantly recognisable, although rather cruelly portrayed, since she was the only lady present. Guessing which was meant to be Churchill, without turning it over to read the backstamp, was aided by the usual props of a spotted bow tie and a cigar! £20.

Character jug moulds

Why does the 1939 Shorter & Son character jug look a lot like the 1990 Staffordshire Fine Ceramics character jug? Answer, because they are from the same mould. Shorter & Son went out of business 1974 and some of their moulds were later acquired by Staffordshire Fine Ceramics of Tunstall.

The moulds created by Shorter & Son in 1939 for their character jug which honoured Churchill's appointment as First Lord of the Admiralty were destined to become very well used. Fielding's acquired Shorter's in 1964 and used the moulds again to make a jug with a musical movement in the base. When Fielding's were taken over in 1976 many of the Shorter moulds were acquired by Staffordshire Fine Ceramics who produced three new versions (a) with added cigar, (b) with top hat and (c) with top hat and spout to form a teapot. In the late 1990s the moulds were purchased by Cortman's of Burslem who produced a wide variety of new colourways.

Shorter & Sons commemorative jug. 1939

Staffordshire Fine Ceramics jug. c1990

Cortman jug. Late 1990s

Cortman jug (variant). Late 1990s

Chartwell

A small stream rises from a spring on the side of a short valley in the Kentish hills south of Westerham – the Chart Well. In the middle of the fourteenth century local archives record that the land containing the Chart Well was in the ownership of one William-at-Well. Over almost 500 years the property passed through the hands of just four families until, in 1848, it was purchased by John Campbell Colquhoun. The building then on the site, a fairly modest farmhouse, was greatly enlarged by Mr Colquhoun into a solid Victorian country manor house.

By 1922 the manor house, and 80 acres of surrounding land, had been unoccupied for

many years and was in a considerable state of dereliction. It was put up for auction by the family of John Colquhoun but failed to reach the reserve price of £6,500. Winston Churchill purchased Chartwell Manor for £5,000 in September 1922 a few days after the birth of his youngest daughter, Mary (Lady Soames). Churchill was then forty-seven and Colonial Secretary, but within a month had undergone an operation for appendicitis and lost his Parliamentary seat and his ministerial post when defeated in the general election at Dundee. Clementine, who had been in an advanced state of pregnancy when first informed of Winston's intentions, was not at first best pleased with the impending purchase. She felt that she had not been properly consulted. She was appalled by the near derelict state

of the property and concerned that Winston could neither afford the purchase price nor the cost of the necessary and extensive restoration.

The architect, Philip Tilden, was appointed to carry out what amounted to a virtual rebuilding of Chartwell. In his memoirs *True Remembrances* (*Country Life* 1954), Tilden describes the despair he felt after his first visit and his discovery of the extent to which damp and decay had made *'such an inroad into the very bones of the building'*. He went on to find out that while his clients' enthusiastic interference in the restoration programme was totally uncoordinated, it was also exhilarating and exasperating! He recalled one frantic Saturday afternoon, with the restoration

work almost complete, when Winston suddenly cast a doubt over whether the overflow pipes from the baths were big enough to take the volume of water should both taps be left running. *'My dear Mr Tilden,'* said Winston, *'have you not conceived that it is possible for a man, or woman for that matter, to be so engrossed upon some matter of such absorbing interest that he or she might leave the taps disgorging at full flow and thereby imperil the structure by the infiltration of water through the plaster ceilings?'* There followed a divertissement of an hour or so whilst everyone rushed from bathroom to bathroom, turning all taps full on, whilst checking for leaks through the ceilings.

The family moved into Chartwell in 1924. The restoration had cost £18,000. Sir Martin Gilbert has written that the total cost of the property and its refurbishment was paid for from the £40,000 advance Churchill received for *The World Crisis* – a phenomenal sum of money in those days. Winston was nearly 50 and Chartwell was to be his principal home until his death over 40 years later. One of his objectives in buying Chartwell, according to Philip Tilden, had been to upstage his friend Lloyd George. Lloyd George's house at Churt had a fish pond, fed by a stream that issued from the hillside. Winston must have a lake – no, two lakes! By building a series of dams he would produce an expanse of water greater, and far more impressive, than that at Churt.

At the end of October 1924 Churchill was re-elected to the House of Commons as MP for Epping and, early in the following month, was appointed Chancellor of the Exchequer in Stanley Baldwin's government – an office he was to hold until 1929. It was a turbulent period to be in charge of the nation's finances but Churchill seemed to revel in the succession of political predicaments and still find time lead a full family life at Chartwell. Contemporary photographs show him, with one or other of his children, riding, swimming, building a snowman and laying bricks.

The Labour Party won the general election of May 1929 and it was to be more than ten years before Churchill held office again.

Top: A view of the house from the southeast. Churchill's principal home from 1924 until his death. *(Photo courtesy The National Trust).*

Left: Churchill's study at the very heart of the house, perhaps the most evocative of all the rooms at Chartwell. It remains essentially as Churchill left it for the last time in October 1964. This was his workshop, where he wrote or dictated his books, his speeches, his letters, his memoranda. From the rafters hangs his standard as a Knight of the Garter.

Above: The Oscar Nemon statue of Winston and Clementine is the latest major addition to the glories of Chartwell, located at the end of the lake but out of sight of the house. The National Trust were anxious that nothing should intrude upon the view which Winston would have had across the grounds. Unveiled by HM Queen Elizabeth the Queen Mother on 13 November 1990, it marks the 50th anniversary of Churchill's appointment as Prime Minister and the 25th anniversary of his death.

In some respects those 'wilderness years' were to be his most creative decade at Chartwell. He spent much of the time writing books, including *My Early Life* (1930), *The Eastern Front* (1931), *Thoughts and Adventures* (1932), *Marlborough* (1933) and *Great Contemporaries* (1937). Visitors ranged from Charlie Chaplin to the former French Prime Minister Léon Blum, from the clandestine visits of Ralph Wigram to a team of journalists from *Picture Post*.

A journalist working for the *Sevenoaks Chronicle*, Percy Reid, lived in Westerham from the mid-1930s, working as a reporter to most of the London national newspapers and news agencies. Opportunities to boost his salary were considerable with Winston Churchill living on his patch, so to avoid making fruitless journeys up the steep hill from Westerham, Reid devised a method of finding out when Churchill was at home.

The local newsagent, Mr Bodger, had a contract to deliver the national newspapers to Chartwell whenever Churchill was there, and this included the official organ of the Communist Party, the *Daily Worker*. Mr Bodger remarked that it was the only copy of that particular paper he ever sold locally. So Reid deduced that whenever he saw the *Daily Worker* displayed for sale outside the newsagents shop, then it had to be the copy not delivered to Chartwell that day and therefore Churchill was not at home.

The main house at Chartwell was closed during World War II. It was considered too easily identifiable from the air and too close for comfort to the invasion-prone Kent coast. However, Churchill did make rare visits during the war years to stay in the cottage he had built himself in 1928.

After losing the 1945 election Churchill feared that his reduced income would no longer allow him to maintain Chartwell. Lord Camrose suggested that a consortium of Churchill's friends should purchase the property for £50,000. Churchill could then continue to live there, for a nominal rent of £350 per year, for the rest of his life, after which Chartwell would pass to the National Trust as a permanent memorial. Churchill was delighted. He remained in residence until three months before his death.

In the summer of 1976, the National Trust presented a series of son et lumière performances at Chartwell in aid of the White Cliffs of Dover Appeal. Churchill, as Lord Warden of the Cinque Ports from 1941 until his death, would surely have been happy to know that the proceeds of the son et lumière festival in the grounds of his beloved Chartwell would be devoted to safeguarding those cliffs on which he stood defiantly in 1940. The part of Churchill was played by Nigel Stock, Barbara Jefford played Clementine and Harold Macmillan and Sarah Churchill played themselves.

On 16 October 1987 a wind of hurricane force blew across much of southern England. One of the greatest storms ever experienced in England was responsible for blowing down 15 million trees, some of them over 400 years old, upending telephone lines, cutting off electricity supplies, blocking roads and even tossing ships onto the shore. The storm wreaked terrible devastation at Chartwell where one

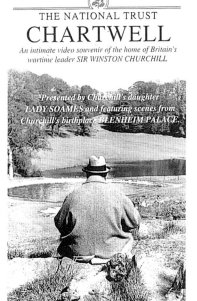

An evocative photograph of Churchill looking out over the lake at Chartwell adorns the cover of a National Trust video souvenir.

of its great glories, the spectacular horse-shoe of beech trees, was snapped and stricken like matchwood. Winston S Churchill Junior wrote: 'It was a mercy that my grandfather was no longer around to witness the scenes of devastation in the valley that he loved so much ... he would have been unconsolable'. In the wake of the storm Prime Minister Lady Thatcher visited Chartwell to plant some new trees.

Above: Lady Thatcher poses behind Oscar Nemon's statue of Winston and Clementine.

Top: Chartwell painted by International Churchill Society member Howard Pedraza.

Chequers

Chequers is just over a mile northeast of Princes Risborough in Buckinghamshire. The 16th century mansion standing in extensive grounds was offered to the nation in 1917 by Sir Arthur Lee, Conservative MP for Fareham, Hampshire (who in the following year became Baron Lee of Fareham), on the condition that it should become the official country home of the Prime Minister. Political and legal problems delayed the drawing up of a suitable trust deed to cover the transfer of the property, and its subsequent upkeep. The deed of gift was signed on 8 January 1921 and Lloyd George moved in on the same day!

Less than a month later Lloyd George invited Winston Churchill to join him for the weekend. Winston was accompanied by his two-year-old daughter Marigold. He wrote to Clementine: *'My darling, Here I am. You would like to see this place. Perhaps you will some day! It is just the kind of house you admire – a panelled museum full of history, full of treasures – but insufficiently warmed – anyhow a wonderful possession...'* Winston made his second visit in June that same year, but Clementine did not *'get to see the place'* until June 1940 when she accompanied her husband on his first entitled visit as Prime Minister. Thereafter, except when the moon was high (see Ditchley Park), Chequers

was the Churchills' principal weekend retreat throughout the war. The weekends were far from being relaxing and restful. They were working weekends, with the family and friends usually greatly outnumbered by cabinet ministers, service chiefs, civil servants and various advisers who had been invited to dine and sleep. The legions of security staff, secretaries, phone operators, chauffeurs, messengers and so on, made the place resemble a busy hotel. The small number of domestics supervised by Miss Grace Lamont, was augmented by volunteers from the ATS and WAAF, a practice which continues even today.

On the weekend following the declaration of results for the 1945 election, Winston and Clementine, and most of the family, gathered at Chequers. The atmosphere was subdued. After dinner on Sunday 29 July, everybody signed the visitors book. Winston was last to sign and, beneath his name, he added *'Finis'*. A postscript which, although understandable in the circumstances, turned out to be profoundly inaccurate!

High on the east wall of the Great Hall at Chequers was Rubens' painting of *The Lion and the Mouse* based on Aesop's fable. The tiny mouse, gnawing at the net ensnaring the lion, was barely visible from floor level. One evening, Churchill sent for his paints and brushes and, using a ladder, ascended to highlight the mouse! In 1974

Stained glass window in the Long Gallery.

the picture was loaned to the Churchill Centenary Exhibition at Somerset House and cleaned, before being returned to Chequers. Alas, Churchill's additional brushwork had been removed. Not even a Prime Minister/Honorary Academician Extraordinary should tinker with a Rubens!

The Long Gallery on the first floor at Chequers runs for almost the entire length of the north front. The walls are lined with bookshelves holding around 5,000 volumes including the biographies of all the Prime Ministers who have resided at Chequers. At the west end of the gallery is a stained glass window initiated by Lord Lee and containing the heraldic bearings of all previous occupants of the house including every Prime Minister since Lloyd George. Churchill's window records his two periods of residence: May 1940 to July 1945 and October 1951 to April 1955.

Left: The Lion and the Mouse painted by Sir Peter Paul Rubens (1577-1640).

Right: A scarce good-quality wartime card, printed on thick glazed stock, with a portrait of Churchill but no indication of the artist. The reverse is printed with a standard layout and the publisher's code GPD 365/21/6.

During his 1951-55 premiership Churchill was a less frequent visitor to Chequers. He preferred Chartwell although Clementine, who was very fond of Chequers, recognised that its larger size, together with its flexible arrangements with domestic staff, made Chequers more suitable for entertaining on the Churchillian scale. The family spent all four Christmases of Churchill's second premiership at Chequers. The weekend of 25-27 March 1955 was to be Winston's last at Chequers. He resigned on 5 April.

Clementine paid another visit. Aged eighty-six, in November 1971 the Prime Minister of the day, Edward Heath, invited her to lunch. His invitation had been extended to allow her to see Winston's own painting, which she had presented to Chequers, hanging in the house. She took delight in pointing out where Winston had climbed, paintbrush in hand, to highlight the little mouse on the vast Rubens painting of *The Lion and the Mouse*. Also, she could see the growth of the avenue of beech trees, planted sixteen years earlier, which had been presented by Winston and herself.

Christmas cards

From Christmas 1940 onwards, as a change from the usual scenes of snow, holly and robins, it was possible to send seasonal greetings to your friends on a card bearing

Photography by Mark Fiennes, reproduced by kind permission of the Trustees of Chequers Estate.

THE RT. HON. WINSTON S. CHURCHILL

With every good wish Christmas 1944

For Freedom

a portrait of Winston Churchill. So popular was the man that the cards sold in their thousands. Unfortunately many of the cards were printed on poor quality paper which had to conform to the 'Authorized War Economy Standard', *so* after more than fifty years they have become badly discoloured, spotted and foxed.

Frank Salisbury's *Blood, Sweat and Tears* (p.104) portrait of Churchill appeared on a wartime Christmas card published by Harrison & Sons. Salisbury (1874-1962) had been commissioned to paint the portrait in 1943 for the Constitutional Club. It is interesting to note that 36 years later, in 1979, when Margaret Thatcher was Prime Minister, she requisitioned the portrait from the club to hang at 10 Downing Street and it remained there until the fall of the Conservatives in 1997, when it was removed by the incoming administration and was sold at Sotheby's for £151,000.

Churchill College, Cambridge

When Churchill resigned his second premiership in April 1955 he left, almost immediately, for a holiday at the *Villa Politi* in Sicily accompanied by his wife, Lord Cherwell and Jock Colville. One day Churchill, Cherwell and Colville were discussing a range of topics when Churchill remarked that he regretted having not taken up Cherwell's recommendations to improve the training of British technologists, while Prime Minister. Cherwell and Colville replied that it wasn't too late and Colville volunteered to raise the money to establish an institute similar to the Massachusetts Institute of Technology. Within five years Churchill College, Cambridge was founded. Churchill himself contributed £25,000 and a public appeal for £3.5 million was launched. Sir John Cockroft, the physicist and former Director of the Atomic Energy Research Establishment, was appointed as its first Master and on 17 October 1959 Churchill flew to Cambridge to mark the occasion by planting an oak tree on the proposed site of the college. The formal opening of the college was performed by the Duke of Edinburgh on 5 June 1964. Winston was not well enough to attend so was represented by Clementine and Randolph.

Churchill College was the first Oxbridge college to admit both male and female undergraduates. Designed by Richard Sheppard, the uncompromisingly modern building is in stark contrast to most of the venerable Cambridge colleges. Its edge-of-town location sets it apart from the long established institutions. It gains advantage from its comfortable and functional accommodation – not least in the attractive and well-appointed halls of residence.

Amongst the works of art in the college are, in the Dining Hall, a copy by John Leigh Pemberton, of the 1916 portrait of Churchill by Sir William Orpen and a very large bronze bust sculpted by Oscar Nemon. The College library is dedicated to Ernest Bevin (a Labour member of Churchill's wartime coalition government) and was paid for by a £50,000 donation from the Transport & General Workers' Union.

The purpose-built Churchill Archives Centre was added in 1973. Funded by a group of prominent Americans, including every US ambassador to London from 1925 to 1973, the centre holds Churchill family documents and those of many other personalities from the Churchill era.

Above: The 1963 Oscar Nemon bust of Churchill at the entrance to the Dining Hall, presented to the college by HM Government.

Top: Ten connecting courts of three-storey brick and concrete in the style of the 1960s.

Right: Churchill by John Leigh Pemberton.

Churchill crown

Silver-plated crown mounted on a hallmarked silver chain. Enamelled crown mounted on a silver plated belt buckle. Enamelled crown on a gold plated chain.

The Churchill commemorative crown coin was announced on 16 March 1965, just seven weeks after Churchill's death. Only four commemorative coins had previously been issued in the UK and this would be the first to feature the head of a commoner on the same coin as the monarch. Mary Gillick's portrait of HM the Queen on the obverse would be the same as that on all the coinage issued since 1953, but the reverse design would be specially commissioned from Churchill's favourite sculptor, Oscar Nemon.

The Royal Proclamation authorising the design of the coin was signed by the Queen on 3 August 1965. Lady Churchill started the coining press at the Royal Mint in September and was presented with the first Churchill crown to be struck. Later the Queen visited the Royal Mint and struck a further example of the coin which was also presented to Lady Churchill. Distribution of the coins began on 11 October 1965 and production continued until the summer of 1966 to satisfy demand.

Reaction to Nemon's effigy of Churchill was mixed and Nemon himself was said to be dissatisfied with the design complaining of having been rushed to meet the Royal Mint's deadline. 19,640,000 Churchill crowns were struck – more than enough to ensure that the coin, in spite of the aspirations of certain dealers, would never have a rarity value.

The Churchill crown does not carry a statement of its face value but continues to be legal tender and is worth, as it has always been, just five shillings or twenty-five pence. To add value jewellers and enamellers have plated Churchill crowns with silver or gold and mounted them on such objects as trinket boxes, pin trays, pendants and belt buckles.

Churchill Homes for Elderly People

When Leader of the Opposition after 1945, Churchill gave his patronage to a charitable enterprise, managed by the Church Army, which provided sheltered accommodation for the elderly, known as The Churchill Homes for Elderly People. By November 1954, a week before Churchill's 80th birthday, forty-six Churchill Homes had been established. Clementine, an active supporter of the project, visited Sevenoaks, eight miles from Chartwell, to open the forty-seventh house. She wrote to Winston: *'One of the old lady*

residents gave me this blotter for you. It seems that 500 old ladies live in the 47 Churchill Houses sprinkled up and down the country... The waiting list for a room in a Churchill House is over seven thousand!' (Signed) *Your devoted old Clem-Pussy Bird.'*

The residents had subscribed to an 80th birthday gift for Winston, which they had presented to Clementine. It was a silver blotter inscribed, *'To the Right Hon. Sir Winston Churchill KG OM CH MP on his 80th birthday, 30th November 1954, with affectionate greetings from the tenants of all Churchill Houses, Church Army Housing.'* The silver knob of the blotter is engraved with the initials *'WSC'*.

Churchill was delighted with the gift and wrote to Miss DE Richardson, one of the organisers of homes. *'The beautiful silver blotter will be constantly on my desk and will be a reminder to me of the good-will so kindly expressed in the message of greetings inscribed upon it.'* To this day the blotter remains where Churchill placed it on his desk in the library at Chartwell.

Churchill tank

Closing a debate in the House of Commons on 2 July 1942 the Prime Minister, Winston Churchill, said: *'This tank, the A22, was ordered off the drawing-board, and large numbers went into production very quickly. As might be expected, it had many defects and teething troubles, and when these became apparent the tank was appropriately rechristened the* Churchill. *These defects have now largely been overcome. I am sure that this tank will prove, in the end, to be a powerful, massive and serviceable weapon of war.'* Churchill's impish sense of humour lightened the mood of an otherwise solemn debate and his concluding prognosis proved to be entirely accurate.

The tank was designed by Vauxhall Motors, who were instructed to transfer it from the drawing-board into production within one year, so that the A22 *Churchill* could be delivered to Army units in June 1941.

The early problems were resolved and by the time the tank was committed to action in the following year it was fully operational.

It was to become the most successful British tank of World War II. As an infantry battle tank it was developed into eleven different marks – with varying armament, turret design, armour and performance. There were also two specialised versions. The *Churchill AVRE* (Assault Vehicle: Royal Engineers) carried a 290mm Petard mortar in the turret instead of the usual howitzer, which fired a 401b bomb – known as *General Wade's Flying Dustbin* – capable of cracking open concrete fortifications. The *AVRE* could also carry a large fascine for filling in anti-tank ditches, a 30ft box girder bridge and a roll of steel mesh which could be unrolled ahead of the tank to provide a firm track over soft ground. It was undoubtedly a versatile vehicle, with the dual capability of construction and destruction. It was much loved by its crews and envied by the Americans, for its ability to traverse terrain which brought other tanks to a standstill.

Perhaps the most famous specialised version of the A22 *Churchill* – or most infamous according to the Wehrmacht – was the *Crocodile*. The *Croc* was an adaptation of the Mark VII *Churchill* equipped with a flame-throwing device capable of projecting a jet of blazing fluid up to 120 yards. The fuel, pressurised with a nitrogen propellant, was carried in a two-wheeled armoured trailer towed behind the tank and the flame-thrower was fitted in the space normally occupied by the hull machine gun. When all the flammable material had been used the trailer could be jettisoned and the parent vehicle would then fight on as a conventional tank. The Germans soon came to fear and hate the *Crocs* and complained that they were inhuman. The official reply was that they were no more inhuman than many of the atrocities being committed by the complainants. On balance the *Crocs* probably saved lives since all but the most single-minded Nazis took to surrendering whenever they saw one coming over the horizon! The armament of the *Croc*, in addition to the flame-thrower, consisted of a 75mm howitzer, a 7.92mm Besa machine gun and a two-inch bomb thrower for firing smoke bombs. Five men made up the crew:

three in the turret – the commander, gunner and wireless operator, and two in the hull – the driver and co-driver/flame gun operator. It was a tight fit and once installed there was no room to fidget! The *Croc*, excluding trailer, weighed 40 tons, was 24½ feet long, just over 11 feet wide and eight feet high. Maximum road speed was 12½ mph. The *Croc* was successfully deployed in Italy and northwest Europe and in 1950 a squadron fought in the Korean War.

A Crocodile
(1:35 scale Taiya model)

Cigarette and trade cards

Cigarette cards were first introduced in 1878 in the USA, but did not arrive in Britain until 1901, when the American Tobacco Company acquired the Liverpool factory of Ogden's. They were virtually killed off when paper rationing abruptly ended their use at the start of World War II.

There was a brief attempt to re-introduce them after the war which was unsuccessful although similar looking trade cards appeared in packets of custard powder, tea, sweets and various other confectionery and grocery products.

Churchill featured on more than thirty cards between 1901 and 1939. Original cards are highly collectable, although beware, modern reproductions abound. Genuine cards from Ogden's *Boer War* series can cost £9 each in good condition. In 1910 some cigarette manufacturers introduced printed silk pictures but these had a brief life and had been phased out by 1925.

Churchill featured prominently on cigarette cards during the 1920s and 30s. The 30s were the heyday of cigarette cards and Churchill, although he was out of office, was rarely out of the public eye. After World War II several manufacturers made desultory attempts to revive cigarette cards before deciding that they had had their day.

Trade cards had limited success. One of the most interesting series was by *Mirrorpic* for AB&C chewing gum, a set of 55 photographs, 3 x 2 inches, depicting scenes from Churchill's life, but the print quality was very poor. Other trade cards were issued by Lingfords Baking Powder, Lyons Maid Ice Cream and Brooke Bond Tea.

Boer War
Ogden's Guinea Gold Cigarettes. 1901

Modern Statesmen
Hignett's Butterfly Cigarettes. 1906

Celebrities of the Great War
Major Drapkin Cigarettes. 1916

Leading Generals of the War
Ogden's Tab Cigarettes. 1901

Celebrities, Cohen Weenen Sweet
Crop Cigarettes. 1901

Famous People
Lyons Maid. c1960

Great War Leaders [[silk]
Godfrey Phillips Cigarettes. 1918

Famous Escapes
Mars Confections. c1955

War Series
B Muratti & Sons. 1916

Famous Escapes
Carreras Turf Cigarettes. 1926

Britain's Defenders
Will's Capstan cigarettes. 1915

Straight Line Caricatures
John Player & Sons. 1926

Notable MPs
Carreras Black Cat Cigarettes. 1929

Personalities of Today
Godfrey Phillips cigarettes. 1932

British War Leaders,
Lingfords Custard Powder. 1950s

Celebrities of the Great War
Major Drapkin Cigarettes. 1916

In the Public Eye
Godfrey Phillips Cigarettes. 1935

War Celebrities
B Morris & Sons Cigarettes. 1916

Empire Personalities
Ardath State Express Cigarettes. 1937

Notabilities
British American Tobacco. 1917

Famous People
Brooke Bond Tea. 1960s

Cigarette lighters

This large and heavy 8½ inches high bust is a cigarette or cigar lighter. It was modelled during World War II by Peter Lambda, then thirty years of age, who was later to gain fame as a sculptor. It is signed with Lambda's PL monogram and *'VBV'*, presumably the caster, moulded in hard plaster and painted in an overall flesh colour. It is a strike lighter, a popular design during the 1920s and 30s, manufactured by that well-known maker, Tallent. The head is hollow and stuffed with cotton wool which is saturated with lighter fuel inserted through a screw aperture at the back. The 'cigar' is the handle of the striker which is a sharpened half-hollowed steel tube with a wick running through the centre. The wick becomes impregnated with petrol vapour and when the striker is drawn across the cerium strip on Churchill's midriff, hey presto, you have your light. The flame could sometimes be more than big enough to light the largest cigar – and, if you weren't careful, singed your eyebrows!

During the 1980s and 90s these lighters were fetching up to £60 in the UK and $250 in the USA. Everything changed in July 1998 when in an auction at Sotheby's, London the bidding reached £517.

Cigarette lighter modelled by Peter Lambda,

Cigar boxes

Top: A nine carat gold cigar case engraved with an outline of Aristotle Onassis' yacht Christina, six Caribbean islands and the inscription 'Happy Birthday from Ari, 30 November 1960'. The case, by Cartier, was given to Churchill, on his eighty-sixth birthday, by the Greek tycoon on whose luxury yacht he had cruised eight times since 1956. The cigar case was sold by Sotheby's in 1998 for £43,300. *(Photo courtesy Sotheby's).*

Bottom: A cedar wood cigar box with poker work decoration. It originates from India, Havanas Syndicate Woriur Madras, and was made during World War II. Inside the lid is the inscription: *'Churchill's Specials. His cigar is as inseparable as Chamberlain's umbrella. It is the terror of the Dictators. It is the secret of Churchill's power. Try it and see!'*

Cigars

Among the many quotations attributed to Churchill are: *'Tobacco is bad for love, but old age is worse.'* and *'Smoking cigars is like falling in love; first you are attracted to its shape; you stay with it for its flavour; and you must always remember never, never, let the flame go out'.*

Churchill's cigar became as great an icon as his V-sign. His daughter, Lady Soames, once remarked that sculptors and modellers had overdone her father's addiction to cigars, but in her book, *A Churchill Family Album* (Allen Lane, 1982) it is noted that more than half of her selection of photographs of her father taken between 1940 and 1945 have him either smoking or holding a cigar.

Churchill toby jugs, busts and figurines are available with cigar or sans cigar in roughly the same proportion. *'Churchill'* became, and remains, a brand name for cigars used by manufacturers around the world.

It is well known that Churchill's favourite cigars were the Cuban *Romeo y Julieta* brand and, by one means or another, he managed to secure a supply of these throughout World War II. On one occasion a large cabinet from the Cuban ambassador was deemed to be suspect by the Downing Street security staff and, much to Churchill's disgust, ordered to be blown up!

Churchill's former secretary, Jock Colville, observed that his master received many gifts of cigars: *'He usually accepted them. If they were not to his taste, they came in useful to give away!'*

In April 1996 at Christie's, London, an 18ct gold cigar case containing two *Don Jonquin* cuestas, formerly Churchill's property, was sold for £3,785. At Sotheby's in July 1997, a buyer paid £4,830 for a cigar case which had been carried to the trenches in France by Churchill during World War I. But things reached a new height in July 1998 when a 9ct gold cigar case, which had been given to Churchill as an eighty-sixth birthday present by Aristotle Onassis, sold for £43,300 at Sotheby's, London .

Cedar-lined cigar casket. One of the finest pieces commemorating the Churchill Centenary in 1974 was a magnificent cedar-lined cigar casket made by Paragon China in a limited edition of 500. Highly collectable. In auction, caskets have made over £1,000 in the UK or $2,750 in the USA.

More modestly priced at £3.99 was the colourful printed tinplate cigar box from Grumbridge's of Bedford in the mid-1990s.

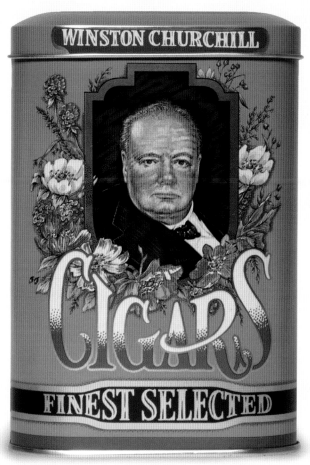

A Swiss manufacturer has placed Churchill's portrait in gold foil on the inside of the box lid.

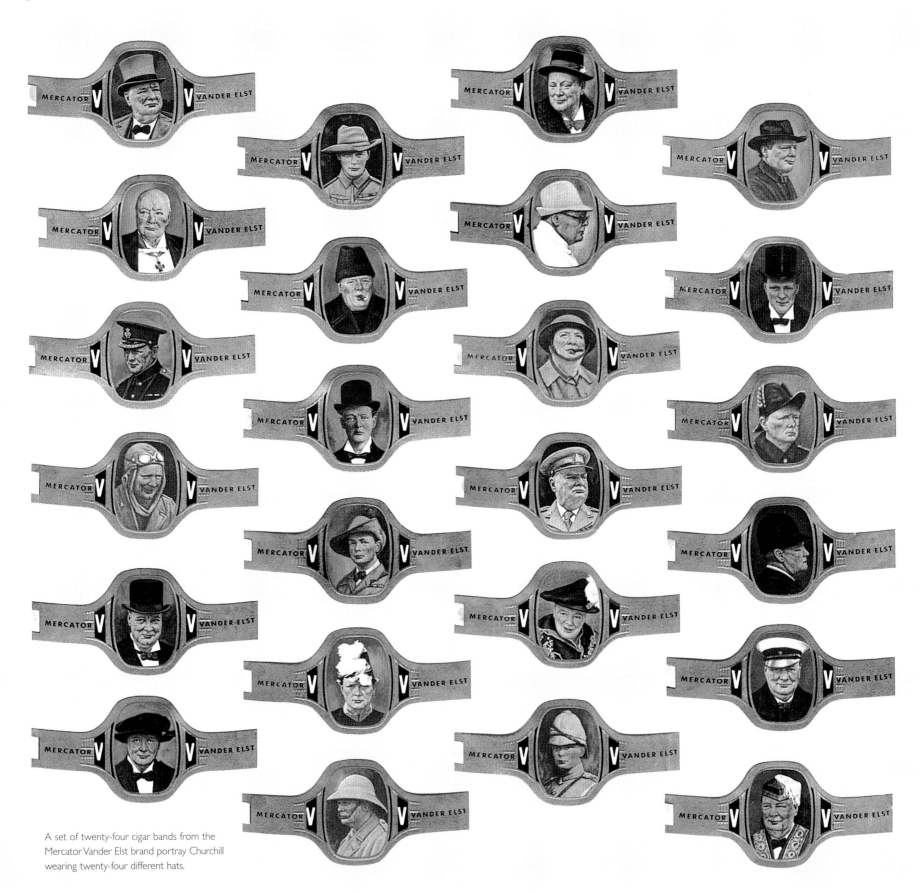

A set of twenty-four cigar bands from the Mercator Vander Elst brand portray Churchill wearing twenty-four different hats.

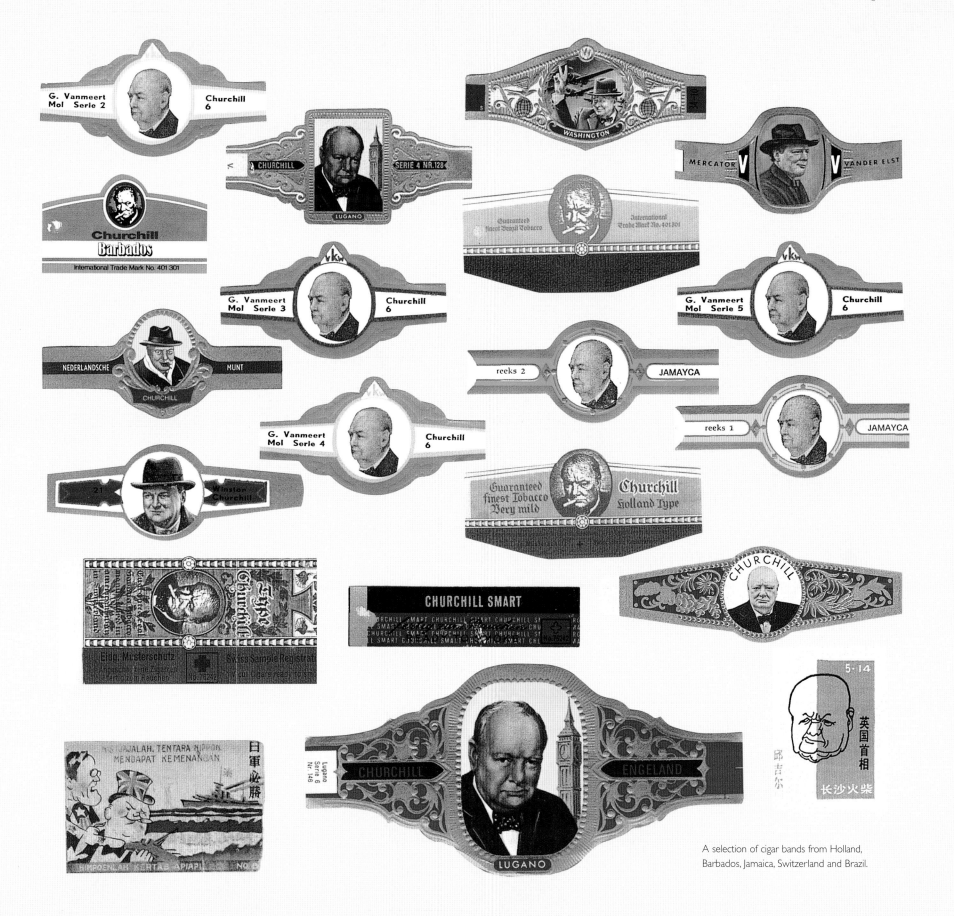

A selection of cigar bands from Holland, Barbados, Jamaica, Switzerland and Brazil.

Claverton Manor, Bath

Claverton Manor was built by Sir Jeffry Wyatville in 1820. It is now the home of the American Museum in Britain. It is the first museum of Americana to be established outside of the United States. On Monday 26 July 1897 Winston Churchill, whilst on three months army leave, made his official maiden political speech to a rally of the Primrose League in the park at Claverton Manor, when he was twenty-three. There was some comment in the evening and weekly newspapers, mostly favourable. *'He seems to be a young man of some ability ... anxious to take a part in public affairs,'* wrote the *Eastern Morning News*. The event is commemorated on a plaque by the front door of the manor.

Coasters

Ceramic coaster by H&R Johnson proclaims: *'Give us the tools and we will finish the job.'*

Bronze-effect felt-backed coaster on sale in the Blenheim Palace gift shop in the 1980s.

Commemorative and first-day covers

The United States was first with a memorial stamp when Churchill died. The 5 cents stamp, based on Yousuf Karsh's 1941 photo was issued in April 1965, three months ahead of the British issue. This cover, postmarked *Fulton, Missouri, was* the location of Churchill's 1946 'Iron Curtain' speech.

The Australian memorial stamp was issued on 24 May 1965 and also made use of the Yousuf Karsh photograph. New Zealand issued its memorial stamp to the same design, but in a 7d denomination, on the same day.

The first of the Churchill memorial stamps not to be based on the Karsh photo was the Cameroun issue on 28 May 1965. All the other West African republics issued individually designed stamps but on a very similar cover until December 1965.

In 1968 West Germany issued a stamp portraying Churchill, in a set of four to commemorate Chancellor Konrad Adenauer, who had died the previous year. Adenauer, Churchill, Robert Schuman of France and Alcide de Gasperi of Italy, had been protagonists of post-war European unity and the founding fathers of the European Union.

Jersey was under German occupation during the war, celebrated the 25th anniversary of its liberation on 9 May 1970. The five pence Churchill stamp quotes from his Victory broadcast of 8 May 1945: *'...and our dear Channel Islands are also to be freed today.'* The cover illustrates the lowering of the swastika and the raising of the Union Jack.

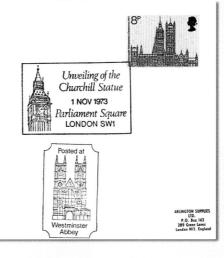

The controversial statue of Churchill in Parliament Square, London by Ivor Roberts-Jones, was unveiled by Lady Churchill on 1 November 1973. Her daughter, Lady Soames described the statue as: *'... combining a sombre likeness with considerable allegorical illusion.'*

BRUNEI

CHURCHILL
MEMORIAL
EXHIBITION

NOVEMBER 23, 1973

FIRST DAY COVER

The Sultan of Brunei was a keen Churchillophile. In the capital of his tiny 2,000 square-mile, former British protectorate in NW Borneo he built a museum devoted to the memory of Winston Churchill. Dominating the approach to the museum was a seven-foot tall bronze statue of Churchill atop a ten-foot tall black granite plinth, sculpted by Astrid Zydower, which features on the 50 sen stamp.

The Churchill Centenary Exhibition was held in Somerset House, Strand, London from 10 May until 14 October 1974.

The Churchill Centenary postage stamps were issued on 9 October 1974. There was a huge choice of first-day covers. This cover, illustrating the Churchill coat of arms, was cancelled at Blenheim Palace, Churchill's birthplace.

A first-day art craft card available to Members of Parliament with a special House of Commons cancellation. Most were posted in an outer envelope for protection and security.

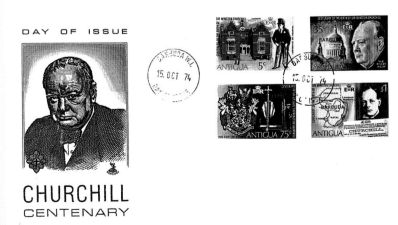

A commonplace cover but a better than average set of Centenary stamps from Antigua, Leeward Islands overprinted for use on Barbuda – a tiny island of just 62 square miles. Several catalogues give the date of issue of the Antiguan stamps as 20 October with the Barbaduan overprint as 20 November, but this is dated 15 October.

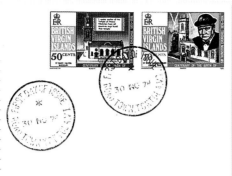

A 'silk' from the British Virgin Islands portrayed Churchill sitting at his easel painting. A pleasant commemoration of the Centenary, with a pair of stamps postmarked 30 November 1974 which depict the former church of St Mary, Aldermanbury, London, now doing service as the Winston Churchill Memorial and Library at Fulton, Missouri in the USA.

The Falkland Islands waited until Churchill's 100th birthday – 30 November 1974 – before issuing their centenary stamps. Little did we all realise that a mere eight years later they would experience: '... *fighting on the seas and oceans ... in the air ... on the beaches ... on the landing grounds ...*' as a prelude to their own 'Finest Hour'.

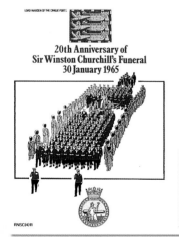

The 20th anniversary of Winston Churchill's funeral commemorated on 30 January 1985 by the Royal Navy. The cover is signed by Rear Admiral Oswald, the officer in charge of the gun carriage which carried the coffin, and Winston S Churchill Junior, Churchill's grandson. Postmarked by the British Forces Postal Service.

An Arlington 'silk' commemorating the 40th anniversary of VE Day on 8 May 1985.

A Benham's limited edition 'silk' cover from their 50th anniversary of World War II collection. This marks the 50th anniversary of the British Forces Broadcasting Service, in November 1993, by picturing Churchill at the microphone speaking on the first anniversary of the formation of the Home Guard.

'Winston is back!' The International Churchill Society commemorates the 50th anniversary of Churchill's election as Prime Minister for the second time on 26 October 2001,

Confectionery

I am not sure whether the quaint spelling – 'sigaar' – has to do with an attempt to mimic Churchill's pronunciation or the whimsical intricacies of EU food labelling directives.

This milk chocolate cigar – 12 inches long x 2 inches diameter and weighing 150 grammes – was a boxed, gift-wrapped, labelled product of the Netherlands and available at all branches of British Home Stores a few years ago.

Cuff links

Churchill commemorative cuff links range from those in solid gold or silver from high-class Bond Street jewellers to the more affordable sets illustrated here.

Top: Based on Nibs *Winnie* cartoon in *Vanity Fair* of 8 March 1911. Enamel on gold-plated mounts.

Below: From Wedgwood for the Churchill Centenary in 1974. Arnold Machin's 1940 dark blue jasper portrait cameos in gold-plated Stratton mounts.

Dagger

A full-size replica of a British Army fighting dagger, with its 7-inch blade, crafted in polished stainless steel by Wilkinson Sword to commemorate the 50th anniversary of the Battle of Alamein. Engraved on one side of the blade: *'In honor of the North African campaigns, The Desert War, 1940-1943 – Egypt, Libya, Algeria, French Morocco and Tunisia'* – and, on the other: *'At last we're on our way – Roosevelt.' 'This is the end of the beginning – Churchill.'* A functional and lethal item.

Decoupage

The art of decorating a surface with shapes or illustrations cut from other materials is another way of creating attractive, and possibly unique, pieces of Churchilliana.

Rare, and possibly unique, is this cartoon portrait incorporating a collection of parts from clocks and watches. Signed: *G Burgess, London,* framed and glazed.

This appealing framed and glazed picture is almost certainly a piece of private enterprise rather than a commercially produced product. A youthful looking and uncommonly hirsute Churchill standing in front of the Union Jack is made from shapes cut from coloured metallic foils and stuck to a black card background.

Ditchley Park

During the early part of World War II it was considered that the Prime Minister's official country residence at Chequers was too conspicuous at full moon and might be a prestigious target for the Luftwaffe. The long broad straight gravel drive at Chequers made a clear landmark in bright moonlight pointing almost like a direction sign to the house. Churchill, whilst not wishing to evade the dangers faced by the population at large, accepted the extreme vulnerability of Chequers and told Attlee that whilst he *'did not object to chance,'* he felt *'it would be a mistake to be the victim of design.'*

Ronald Tree MP offered the Prime Minister the use of his house at Ditchley Park, near Oxford, which was then surrounded by a park of mature trees and therefore less conspicuous from the air, even if the Luftwaffe had known that Churchill was there. Churchill knew the house, since he and Clementine had been there in 1937 when Ronald Tree was one of the small

group of MP's who had shared his concern about the German menace, and as a result remembered the quality of its cellar!

Churchill first went to Ditchley, in lieu of Chequers, on 9 November 1940. He was accompanied by Clementine and daughter Mary. Ronald Tree and his wife Nancy were American by birth but had taken up Anglo-American citizenship. Ronald, who had edited *Forum Magazine* in New York 1922-26, had been MP for the Harborough division of Leicestershire since 1933 and having been PPS to Sir John Reith and Alfred Duff-Cooper was then PPS to Churchill's protégé, Brendan Bracken. He had acquired Ditchley Park in 1933 after the death of the 17th Viscount Dillon. The Dillons were an ancient Irish Catholic family with estates in Ireland as well as Ditchley and the new Viscount, then at Sandhurst and about to embark on an army career, made his home at Drogheda.

Ditchley had been the home of the Dillon and Lee families for over 300 years and when Ronald Tree bought it he described it

Angela Conner's fine bronze of Winston Churchill, on the terrace at Ditchley Park, unveiled in June 1994 by British Foreign Secretary Douglas Hurd and US Secretary Warren Christopher.

as presenting *'an unforgettable picture of magnificence and accumulated junk'*. By 1940 the junk had been cleared and the magnificence fully restored. For Churchill's first visit telephone lines, with a scrambling system, were installed. Accommodation was provided for the Prime Minister's staff and secretariat as well as billets for a full company of the Oxford and Bucks Light Infantry who would guard the house! To Ronald Tree's relief, when Churchill left on the following Monday he said that he had been very satisfied and would be back the following weekend *'high moon or no high moon'!*

Churchill had, in fact, just left Downing Street for Ditchley Park the following week-end when he opened a top-secret message which had been handed to him as he was getting into the car. He told the driver to turn back. An Enigma decrypt indicated the prospect of a heavy raid on London that night. Churchill said that he was not going to spend the night *'peacefully in the country while the metropolis was under heavy attack'*. In the event three hundred German bombers that night attacked Coventry – thirty miles from Ditchley. Churchill did, however, return to Ditchley at regular intervals over the next two years. The last weekend occasion was on 26 September 1942 when he was again accompanied by Clementine and Mary. It happened to be Ronald Tree's birthday, the United States had now entered the war and Churchill was in high good spirits: all the ingredients of a good party which, by Ronald Tree's account, it apparently was! Churchill's last ever visit to Ditchley, for lunch, was in March 1943. The driveway at Chequers had been turfed over, the defences were more sophisticated and risk of attack was considered minimal with the attentions of the Luftwaffe targeted on the Russian front.

Ditchley Park is now owned by the Ditchley Foundation an Anglo-American educational trust which seeks to further transatlantic accord through a programme of seminars and conferences. The Chairman of American Ditchley is the Hon Cyrus Vance. The house is open to the public by prior appointment with the Bursar: The Ditchley Foundation, Ditchley Park, Enstone, Chipping Norton, Oxfordshire, OX7 4ER.

The Churchill connection was for more than fifty years modestly discreet and low-key consisting only of a very small plaque recording that this was where Churchill met President Roosevelt's emissary, Harry Hopkins, to work out the Lease-Lend Agreement. However, in June 1994 US Secretary Warren Christopher and UK Foreign Secretary Douglas Hurd unveiled a fine 38-inch high bronze bust of Churchill by the distinguished sculptress Angela Conner which now stands in a prominent position and more adequately marks the role of Ditchley Park during a critical phase of World War II. A second copy of the bust was auctioned at Sotheby's in July 1999 with a pre-sale estimate of £10,000-15,000 but failed to meet the reserve price.

Doorknocker

How better to announce your arrival than by knocking Churchill's head against the door to the House of Commons? This unusual doorknocker was made at the now defunct BEL foundry in Birmingham in the late 1960s. The 8-inch high knocker, containing two pounds of solid brass, can be found around the UK secondary market for £20-£30 but the transatlantic shipping cost of such a weighty piece is presumably a factor in the US price of $200+.

Doorstop

This solid cast-iron doorstop is 16 inches high and weighs 20 pounds. It was first cast at a Stourbridge foundry in the mid-1950s but after the foundry closed down the mould was acquired by a craft hobbyist who continued to cast examples until the mid-1990s. Nicely detailed, it incorporates a well recognisable Churchillian expression, a cigar, a V-sign, the sash and star of the Order of the Garter, the collar badge of the Order of Merit and a bar of medals. Mostly found in the traditional black-painted cast-iron finish but also in brass and full-colour enamels. Whist these doorstops were being offered around the UK craft fairs at £20 in the 1990s I heard that prices as high as $400 were being charged in the USA!

Downing Street

On 22 September 1735, 10 Downing Street became the official residence of Sir Robert Walpole, Britain's first Prime Minister. Between 1735 and 1902 the house was variously occupied by Prime Ministers, First Lords of the Treasury, Chancellors of the Exchequer and sundry other officials. From 1847 to 1877 there was no tenant at all and the house was used simply as offices with an occasional official function in the state rooms. Since AJ Balfour, who

was already resident as First Lord of the Treasury, became Prime Minister in 1902 all Prime Ministers, who have also been First Lords of the Treasury, have lived in the house.

The present day 10 Downing Street is in fact an amalgamation of two originally separate houses. The front and most famous section, with its black door overlooking Downing Street, was not connected to the larger and more sumptious Bothmar House (the 'house-at-the-back') which had its entrance on Horse Guards Parade, until 1735. Both houses were built in the 1670s but considerable re-building continued into the next decade to rectify structural faults, caused by building on marshy ground and some shoddy work by a 17th century jerry-builder. The conversion of two houses into one was carried out for Sir Robert Walpole before he took up residence.

Churchill became the thirty-first Prime Minister to live at 10 Downing Street when he succeeded Chamberlain in 1940 but his tenure, during his first term of office, was much interrupted by the need to live and work in the more secure environment of the 'Annexe' at Storey's Gate. He returned for a second term from 1951 to 1955, but all the Prime Ministers who have followed him testify that his tremendous personality as a dynamic wartime leader is still tangibly present in the house.

Churchill's portrait hangs alongside those of all other former Prime Ministers on the main staircase. However, for many years there was a second portrait of Churchill, *Blood, Sweat and Tears* by Frank Salisbury, hanging in the ante-room of the Cabinet Room. A plaque in the Garden Room marks the fourteen occasions on which Churchill entertained King George VI in that room during the war years. Churchill made his celebrated VE-day broadcast, from the Cabinet Room on 8 May 1945 – the one which he said gave him the greatest personal satisfaction.

He preferred to use the Cabinet Room as his office and successive Prime Ministers up to the present day have been aware that their chair at the cabinet table, the only one that has arms, was 'Churchill's seat'.

In his second term as Prime Minister, Churchill was able to live in greater style at 10 Downing Street. He resumed using the Cabinet Room as his office, whilst Clementine transformed the White Drawing Room into her personal boudoir. She hung one of her favourite paintings by Winston and it is still there! This time Churchill's tenancy embraced the Coronation and, although in his late seventies, he insisted on taking an active part in the planning.

On 4 April 1955 the Churchill's entertained HM the Queen and the Duke of Edinburgh to dinner in the State Dining Room. There were fifty guests including members of his family, close friends, the three party leaders and the Speaker of the House of Commons. Next day Winston Churchill resigned. A plaque in the Garden Room reads: *'In this room during the Second World War His Majesty the King was graciously pleased to dine on fourteen occasions with the Prime Minister, Mr Churchill ... on two of these occasions the company was forced to withdraw into the neighbouring shelter by air bombardment of the enemy.'*

Churchill's painting, *Long River, Alpes Maritimes,* on loan from the Tate Gallery, hangs in the first-floor study. The wine cellar always holds a stock of *Pol Roger* Champagne *Sir Winston Churchill Cuvée* for special state occasions.

Left: Architectural model-maker Timothy Richards of Bristol made this model of the famous doorway of 10 Downing Street. The 8 inches × 6 inches model, in plaster and delicate wrought iron work, is accurate in every detail. For the photograph I have inserted an in-scale pewter figure of Churchill giving his V-sign. The famous black front door opens on a treasure trove of Churchilliana.

Below left: The entrance to 10 Downing Street.

Below: Sir Winston and Lady Churchill welcome HM the Queen to 10 Downing Street on 4 April 1955.

Dressed dolls

Peggy Nisbet's hobby was making and dressing dolls. In 1952 she made a doll of Queen Elizabeth II in her coronation robes and showed it to a buyer at Harrods. He ordered 300 and, at the age of forty, Peggy began her new career and became Britain's premier maker of handmade historical dolls.

In 1953 she made a Winston Churchill doll, in the robes of a Knight of the Garter. She used authentic silk, satin, barathea and taffeta, embroidered with gold thread, a miniature breast star, collar badge and a genuine ostrich feather plume in the cap. Exhibiting at the British Fair in New York in 1962 she presented a doll to Randolph Churchill and asked him to give it to his father, but she was never sure if he did. Later, Mrs Nisbet made a doll of Churchill dressed in a grey worsted suit with a waistcoat, spotted bow tie and gold watch chain but the thickness of the genuine worsted prevented a tidy fold to the collar and lapels of the jacket and the doll was less successful. However, these are two rare and sought after items of Churchilliana.

The Dutch are famous for their pottery ornaments depicting boys and girls dressed in national costume adopting a variety of winsome poses. This one, probably rather hurriedly and therefore somewhat crudely made in 1945, celebrates the liberation of Holland. The Dutch boy has been replaced by Churchill, smoking a cigar and with his left arm raised in a V-sign, clearly enjoying being embraced and kissed by a grateful and buxom Dutch girl.

Above: Dutch boy and girl, c1945.

Left: A Peggy Nisbet doll of Winston Churchill in the robes of a Knight of the Garter from the 1950s.

Drinkers' requisites

Winston Churchill was a high-profile tippler. Once, when challenged over his habit of indulging in drink, he remarked: *'All I can say is that I have taken more out of alcohol than it has taken out of me.'* It was inevitable that he should be associated with all manner of drinkers' requisites.

One of the many designs of drinking goblet etched with Churchill's portrait.

A leather-covered stainless steel hip flask as sold at the Cabinet War Rooms souvenir shop.

Bottle opener and bottle pourer, c.1950 (see page 26).

A well-modelled pewter figure mounted on a cork to form a bottle stopper.

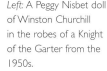

A one-pint engraved polished pewter tankard as sold for around £20 in the Blenheim Palace souvenir shop in the 1980s.

Churchill's Pride beer mat. During World War II a small Lincolnshire brewery supplied a strong ale to many of the RAF stations. Rediscovered in 1990 it was brewed to mark the 50th anniversary of the Battle of Britain.

Drinks

A china bust sold containing 25ml of Scotch Whisky. Marketed by the Trevelyan Manufacturing Company of Bovey Tracey, Devon and sold, amongst other places, at Blenheim Palace.

Below: A flagon of Lindisfarne Mead, made and sold by the monks at St Aidan's Winery on Holy Island. The label on the back of the flagon announces that it is number six in a series of English historical characters and goes on to give a brief outline of Churchill's life.

Dundee

Whilst he was MP for NW Manchester in 1908 Churchill was appointed to the Cabinet as President of the Board of Trade. Having obtained Cabinet office he had, according to the rules of the day, to seek re-election to Parliament. Much to his surprise he was defeated in the by-election. The large Jewish vote in his constituency had been disaffected by the Liberal government's Aliens Act and local Catholics were incensed by his stance over Home Rule for Ireland. Within less than three weeks Churchill found himself a 'seat of convenience' at Dundee and on 9 May 1908 polled over 7,000 votes to easily

overcome his Conservative and Labour opponents. He told his mother he had secured, 'a life seat'. In fact he remained MP for Dundee until 1922.

Scotland's third largest city, 440 miles north of Westminster, was in those days only practically accessible by the rather joyless overnight sleeper train from King's Cross, so Churchill never became a frequent visitor to his new constituency. In any case it was a less than joyful place to arrive at before dawn with its tall, dark and grimy jute mills and tenement blocks and much unemployment, poverty and drunkenness. The Dundee electorate seemed honoured to be represented by a high-profile cabinet

minister and fully prepared to overlook Churchill's long absences. He became Home Secretary in 1910, First Lord of the Admiralty in 1911, Chancellor of the Duchy of Lancaster in 1915, Minister of Munitions in 1917, Secretary of State for War and Air in 1919 and Secretary of State for the Colonies in 1921. Even his political nadir over the Dardanelles affair in 1915 did not cause as much consternation in Dundee as it did in Ayrshire where his appointment as Colonel of the locally raised 6th Royal Scots Fusiliers at the Western Front almost caused a mutiny. The battle-hardened infantrymen from SW Scotland, veterans of the Battle of Loos, were incensed at having imposed upon them, as they saw it, a failed politician linked with the loss of thirty-four thousand lives and an over-promoted, untrained, improperly dressed former cavalry officer subsisting on luxury food parcels sent from Fortnum and Mason.

Winston Churchill, President of the Board of Trade and MP for Dundee, 1908.

It seems surprising to some that a quintessentially aristocratic Englishman should have survived for so long as an absentee MP of a massively under-privileged Scottish industrial city, but the fact is that much of Churchill's political energy during his fourteen years as Dundee's Liberal MP was expressed in a personal class war against Conservative capitalism. With Lloyd George, he laid the foundations of a Welfare State and introduced Old Age Pensions and Unemployment Insurance. These measures were popular in this predominantly working class constituency and were not offset, as elsewhere, by the

introduction of progressive Income Tax, as few of Churchill's Dundee electorate earned enough to pay Income Tax anyway! However, Churchill's unlikely relationship with the people of Dundee became strained by the events of World War I.

The longed-for victory over Germany brought not peace and progress, but bitter disillusionment, due to the decimation of a generation in its youthful prime. The people of Dundee saw their MP drifting to the political right and gaining a reputation as a warmonger. Local indignation reached a peak when, after making much of the fact that the war was over in his 1918 general election campaign, Churchill should then take the appointment of Secretary of State for War! In the 1922 general election Churchill came fourth in the poll behind the Prohibitionist, the Labour candidate and his fellow Liberal.

This postcard, dating from 1908, reflects the speed with which Churchill found a new constituency, having lost his seat in NW Manchester. The caption reads:

The worries of Winston C.
The wiley Scot outwiled.
Poor Winston C – he lost the seat,
The one he'd set his heart on.
So as they wouldn't have him there,
He tried the land of Tartan.
Got him at last?
But eh mon it's been a stroogle!

Enamelled objects

Copper trinket boxes

The art of enamelling trinket boxes dates from the 18th century. Enamels are applied by hand and the cost of up to six firings makes these objets d'art very expensive. Bilston and Battersea Enamels, the makers of *Halcyon Days* boxes, have produced two pieces of Churchilliana: an edition of 500 for the Churchill Centenary in 1974, and in 1990 an edition of 1,000, marking the 50th anniversary of the Battle of Britain. The company runs a 'sale and wanted' register for discontinued lines and one of their *Churchill Centenary* boxes was sold via that facility a few years ago for £300.

Medallions

An unknown enameller has applied his craft to this. The 56mm diameter 1965 Churchill Memorial Medal in silver, designed by Frank Kovacs and struck by Spink, one of many to mark the death of Churchill was distinguished in that the design on the reverse was a reproduction of David Low's famous 1940 cartoon captioned: *'Very Well, Alone.'*

Signs

Enamelled advertising signs were common on the walls of corner shops and railway station platforms during the first half of the 20th century.

A trinket box by Kingsley Enamels, who work mainly on commissions from up-market retailers or mail-order traders selling high-priced items by subscription.

1965 *Churchill Memorial Medal*, designed by Frank Kovacs and struck by Spink.

Epping and Woodford

After losing his seat at Dundee in 1922 Churchill was absent from the House of Commons for almost two years. He fought and lost elections in West Leicester and the Abbey Division of Westminster before returning to Parliament in October 1924 as the Independent Constitutionalist anti-Socialist MP for Epping. He called it his *'semi-rural constituency among the glades of Epping Forest'* and effectively it became his base for the rest of his political career. He defended and retained the Epping seat in 1929, 1931 and 1935 and again in 1945. When boundary changes occurred, he stood for the new Woodford Division, a safer seat, which he retained till his retirement in 1964.

Directly after his return to Parliament in 1924, Churchill was appointed Chancellor of the Exchequer – a position he was to hold for five years. He was fully engrossed in national issues: the General Strike, the return to the Gold Standard, pensions for widows and orphans, unemployment and the Depression.

Constituency issues continued to receive scant attention. Churchill's rare whistle-stop tours or appearances at Conservative summer fêtes in Epping kept the local voters content. They enjoyed their MP's high profile and were prepared to overlook his limited parochial presence. He was popular, respected and even regarded as a political 'Colossus'.

However, the general election in May 1929 swept the Conservatives from office and Churchill was destined to spend ten years in the political wilderness as a back-bencher. Increasingly isolated from his party, first over Dominion status for India and then over rearmament and the Hitler threat, he faced considerable hostility at several constituency meetings. He ruffled many feathers with his attacks on Neville Chamberlain's policy of appeasement and some local branches passed resolutions of censure. There was a determined attempt to unseat him after what many supporters thought was an injudicious Munich speech and he later said that if he had lost the support of the local executive council he would have resigned his seat and stood as

Chancellor of the Exchequer and MP for Epping and Woodford, 1924.

an Independent at a by-election, putting the Conservative interest in jeopardy and his own hold on the constituency. Staunch friends managed to retrieve the situation which he later regarded as one of the major political crises he had faced in his career.

Churchill's 'wilderness years' have given rise to a rich crop of learned theses from historians and political biographers. He has been variously described as a seer and saviour, or as a warmonger who provoked Hitler into inflicting another war on a British population still bearing the scars of the last one.

In 1933 the Oxford Union supported by a large majority the motion: *'That this House refuses in any circumstances to fight for King and Country'.* Churchill's response that: *'I think of Germany with its splendid clear-eyed youth marching forward on the the roads of the Reich singing their ancient songs, demanding to be conscripted into the army ... burning to suffer and die for the fatherland,'* was widely misinterpreted.

However, as he had so often done before, Churchill survived and was available for recall in 1939 and to achieve his 'finest hour' in 1940. As wartime Prime Minister, postwar Leader of the Opposition, Prime Minister again, and finally revered elder statesman Churchill served the Woodford constituency until he was within a few weeks of his ninetieth birthday.

Face masks

Face masks, or wall masks, are simply flat-backed high-relief portrait busts made for wall hanging. Many are of fine quality. Eric Owen designed a striking face mask of Churchill for Minton in 1941 which made $1,250 in a US auction in the 1980s.

Face mask in varnished plaster and unmarked. It is unusual in that it has Churchill smiling broadly. Possibly dates from 1945 – between 8 May (VE Day) and the declaration of the result of the general election on 25 July!

Face pots

Face Pots from Peggy Davies Ceramics are a series of two-piece porcelain pots, 2½ inches in diameter, featuring an upturned face of a famous personality on the lid. Inside the pot is the name of the subject and an apposite inscription.

Face pot inscribed: *'Churchill – We shall never surrender'* and the date of manufacture. UK price £25.50; US $45

Fakes and forgeries

Wedgwood is plagued by fakes of its more valuable pieces, but even less expensive pieces of Churchilliana can be targeted. A bronze and green resin copy of the genuine Wedgwood blue jasper 1974 portrait medallion fooled some collectors into parting with serious money around 1990.

The Staffordshire Fine Ceramics character jug was on sale in London W1 and at Heathrow Airport in the early 1980s for around £25. It is a replica of a Shaw & Copestake (SylvaC) jug. The poor quality fake below is obvious when there is a benchmark, but was fooling some of the people for some of the time.

Figurines

Full-length figurines or statuettes represent a significant sector of Churchilliana. Quality and artistic merit have been just as variable as for all other forms but, perhaps, the spread between cheap and cheerful and extortionate and excellent has been wider. Maquettes of most of the full-size public statues around the world have been offered by the sculptors concerned.

1. Michael Sutty Porcelain. 1988

The earliest representation of Churchill, a newly commissioned Second Lieutenant of the 4th Hussars in 1895. Mr Sutty, a leading military modeller, based the figure on the photograph which appears as the frontispiece to volume 1 of the official biography. Highly detailed and accurate in every detail the figure is hand-painted with extensive use of gilding. Part way through his planned limited edition of 250 of this figure Mr Sutty's business went into receivership largely because of the high overhead cost of his Burlington Arcade showroom. Around 100 figures were sold, at £500 in the UK and $1,000 in the USA.

2. Sureda, Spain. 1980s

A well-modelled, but woefully inaccurate figure of Churchill from a Spanish pottery. The Royal Air Force uniform is completely wrong and the face looks nothing like Churchill's. Were it not for the cigar, the V-sign and the inscription: *'Winston S Churchill, Inglaterra (1874-1965)'*, it could be anybody. Around £50 in the UK.

3. Peter Hicks. 2001

'Winston ... December 1941'. A 13-inch high cold-cast resin bronze figurine created by Peter Hicks of Seend, Wiltshire for members of the International Churchill Society. The sculpture marked the visit of the United States Navy's newest warship, the *USS Winston S Churchill*, to Portsmouth in August 2001 and also the 60th anniversary of Churchill's second wartime visit to the United States to meet President Roosevelt. The figurine portrays Churchill in his Royal Yacht Squadron cap and reefer jacket, his habitual form of dress when aboard HM ships or visiting RN shore establishments. Price to UK members was £126.

1. Michael Sutty Porcelain. 1988

2. Sureda, Spain. 1980s

Winston S. Churchill
Inglaterra (1874 - 1965)

3. Peter Hicks. 2001

4. Bairstow Manor Pottery. 1999

5. Royal Hampshire
Art Foundry. 1995

6. Royal Hampshire
Art Foundry. 1995

7. Ashmor Fine China
Worcester. 1990

8. Spode. 1941

9. Newport Pottery
World War II

10. Carver unknown. c1955

13. Chingleput
High School
India. 1942

12. Bovey Pottery
Devon
World War II

14. Maker unknown
c.1955

15. Corgi
Classics Icon

4. Bairstow Manor Pottery. 1999

'Churchill – Lord Warden of the Cinque Ports'. A 1999 offering from Bairstow Manor Pottery, modelled by Ray Noble. Churchill had been appointed Lord Warden of the Cinque Ports in 1941 although the formal investiture was postponed until 1946. He was delighted by the appointment, a gift of the King, and wore the elaborate full-dress uniform whenever he felt the occasion warranted it – for example at the coronation of Queen Elizabeth II. 10 inches high, hand painted, in a limited edition of 750. Values as for *'Winston the Politician'* on page 70.

5. Royal Hampshire Art Foundry. 1995

In polished pewter on a wooden plinth this highly detailed figurine portrays Churchill in 1898 as a Lieutenant of the 21st Lancers at the battle of Omdurman. Churchill gives a most graphic account of that battle in his book *My Early Life.*

6. Royal Hampshire Art Foundry. 1995

Polished pewter on a wooden plinth depicting Churchill in his wartime naval uniform, including the cap of the Royal Yacht Squadron, adopted whenever visiting a RN shore establishment or making a voyage on one of HM ships. The figurine was on sale in the souvenir shops at the Imperial War Museum and the Cabinet War Rooms during the 1990s priced at £30.

7. Ashmor Fine China Worcester. 1990

A figurine commissioned by the History in Porcelain Company to raise funds for the Guinea Pigs Club. The modeller, Andrew Turner, portrayed Churchill, in siren suit and steel helmet, standing defiantly on the beach at Dover after the evacuation of Dunkirk. Turner's design was inspired by David Low's evocative cartoon – *Very well, alone* – in the *Evening Standard* of 18 June 1940. A limited edition of 500 was planned but unfortunately after only 21 figures had been completed Ashmor Fine China went into liquidation. The good news is that in 1997 the moulds for the entire range of History in Porcelain figures were acquired by Albany Fine China of Worcester who offered to produce any item from the series

on a 'made to order' basis up to the originally declared limit. The superbly detailed decoration of the 'second edition' figures is by the same artist responsible for the original edition, indistinguishable other than by the 'Albany' backstamp in addition to that of 'Ashmor'.

24-inch high resin bronze maquette of Oscar Nemon's House of Commons statue of Churchill, made £28,750 at Sotheby's in 1998.

8. Spode. 1941

A finely modelled and excellently painted bone china figurine designed by Eric Olsen for WT Copeland/Spode. Some paintwork variations have been observed. The figure was reissued in earthenware as a memorial piece in 1965. Both the original and the 1965 reissue are rare. An unusually wide range of auction prices has been reported – UK £300-£750; USA $900-$1,200.

9. Newport Pottery World War II

The Newport Pottery belonged to the Shorter family and was for many years the base of the renowned Clarice Cliff (Mrs Colley Shorter). There is nothing to suggest that Miss Cliff was involved in the design of this little figure although her signature appears on the contemporary Churchill toby jug produced by another Shorter-owned pottery, Wilkinson's.

10. Carver unknown. c1955

A nice caricature figure carved in wood and simply, but nicely, painted. There are also some later replicas cast in resin which are difficult to distinguish from the original. The originals can usually be found for £40-£50 around the UK secondary market. Replicas should be no more than half that price. A version described as 'hand-carved, painted hardwood' was offered in a US sale for $150.

11. Makers unknown. 1950-55

The 1950 general election, and again in 1951 and throughout Churchill's second premiership, saw a flood of cheap plaster caricature figures in various sizes and poses. Varying from 3 to 9 inches tall they were usually, though not always, crudely painted although many of them accurately captured Churchill's typical posture. One of the smaller ones, A Cleveland Novelty, came in a red cardboard box labelled *'Smoking Statesman – Amusing Novelty – Actually puffs smoke and blows smoke rings when cigar is lit!'* Some were made at home by children from a kit containing a rubber mould, a packet of plaster of Paris, some paints and a brush. From 1953 some superior versions have Churchill wearing his Garter breast badge, sash and medal ribbons. They have survived in their thousands although the soft plaster and brittle paintwork is often scuffed or chipped. In the UK from £5 up to perhaps £30 for one of the best examples; in the USA they have been seen for as much as $125.

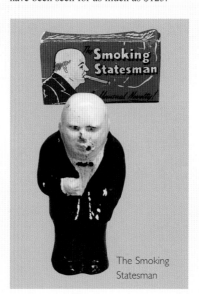

The Smoking Statesman

12. Bovey Pottery, Devon World War II

This small Devon pottery produced a range of stone-coloured earthenware caricature figurines based on the Our Gang series of newspaper strip cartoons. Other subjects included Roosevelt (Frank), Stalin (Joe), Hitler (Hit), Mussolini (Muss), a Soldier, a Sailor, an Airman, an Air Raid Warden and a Land Army Girl, etc, but the Churchill figure outsold them all many times over. Still frequently seen around the secondary market at a wide range of prices – UK £40 upwards; USA up to $125.

13. Chingleput High School India. 1942

An Indian ceramic produced at St Joseph's High School, Chingleput, India and labelled on the base: *'All profits go to His Excellency the Governor's Amenities for Troops Fund.'* The character was probably based on the *Our Gang* series of strip cartoons which must have been syndicated to an Indian newspaper! Scarce. Usually £25-£35 if found in the UK but has been offered at $150 in the USA.

14. Maker unknown c1955

The figurine of Churchill is cast from the same mould as the largest of the plaster figures. Churchill has an extraordinarily long cigar and is accompanied by a bulldog. The casting appears to be in either solid bronze or gunmetal and the entire piece weighs an impressive 21 pounds. It is unlikely that the figurine was made for commercial sale and I suspect it is the work of a skilled moulder in an industrial foundry. A charming figurine – always a talking point.

15. Corgi Classics Icon

Painted pewter scale model of the current waxworks figure of Churchill in Madame Tussaud's exhibition at Marylebone Road, London. Madame Tussaud opened her waxworks exhibition in 1835, since when it has consistently been among London's top tourist attractions. The first waxworks figure of Churchill was unveiled in 1908 when he was thirty-three years of age and has been remodelled no less than thirteen times over the next 57 years to reflect the changes in his appearance as he aged.

16. Heritage China. 1969
A china whisky flask containing 4/5ths of a quart of Ezra Brooks whisky. It was presented to guests at the dedication of the Winston Churchill Memorial and Library at Fulton, Missouri on 7 May 1969. Not the best representation of Churchill you ever saw. He wouldn't have liked the effigy but would perhaps have been mollified by the contents. I am told that a perfect example, complete with its original paper labels, is worth up to £35-£50 in the UK, $150 in the USA.

Capo di Monte. 1974
A superbly modelled and painted seated figurine from the renowned Capo di Monte factory in Italy. Modelled by Bruno Merli for the Churchill Centenary in 1974. The edition size is unknown. Scarce. I know of only two examples in the UK (one is in the collection at Bletchley Park) and I have no record of it coming to auction either here or in the USA.

17. Keith Lee. 1981
Inspired by the Southern IV series and Martin Gilbert's book, *The Wilderness Years*. A much admired and respected cold-cast bronze modelled by Keith Lee. A limited edition of 200. I have not seen this figurine at auction in 20 years.

18. Karin Churchill. 1976
Mrs Churchill (no relation) produced this fine 16-inch high cold-cast bronze figure of her namesake wearing the robes of a Knight of the Garter. The Royal Fine Art Commission had rejected a design with

Churchill wearing garter robes for the statue in Parliament Square. When Ivor Roberts-Jones' *'bronze monster'* was unveiled, Mrs Churchill decided to sculpt something better. Her finely detailed figure was issued as a limited edition of 400 signed and numbered castings, at £250.

19. Peter Hicks. 1999
A 12-inch high cold-cast resin bronze by Peter Hicks of Seend, Wiltshire in 1999 for Members of the International Churchill Society. Titled *'Winston is back'*, the model is based on a photograph of Churchill striding along Whitehall on 4 September 1939 to take up his post as First Lord of the Admiralty. As soon as his appointment was announced, the Board of Admiralty signalled all ships: *'Winston is back.'* Original cost £115 in the UK; $315 in the USA.

20. Ashmor Fine China Worcester. 1985
Commissioned by the History in Porcelain Company to raise funds for the Guinea Pigs Club – a charity to aid airmen burned during World War II and operated on by the pioneering plastic surgeon Sir Archibald McIndoe. The figurine was modelled by Andrew Turner. The limited edition of 350 was later increased to 375, but Ashmor

Carin Studio, N. Carolina, USA. 1997
A scarce figurine from the Cairn Studio, North Carolina in 1997. Cold cast in resin mixed with crushed pecan nut shells. The scroll contains a long quotation from Churchill's *blood, toil, tears and sweat* speech of 13 May 1940. I am told that the figure costs around $650 plus state taxes in the USA.

Fine China went into liquidation in 1992 after only 200 items had been sold. In 1997 the Albany Fine China Company, Worcester acquired the original moulds and sold the figure on a 'made to order basis'. When first offered in 1985 the price of the figure was £535 (USA $1,000) which included a substantial mark-up for charitable causes. Second-edition examples, numbered from 201 up, can be acquired for around £400. In 1993 a low-numbered model from the original production was sold in the USA for $1,500. Second-edition figures carry the Albany and Ashmor backstamps.

21. Royal Doulton. 1985
Designed by Adrian Hughes, Doulton's familiar 'man in a white suit' is still in production and available to order from high street china shops everywhere.

22. Winston's of Harrogate. 1990
A porcelain figure commissioned from Derek Stapley to mark the 50th anniversary of the Battle of Britain. The figure was based on a press photograph of Churchill standing atop the White Cliffs of Dover just as the battle was about to commence. In gloss and matt glaze the figure was offered in a limited edition of 2,500 at £125.

23. Leonardo. 1990s
Matt-glazed porcelain on a varnished wood plinth. From a pottery best known for its animal and bird figures. This figure was available only at Churchill-related locations, rather than high street stores. Well moulded and painted with a face that is a good likeness. Priced around £40 in the UK.

24. A Stadden. 1995
Two-inch high pewter figurines crafted by A Stadden for the 50th anniversary of VE Day in 1995. These finely detailed figures were available in Burlington Arcade, London, in either polished pewter or painted at £115, but could by found on the secondary market later that year for £25-£35.

25. Royal Doulton. 1992
Following the long-running success of their Harry Fenton toby jug, in production from 1940-91, Doulton introduced this superb hand-painted china figure, modelled by Alan Maslankowski. In a limited edition of 5,000, the figure depicts Churchill on a

wartime walkabout over the rubble in a blitzed area of London. A very desirable piece of Churchilliana. Launched at £275. Still available to order from Doulton stockists at £295.

26. Baytree Crafts, Lincolnshire. 1995
Hand-carved wood. A homburg hat, a bow tie, a cigar and a V-sign but whoever can it be? Well the label underneath says, *'Winston Churchill'*. Now you know! All the figures produced by this woodcarver have the same face. Their occupation is indicated by the costume and accessories. UK price £20.

27. Quay Sculptures, Poole. 1980s
Cold-cast bronze mounted on linen in an oak frame. Also available in painted resin. Originally sold at around £60 in UK shops. Seldom seen on the secondary market. Quay Sculptures are no longer in business.

28. Bairstow Manor Pottery. 1999
10½ inches tall figurine modelled by Ray Noble for Bairstow Manor Pottery of Hanley, Stoke-on-Trent. Churchill, in top hat and frock coat, stands on a symbolic book in front of a Union Jack draped Big Ben. A follow-on from the earlier models in *Bairstow's Life and Times of Winston Churchill* series. *'Winston the Politician'*, in a limited edition of 750, was available at £90-£120 in the UK and $150-$200 in the USA. Also available as a toby jug.

29. Bairstow Manor Pottery. 1996
Number 2 in the series – *'Winston the Bricklayer'*. Available in four colourways – with black, blue, brown or grey suit. Also modelled by Andy Moss and in a limited edition of 3,000. On the wall behind the figure is the stone tablet in the garden wall at Chartwell: *'The greater part of this wall was built between the years 1925 and 1932 by Winston with his own hands'*. Available in UK at £95-115 and $140-$160 in the US.

30. Bairstow Manor Pottery. 1995
'Winston the Artist' from the *Life and Times of Winston Churchill* series. Four colourways are available each with a different Churchill painting on the easel. This model depicts *Mediterranean near Genoa – 1945*. Limited edition of 3,000. Created by Andy Moss. Hand painted. Price and availability as for *'Winston the Bricklayer'*.

16. Heritage China
1969

17. Keith Lee
1981

18. Karin Churchill
1976

19. Peter Hicks
1999

20. Ashmor Fine China
Worcester. 1985

21. Royal Doulton
1985

22. Winston's of
Harrogate. 1990

23. Leonardo
1990s

THE
IRON CURTAIN
SPEECH

Heritage

MARCH 5 1946
FULTON, MO

EZRA BROOKS
160

•CHURCHILL•

25. Royal Doulton. 1992

27. Quay Sculptures, Poole. 1980s

WINST
CHUR

WINSTON CHURCHILL
1945
VE DAY 50TH ANNIVERSARY

24. A Stadden. 1995

26. Baytree Crafts
Lincolnshire. 1995

28. Bairstow Manor
Pottery. 1999

29. Bairstow Manor
Pottery. 1996
'Winston the Bricklayer'

30. Bairstow Manor
Pottery. 1995
'Winston the Artist'

Sir Winston Churchill, 10 Downing Street, June 4th 1940

Flora Churchilliana

The first of an impressive list of garden
plants named after Winston Churchill was a
rosy red dianthus (border carnation) first
registered in 1905. It is no longer available,
but a number of later introductions can be
found around garden centres and nurseries,
enabling the enthusiast to assemble an
alfresco collection of Churchilliana.

Narcissus: Sir Winston Churchill
Right: Tall, late-flowering, creamy-white double
flowers with an orange-red cup. Trouble free.
Highly recommended.

Saxifrage: Winston Churchill
Below: A rockery plant with mounds of
dark green mossy leaves from which emerge a
mass of delicate pink and white flowers.

Chamaecyparis Lawsoniana:
Winston Churchill
Below right: A golden evergreen growing
to 8 feet tall in the open garden but equally
happy as a 2-3 feet patio specimen

Aster Novi-Belgii:
Winston S Churchill
Left: An old-fashioned Michaelmas Daisy
growing to 2$^{1}/_{2}$ feet tall. Needs spraying to
prevent attacks of powdery mildew.

Rhododendron Azalea Mollis:
Winston Churchill
Left: Needs a lime-free soil and prefers a
semi-shaded 'woodland' position but quite
happy as a patio specimen.

Fuchsia: Winston Churchill
Below left: Not hardy so must be protected
from frost. Flowers prolifically from June to
October – lavender petals with pink tubes.

Regal Pelargonium:
Winston Churchill
Below: Another plant which needs protection
from frost but does well outdoors in large
bowls or window boxes from mid-June.

Glassware

Churchill memorabilia made of china is available in abundance but oddly enough Churchill has rarely been commemorated in glass although the British glass industry has long been famed for its fine hand-cut and engraved crystal glassware. I illustrate some of the best examples of the genre.

1. Royal Brierley engraved crystal goblet by Thomas Goode & Co, London. 1964

Commissioned to commemorate Churchill's award of the Honorary Citizenship of the United States. 6$^{1}/_{2}$ inches high x 4 inches in diameter the goblet was engraved and signed by Tom Jones in a limited edition of 500. Churchill's portrait, surrounded by a garland of oak leaves, is surmounted by an American eagle and encircled by his achievements and the date of the award. On the reverse are engraved details of his birth, family crests and office as Prime Minister. Churchill died whilst the goblet was in issue and all but the earliest numbers in the edition were additionally engraved with the date of his death. The example illustrated is number 140 and it carries the death date. The original issue price was 30 guineas (£31.50). A goblet was sold at Sotheby's in July 1998 for £253 and in 1991 an early goblet (number 37) without the death date made $650 in the USA.

2. Toasting goblet by Webb Corbett. 1974

Toasting Goblet, 8$^{1}/_{2}$ inches tall, made in a limited edition of 1,000 by Webb Corbett for the *Churchill Centenary* in 1974. Churchill's portrait on the obverse is backed by a view of Big Ben etched on the reverse. Signed and numbered (this is number 666) beneath the foot, the goblets were sold in a smart brass-bound blue leatherette box with a blue and white satin lining and a Certificate of Authenticity signed by the Managing Director of Webb Corbett. An example made £75 at auction in 1994.

3. Tumbler engraved by Carol Moon

A tumbler, marking the 50th anniversary of VE Day, engraved by Carol Moon of Eaton Socon, Cambridgeshire. The inscription around a Union Flag and a 'V' reads: *'1945 – VE-Day 8 May – 1995.'*

4. Half-pint tankard by Stuart Crystal

A half-pint tankard from Stuart Cyrstal. Several variations exist. This one is engraved: *'We shall defend our island whatever the cost may be and we shall never surrender.'* Two Spitfires on the reverse. A variant design bears the inscription: *'Grim and Gay.'*

5. Crystal glass decanter engraved by Carol Moon

An altogether grander piece by Carol Moon celebrating the 50th anniversary of VE Day. A 9 inches high blown crystal glass decanter by Luigi Bormioli in his *Light and Music* design, extensively engraved by Ms Moon. Churchill gives his V-sign alongside the Union Flag and a large 'V' with the inscription: *'VE-Day/8 May/1945/1995 – Never in the field of human conflict was so much owed by so many to so few – 20 August 1940.'* Presentation piece from the Churchill Rooms, Bletchley Park.

6. Amber glass tankard by Wedgwood. 1974

Wedgwood produced a lead crystal paper weight and this chunky little amber glass tankard for the Churchill Centenary in 1974. Both encapsulated a blue and white jasper cameo portrait which had been modelled by Arnold Machin in 1940 when he was a student on a scholarship for sculpture from the Royal College of Art. Wedgwood used few of Machin's designs during the war, as he was a conscientious objector and they feared an unfavourable public reaction. But when he became Master of Sculpture at the Royal Academy and designed the Queen's portrait on postage stamps and coinage, Wedgwood used his Churchill portraits extensively.

7. Crystal glass tumbler by Stuart Crystal

The same Churchill portrait bust as the tankard but with the inscription: *'Put your confidence in us...and under providence all will be well.'* On the reverse is a portrait of Roosevelt and the inscription: *'Sail on ship of state, sail on oh union strong and great...'* Scarce. Probably made for the American market.

8. Crystal goblet by Carol Moon

Cambridgeshire engraver Carol Moon designed this cut glass crystal goblet exclusively for Bletchley Park. After a visit she wrote: *'The moment I came to Bletchley Park I fell in love with the place ... it is with great pleasure that I have engraved this piece of glassware in honour of Britain's greatest statesman – Winston Churchill.'* Around £15 in aid of Bletchley Park funds.

1. Royal Brierley engraved crystal goblet by Thomas Goode & Co, London. 1964

2. Toasting goblet by Webb Corbett. 1974

3. Tumbler engraved by Carol Moon

5. Crystal glass decanter engraved by Carol Moon

7. Crystal glass tumbler by Stuart Crystal

6. Amber glass tankard by Wedgwood. 1974

8. Crystal goblet by Carol Moon

4. Half-pint tankard by Stuart Crystal

A Grog Winston about 24 inches high like this, would set you back £1,500.

WINSTON CHURCHILL

God Save the King and Queen

The King and Queen remained in residence at Buckingham Palace throughout World War II. The palace was, of course, very recognisable from the air and it suffered nine direct hits from the German Luftwaffe.

Hand-painted pewter figures, issued by the Royal Air Force Benevolent Fund, depict Churchill with the King and Queen surveying the damage after the worst of the raids. King George VI had been Patron of the RAFBF from 1936 until his death in 1952. Churchill was a Vice-President of the Fund from 1919 until his death in 1965.

'Grog' Churchill

John Hughes has a Grog shop in Pontypridd, S Wales. It is not a disreputable hostelry serving watered down alcoholic beverages. No, John makes and sells grogs – grotesque caricatures of well-known human figures – as up-market substitutes for the ubiquitous garden gnome. Finely modelled, cast in resin and painted to requirements, grogs come in whatever size is specified. Actors, sportsmen, TV personalities and politicians are all fair game.

Guildhall

The Great Hall in the City of London dates from 1411 but little is left of the original building. Virtually destroyed in the Great Fire which devastated the City in 1666, it was restored by Christopher Wren, provided with a new facade in 1788, badly damaged again during the Blitz of 1940 and given a new roof in 1953. Guildhall contains the administrative buildings of the Corporation of London, a museum, an art gallery and a library housing thousands of valuable books and manuscripts dealing with the history of London and the first and second folios of Shakespeare's plays.

Guildhall is at the centre of the pageantry and ceremony surrounding the election of the Lord Mayor, the colourful procession of the Lord Mayor's Show, the Court of Common Council and the Admission of Sheriffs – all part of the City of London's tradition. The Great Hall, splendidly restored by Sir Giles Scott after wartime bombing, is used for the Lord Mayor's Banquet and other state and civic functions. The walls are decorated with the shields and banners of the livery companies and there are several statues of outstanding people in British history, including a superb sculpture of Winston Churchill.

Oscar Nemon's larger-than-life seated bronze figure of Churchill in the Guildhall is appropriately sited opposite the memorial to those who died in the Boer War, in which Churchill had participated and been taken prisoner. It was the first statue of Churchill, commissioned by the Corporation of the City of London and was unveiled in his presence on 21 June 1955. While sculpting Churchill, Nemon found it necessary to pacify his restless sitter by providing him with a ball of clay. Thus while Nemon sculpted Churchill, Churchill sculpted Nemon. Later, Churchill's clay model was cast and presented to him.

Churchill's bust of Nemon can now be seen in the Studio at Chartwell and there is a letter from Nemon to Churchill in the archives at Churchill College, Cambridge: *'... I beg you not to underrate the artistic value of this work which would be considered by any expert as outstanding for a first attempt.'* In his speech at the unveiling of the statue Churchill said: *'I regard it as a very high honour that the City of London should decide to set up a statue of me in this famous Guildhall... I think that the House of Commons has made a good rule in not erecting monuments to people in their lifetime. But I entirely agree that every rule should have an exception... I greatly admire the art of Mr Oscar Nemon... I also admire this particular example ... because it seems to me such a very good likeness.'*

Churchill had attended many grand occasions at the Guildhall. Apart from the unveiling of his statue, the occasion which probably gave him the greatest personal pleasure was when he was presented with the Freedom of the City of London on 30 June 1943. In his speech of thanks Churchill said: *'You have given me this casket, which contains my title as a Freeman of the City of London. I have not always been wrong about the future of events and if you will permit me, I shall inscribe some of these words within it as my testament, because I should like to be held to account for them in years which I shall not see... This event will always rank in my mind with the very highest days of rejoicing that I have passed in my journey through the world.'* The presentation of the Freedom of the City of London to Churchill was marked by the issue of a special pack of playing cards.

Oscar Nemon's statue of Churchill in the Guildhall. This was the first statue of Churchill, commissioned by the City of London and unveiled in his presence on 21 June 1955.

Handbag mirror

Typical of the patriotic baubles issued between 1940 and 1945 is this *'Souvenir of the World's War.'* It is a small handbag mirror, cheaply printed on card and bound to the mirror glass with passe partout. It has done well to survive intact, though somewhat faded, for sixty years.

Harrow School

We have Winston Churchill's own account of his time at Harrow in his book *My Early Life*. The book covers the first 28 years of Churchill's life and he devotes just ten of its 392 pages to his years at Harrow. Frederick Woods, Churchill's bibliographer, described it as a *'racy, humorous, self-deprecating classic of an autobiography.'* There is little doubt that Churchill was being excessively self-deprecating about his scholastic achievements since whilst there is independent evidence to confirm that he was not always a model pupil there is also ample corroboration of his capacity to learn, and learn thoroughly, when the subject interested him. Latin did not interest him, a lack of concern shared by generations of schoolboys before and since, but history certainly did interest him as did English.

When Churchill became Prime Minister in 1940, the school magazine, *The Harrovian*, printed a poem, *The Influenza*, which he had written when he was just fifteen years old. He had been awarded a House Prize for the poem, which had gone some way towards redeeming his position with both his parents and his teachers who had been less than impressed by his recent attitude and scholastic achievement. It was an accomplished piece of verse and perhaps gave a hint that here was a future winner of the Nobel Prize for Literature.

Churchill was a pupil at Harrow for 4$\frac{1}{2}$ years from 1888 to 1892. For a fuller, and probably more objective account than his own memoir, try to find *Winston Churchill and Harrow* by EDW Chaplin (Harrow School Book Shop 1941). It includes recollections by contemporaries who, although they were then writing with the benefit of hindsight and no doubt a little deference, added a valuable perspective to Churchill's own account.

Churchill was a slight and somewhat puny youth but he won the Public Schools Fencing Championship in 1892. He passed the Army Preliminary Examination at Harrow but was sent to a 'Crammer' for intensive tuition in the hated, but obligatory, Latin before passing into Sandhurst.

Churchill first returned to Harrow eight years after leaving. In October 1900, just before he became MP for Oldham, he gave the boys an account of his experiences in the Boer War, his capture and escape. *The Harrovian* reported his lecture in somewhat breathless idolatry. For the next forty years Churchill's return visits to his old school were rare but in December 1940 he went back to address the boys and take part in the traditional singing of the *School Song*. He was much moved by the experience and thereafter was to return regularly each year for the next twenty years. In fact, his twentieth successive annual visit in November 1960 was to be the occasion on which he made his last ever public speech. In his honour an additional verse was added to the school song:

*Nor less we praise in darker days
The leader of our nation
And Churchill's name shall win acclaim
From each new generation
While in this fight to guard the right
Our country you defend, Sir
Here grim and gay we mean to stay
And stick it to the end, Sir.*

Hat box

In Victorian and Edwardian times a well-dressed gentleman often had a vast collection of hats. A hat for all occasions: see the display of some of Churchill's hats at Chartwell. The well-dressed gentleman

also had a hat box in which to carry his hats whilst travelling. It was robustly made, usually of steel, with a substantial lock to protect the contents against thieves and robbers. It became the fashion to decorate one's hat box with labels from ocean-going liners, inter continental railway trains and the world's best hotels. I came across this hat box, at a a car boot sale, some years ago which had been lovingly adorned with some now slightly faded early photographs of Winston Churchill.

Havengore

On 30 January 1965 the Port of London Authority's survey launch *Havengore* was called upon to perform the solemn duty of carrying the coffin of Sir Winston Churchill, following his State Funeral in St Paul's Cathedral, along the River Thames from the Tower of London to Festival Pier. Churchill's coffin had been hauled on a gun carriage from Westminster Hall to St Paul's and thence through the City of London to Tower Pier in order that a short, but symbolic, river journey should be included as a fitting tribute to a man who had had such a great affection for all things maritime. Twice First Lord of the Admiralty; famously, in his wartime correspondence with President Roosevelt, Former Naval Person; an Elder Brother of Trinity House; Lord Warden of the Cinque Ports; proud wearer, when on his wartime 'naval' excursions, of his Royal Yacht Squadron cap and reefer jacket; Winston Churchill had long considered himself a

Top: Havengore on duty, 30 January 1965. An escort of Grenadier Guards flank Churchill's coffin on its journey along the River Thames.

Far left: June 1997. Owen Palmer surveys the dilapidation of the planking above *Havengore's* plotting cabin prior to restoration work in Chatham Dockyard.

Above left: The original ship's bell from *Havengore* was presented by owner Owen Palmer to Jack Darrah, the driving force behind the Bletchley Park exhibition. The polished wood gantry from which the bell is hung was constructed from deck timbers replaced during the restoration process.

Below left: A water line scale model of the PLA launch *Havengore* carrying Churchill's coffin and its escort of Grenadier Guards along the Thames, after the funeral service at St Paul's Cathedral, on 30 January 1965. The scale model was built by marine modeller Brian Martin of Bere Alston, Devon especially for the Churchill Rooms at Bletchley Park.

sailor. So he was given a sailor's farewell with a water-borne procession matching that previously accorded to Lord Nelson in 1805.

Churchill's coffin rested on a bier erected over a skylight aft of the cabin. An escort of Grenadier guardsmen flanked the coffin whilst close family members were installed below decks in the spacious plotting cabin. The flag of the Lord Warden of the Cinque Ports flew at the bow of *Havengore* and the Blue Ensign of the Royal Navy Auxiliary streamed at the stern. A Royal Marines band played *Rule Britannia*; a nineteen-gun salute was fired; riverside cranes dipped in salute and there was a flypast of sixteen Royal Air Force Lightning fighters. The Captain of *Havengore* was the PLA's River Superintendent and Harbour Master, Commander GV Parmiter.

Havengore was built by Tough Brothers of Teddington in 1956, to an extravagant specification. Eighty-seven feet long, eighteen feet in the beam and with a draft of almost six feet, she had a gross displacement of 89 tons. Her dark blue hull was of flush-jointed teak planks over an oak frame and her superstructure of clear-varnished natural hardwood. Although built to carry out hydrographic surveys for the Port of London Authority *Havengore's* smart appearance had often seen her pressed into service on ceremonial occasions – for example, wreath laying on Remembrance Day, the Lord Mayor's Show and the State Visit of the President of Finland – but there is no doubt her 'Finest Hour' was on 30 January 1965.

More than thirty years later Australian Owen Palmer, and his wife Sally Browne discovered *Havengore*, long unused and laid up in Chatham Dockyard. The once proud vessel presented a sorry sight – peeling paintwork, flaking varnish, sprung and leaking deckboards, broken ports and missing fittings and rails. But a survey established that she was structurally sound and without major defect. Aware of the historical significance of *Havengore* Mr Palmer acquired the vessel, formed the *Havengore Trust*, and set about restoring her to her former glory. It is his intention that *Havengore's* primary role in future

will be to provide disadvantaged children, with the opportunity to take river and coastal voyages and enable them to take part in maritime festivals and acquire a sense of identity and a feeling of pride. When the restoration of *Havengore* has reached a suitably advanced stage, it is planned that ongoing fund-raising activities will enable the vessel to be hired for special functions, river trips, meetings and banquets. It is intended that a permanent display will be mounted in the plotting cabin illustrating *Havengore's* historic connection with Sir Winston Churchill.

HMS Belfast

The largest cruiser operated by the Royal Navy during World War II, *HMS Belfast* had a full load displacement of 14,930 tonnes. Built by Harland & Wolff in Belfast she was completed in 1939 but almost came to early grief being badly damaged by a German magnetic mine in the Firth of Forth on 21 November 1939. Her armament consisted of twelve six-inch (152mm) guns in triple turrets, torpedo tubes and a number of 40mm anti-aircraft guns.

HMS Belfast is best remembered for the important part she played in the Battle of North Cape, in December 1943, when the German battleship *Scharnhorst* was sunk while attempting to intercept an Allied convoy bound for Russia. In action with *HMS Belfast* were the battleship *HMS Duke of York*, the cruisers *HMS Norfolk*, *HMS Sheffield* and *HMS Jamaica* and eight destroyers. The *Scharnhorst* tried to break off the action but *HMS Duke of York* was able to get within range with devastating effect. Of a company of 1,970 officers and men aboard *Scharnhorst* only thirty-six were rescued by the British ships.

HMS Belfast almost secured an even greater place in history! At the approach to D-Day in 1944 Winston Churchill decided that he would like to cross the Channel aboard one of HM ships to observe the preliminary bombardment at close quarters. He asked Admiral Ramsay, the naval Commander-in-Chief, to make a plan. The admiral arranged that Churchill would embark in *HMS Belfast* at Weymouth on the afternoon of the day before D-Day and spend the night aboard her before watching the dawn attack and making a short tour of the beaches. Admiral Ramsay told General Eisenhower of his plan and Eisenhower protested that Churchill was running too great a risk. Churchill replied, stating that whilst we accepted him as Supreme Commander, the Royal Navy was putting up four times as many ships as the United States Navy and he had no authority over the complements of British ships.

However a complication arose. At his weekly audience with King George VI Churchill mentioned that on D-Day he proposed to watch the bombardment of the invasion beaches from one of the cruiser squadron. The King immediately replied that he would like to go too.

Churchill said that he was not unwilling to put the matter to the Cabinet. That caused alarm bells to ring in all high places. General Ismay was opposed to Churchill's plan not so much by the personal risk involved but by the prospect of the Prime Minister being cut off from communication with the outside world at a time when critical decisions might have to be taken. The King was prevailed upon to decide that neither he nor Churchill should go and he wrote from Buckingham Palace on 31 May 1944: *'My dear Winston, I have been thinking a great deal of our conversation yesterday and I have come to the conclusion that it would not be right for either you or I to be where we planned to be on D-Day.'*

Churchill put up every argument he could think of to persuade the King to allow him to go: *'... as Prime Minister and Minister of Defence I ought to be allowed to go where I consider it necessary...'* However, he bowed to the King's wishes, although later, in his book *The Second World War*, he grumbled: *'I may add that the cruiser squadron was ... not exposed to any undue danger. In fact it did not sustain a single casualty.'*

HMS Belfast has been a floating branch of the Imperial War Museum since 1971, permanently moored on the River Thames in London, close to Tower Bridge. The displays and exhibits include much of interest to Churchillians.

HMS Churchill

The Nuclear Fleet Submarine *HMS Churchill* was built by Vickers at Barrow-in-Furness. Her keel was laid on 30 June 1967 and the launching ceremony was carried out by Winston's youngest daughter Mary, Lady Soames, on 20 December 1968. The ship was 285 feet long and with a beam of 33 feet the submarine displaced 3500 tons (standard) and 4900 tons (submerged). Her main propulsion was a nuclear reactor with steam turbines driving a single shaft.

Crewed by 11 officers and 92 petty officers and ratings she was equipped with six torpedo tubes and would normally carry hunting torpedoes. Capable of high underwater speeds *HMS Churchill* could remain on patrol almost indefinitely with the capability of circumnavigating the world without surfacing. Her building cost was of the order of £24-£30 million.

After sea trials in March and April 1970 *HMS Churchill* was commissioned on 15 July in that year. At the time the island of Jersey was celebrating the 25th anniversary of its liberation from German occupation in 1945 and the Jersey Post Office had issued a 5d stamp bearing a portrait of Churchill and the quotation: *'And our dear Channel Islands are also to be freed today.'*

The stamp appropriately featured on a first-day cover marking the first commission of *HMS Churchill*. The cover had a full-colour reproduction of the ship's badge, the ship's motto *'Veteris Vestigia Flammae'* and cancellations by the Jersey Post Office and the Commanding Officer.

HMS Churchill was one of the Royal Navy's *Valiant* class nuclear-powered submarines normally armed with Mark 8 and 21-inch Tigerfish torpedoes. Her sister ships *HMS Courageous* and *HMS Conqueror*, after additionally equipping with Harpoon surface-to-surface missiles, participated in the Falklands War in 1982. Both submarines left their base at Faslane on the Clyde on 4 April. *HMS Conqueror*, under the command of Commander Chris Wredford-Brown DSO RN, arrived off South Georgia on 19 April. Subsequently *HMS Conqueror* was ordered to carry out surveillance of the Argentine cruiser *General Belgrano*.

On 2 May the order came from London to open fire. She fired three Mark 8 torpedoes at the *General Belgrano* scoring two hits; the third torpedo struck the destroyer *Hipolito Bouchard*. The *General Belgrano* sank within 15 minutes with the loss of 321 lives. *HMS Conqueror* dived deep and was hunted for two terrifying hours by Argentine destroyers using sonar and depth charges. Mark 8 torpedoes had been used rather than Tigerfish on the grounds of expense. Tigerfish cost around £$^1/_2$ million, whilst the Mark 8s were conventional vintage torpedoes, circa World War II.

Thus the combination of modern warship and antiquated weapon wrought terrible damage. Perhaps it is as well that the Tigerfish were taken back to Faslane unused. Whilst *HMS Churchill* did not herself participate directly in the Falklands War, it is fitting that her sister ship should have had such a significant role.

After the end of the cold war in 1989, *HMS Churchill* became a victim of defence cuts and was decommissioned and laid up at Rosyth awaiting disposal. *HMS Conqueror* shared the same fate at Devonport. Debate still continues over the safe disposal of all the redundant first generation nuclear-powered submarines. Some nations believe that sinking in deep water is preferable to attempting to remove the nuclear reactor before traditional scrapping.

HMS Churchill spent virtually the whole of her service during the Cold War stalking and observing ships of the Russian Navy. She had the capability to circumnavigate the world without surfacing. As a result she was rarely photographed.

Left: A commemorative cover postmarked *'Jersey, Channel Islands – 15 July 1970'* on the occasion of the first commissioning of the Royal Navy's nuclear fleet submarine *HMS Churchill.* The cover bears the ship's badge of *HMS Churchill,* the cachet of the commanding officer and the special stamp issued by the Jersey Post Office commemorating the 25th anniversary of the liberation of the island from German occupation.

Below: This rare picture of *HMS Churchill* was taken at the Queen's Review of the Fleet at Portsmouth during her Silver Jubilee celebrations in 1977.

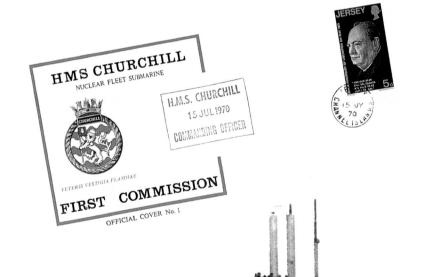

Horse brasses

In 1944 a horse brass depicting the Prime Minister was designed by Harry Richards. It had a portrait bust of Churchill smoking a cigar within large 'V' and surrounded by a laurel wreath. An example was sent to 10 Downing Street for approval, but the reply came back that the horse brass should not be put into production until the war was over and the brass no longer needed for munitions! However, it is known that at least one further first edition casting was made and sent to President Roosevelt, disregarding the Prime Ministerial ruling. When Mr Richards' design did eventually go into mass production it was widely copied. Many foundries used low-grade brass to make poor quality castings. When Churchill died, Mr Richards' design was reintroduced and a much crisper casting, inscribed: *'Sir Winston Churchill, 1874-1965'*, was issued in better quality metal. 1995 saw another reissue of the Richards design, often paired on a leather martingale strap, with contemporary brasses marking the 50th anniversary of VE-Day. The anchor-shaped horse brass is from the Sail Training Association, sold as a souvenir of the schooner *Sir Winston Churchill* and appropriately marks Churchill's two terms as First Lord of the Admiralty.

Hoskins Churchill's Pride

This strong beer, allegedly first brewed in Lincolnshire during World War II exclusively for the Royal Air Force, was revived in 1990 to commemorate the 50th anniversary of the Battle of Britain.

Promotional items included a crystal glass paperweight and a coaster.

House of Commons

The House of Commons is within the Palace of Westminster, still officially a Royal Palace, as it has been for nine hundred years. The last king to live there was Henry VIII, in 1512. Very much the working heart of British Government, the House of Commons has been the model for the legislatures of many countries around the world. Busy and bustling with activity as it goes about its day-to-day business, it is regularly the scene of grand ceremonial on occasions like the State Opening of Parliament. Each November the Queen drives from Buckingham Palace to the Sovereign's Entrance beneath the Victoria Tower. Donning her crimson robe and the Imperial State Crown she walks in procession to the Chamber of the House of Lords where the lords and judges await her. The Gentleman Usher of the Black Rod then summons the House of Commons and upon their arrival at the Bar of the House, the Queen reads her speech from the Throne, setting out the parliamentary programme arranged for the new session.

Even the daily sittings of the House of Commons are not without a historic ritual, being preceded by the Speaker's procession from his, or her, residence within the palace to the Commons Chamber. A police inspector calls *'Hats off, Strangers'* and all the MPs and officers bow to the Speaker who, in robes of office, is accompanied by the Trainbearer, the Chaplain, a Secretary and the Sergeant-at-Arms carrying the Mace. The latter is placed upon the Table of the House whenever the House is sitting and is put on hooks 'below the table' when the House goes into Committee.

The present Chamber of the House of Commons was designed by Sir Giles Gilbert Scott and was opened in 1950. It replaced the Chamber designed by Sir Charles Barry, first used by the Commons in 1852, and destroyed by German bombing in 1941. The Commons had acquired its first permanent home in 1547, when St Stephen's Chapel was made available. The chapel was used until 1834 when it was destroyed by fire. The present Chamber is almost a replica of Barry's though its decoration is less ornate, and larger galleries have been

Dominating the Lobby of the House of Commons is Oscar Nemon's massive bronze statue of Winston Churchill, standing alongside the Churchill Arch. It was unveiled by Lady Churchill in December 1969.

Left: The Churchill Arch, which forms the main entrance to the Chamber of the House of Commons. It was built, at Churchill's suggestion, with scarred and blackened stones from the debris of the old chamber, bombed on 10 May 1941.

Below: The Chamber of the House of Commons. Government benches are on the left, Opposition on the right. Beneath the clock is the Speaker's chair and above is the Press Gallery.

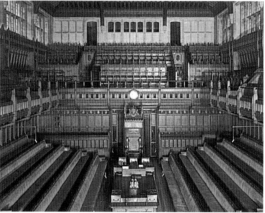

Baldwin and all those who have served in the office of Prime Minister. Most of all you will find memorabilia connected with Sir Winston Churchill. The House of Commons was Churchill's second home. With a break of just two years he was an MP from October 1900 till October 1964, and his spirit is everywhere.

The arch above the doors forming the main entrance to the Chamber is built of stones bearing the scars of the bomb damage which destroyed the old chamber in 1941. Fire blackened, they were re-incorporated into the new arch. On 25 January 1945, in a speech to the House of Commons, which had been sitting in the House of Lords since its own Chamber was destroyed in the air raid of 10 May 1941, Churchill said: *'I venture to add a suggestion of my own... I hope very much that the archway into the Chamber from the Inner Lobby ... which was smitten by the blast of the explosion ... will be preserved intact as a monument of the ordeal which Westminster has passed through.'* The preserved arch came to be known as the Churchill Arch.

Churchill wrote to his son, Randolph, then serving with the Commandos in the western desert: *'Our old House of Commons has been blown to smithereens. You never saw such a sight. Not one scrap was left except for a few of the outer walls.'* Somebody had the idea, it may have been Churchill, that the pieces of broken stone could be made into souvenirs and sold in aid of the Red Cross. Sir Vincent Baddeley, a retired civil servant who had worked for Churchill while at the Admiralty from 1899 to 1935, then a director of the Alliance Insurance Company, was appointed to make the arrangements. The London Stonecraft Company selected the smaller pieces of stone, approximately 5 x 4 inches, to create paperweights and deliberately left the stone untrimmed, but backed with green baize and carrying a $2^1/_2$ inch diameter portrait medallion of Churchill cast in lead from the damaged roof. Larger pieces of stone were carved into ashtrays, book ends and tobacco jars. Some had lead medallions displaying a view of Big Ben instead of Churchill and I have a pair of book ends embellished with portrait medallions of Churchill and Roosevelt. Each piece was sold with a certificate

provided for visitors. In October 1943 Prime Minister Winston Churchill moved that a Select Committee be appointed to consider and report on plans for rebuilding the Commons Chamber. Churchill said: *'We have now to consider whether we should build it up again, and how, and when. We shape our buildings and afterwards our buildings shape us. Having dwelt and served for more than forty years in the late Chamber, and having derived very great pleasure and advantage therefrom I, naturally, would like to see it restored in all essentials to its old form, convenience and dignity.'* When the Select Committee presented its Report to the House in January 1945 Churchill remarked that he was *'... extremely gratified to see that the main principles which I ventured to submit*

to the House eighteen months ago have been confirmed by the committee in such emphatic terms'. He was anxious that nothing should delay the rebuilding and suggested that with a vast labour force of 130,000 men working on war damage repairs in London that a hundred could be spared to rebuild the Commons Chamber.

Following tradition, there are only 437 seats in the new chamber, although there are 630 MPs. The restriction is deliberate as the House is not intended to be a forum for set orations and large audiences, but a specialised debating chamber where a small, intimate, conversational atmosphere is usually more appropriate. As well as providing an often crowded, noisy and heated debating chamber for the elected

Members of Parliament and a usually more decorous and restrained, forum for members of the House of Lords, the Palace of Westminster also houses thousands of civil servants and others concerned with the administration of government. On the one hand an entirely progressive and up-to-the-minute assembly and on the other, possibly the world's greatest museum of democracy, preserving many time-honoured rituals. Somewhat cathedral-like in its architecture, the Palace is also a shrine to many of those prominent in the history of British politics. You will find busts, statues, pictures and other objects commemorating Sir Robert Walpole, Lord North, William Pitt, the Duke of Wellington, Earl Grey, Sir Robert Peel, Benjamin Disraeli, William Gladstone, David Lloyd George, Stanley

A paperweight made of
stone and lead from the
bomb-damaged House
of Commons.

signed by Sir Vincent Baddeley: '*I hereby certify that this stone was part of the structure of the Houses of Parliament, damaged by enemy air raids on 10 May 1941.*' The souvenirs clearly sold in considerable numbers and many examples have survived. Most can be picked up for just a few pounds but those which still have their Certificate of Authenticity may attract a large premium.

Beneath the arch to the Chamber are heavy double doors which are locked against Black Rod during the colourful ceremonial when the Queen opens a new session of Parliament. Oscar Nemon's giant bronze statue of Churchill, catching him in a characteristic oratorical posture, stands beside the arch. The toecap on Churchill's left shoe has been worn to a smooth shine through being constantly touched as a talisman by MPs entering the Chamber.

Sir Oswald Birley, the noted portraitist, became a friend of Churchill and painted four pictures of him when he was Leader of the Opposition between 1946 and 1951. One, a near full-length seated study, now hangs in the House of Commons. Not one but two of Churchill's own paintings hang in the House. Two of his pictures, which had been exhibited on the World Tour in 1958 and at the Royal Academy in 1959 – *Mimizan Lake c.1922* and *Venice 1951* – were placed on permanent loan by Lady Churchill and have been there ever since.

The State Rooms in Speaker's House contain a marvellous collection of pictures, bronzes and porcelain including several Churchill commemorative pieces. These are understood to include a richly decorated crimson and gilt vase made by Spode in 1965 and a porcelain figure of Churchill standing outside 10 Downing Street, with right arm raised in the V-sign. The latter, ten inches tall and superbly modelled and painted, was made by Ashmor Fine China of Worcester in a limited edition to mark the 40th anniversary of VE Day.

In October 1950, when speaking at the first session in the newly re-built Chamber, Churchill described himself as '*a child of the House of Commons*'. Surely he must be its favourite son.

28 Hyde Park Gate, the Churchill's last London home from 1945-1965

Hyde Park Gate

During the winter of 1944-45 Clementine Churchill quietly began house hunting in London. She cherished the thought that when the war was over, and the coalition government dissolved, Winston would retire. After all he had just celebrated his 70th birthday. It is unlikely that Winston shared his wife's thought but, in any event, he was still totally absorbed with the prosecution of the war and the problems he knew would accompany the peace.

In January 1945 Clementine found a charming and secluded house with a delightful garden at 28 Hyde Park Gate,

a quiet cul-de-sac off Kensington Road about a quarter of a mile west of the Royal Albert Hall. She wrote to her daughter, Mary: '*Yesterday afternoon I took Papa to see the little house I covet. He is mad about it, so now I must be careful not to run him into something which is more than he can afford.*'

When the shock result of the 1945 general election was declared in July the Churchills became effectively homeless. Chartwell had been closed down during the war and a lot of work was necessary to make it habitable again. They had to vacate 10 Downing Street with customary haste to

allow the Attlees to take up residence. Their daughter Diana and her husband Duncan Sandys came to Winston and Clementine's immediate rescue by lending them their flat in Westminster Gardens until they found permanent accommodation. Churchill himself had not really paid close attention to 28 Hyde Park Gate during his visit in January, his mind had been on other things, but another visit made him enthusiastic and negotiations commenced forthwith.

The raised ground floor comprised a large drawing room and dining room with a long third room which would provide an ante-room or study. A graceful curved staircase led to the first floor consisting of two commodious bedroom suites described in the agents particulars as '*some of the finest accommodation in a London home.*' On the second floor was a further bedroom suite, three single bedrooms, another bathroom and a maid's room. A large basement area contained a kitchen, scullery, larder, two pantries, a wine cellar and a staff sitting room. The walled garden was screened by trees and flowering shrubs with a York stone terrace and paths around a pleasant lawn.

Fortunately little needed to be done to the house other than some redecoration and the Churchills were able to move in at the beginning of October 1945. Immediately an unexpected problem arose. Clementine had visualised the need for a comfortable house for an elderly, retired couple. She had not allowed for the large secretariat which Winston needed to support his continuing political life as Leader of the Opposition and his immediate major project – his book *The Second World War*. Fortuitously the house next door, number 27, had just come onto the market. It was of similar size, design and construction to number 28 and was duly purchased. The required office accommodation was created on the ground floor and the basement, while the top two floors were converted into a flat, which was let to provide income to defray the cost of living in two houses.

When Churchill became Prime Minister again in 1951 and returned to 10 Downing Street, 28 Hyde Park Gate was let to the Cuban Ambassador. When Winston resigned in 1955 and he and Clementine went back to Hyde Park Gate neither of them was in the best of health. Winston's life-style for a man of eighty was of concern to his doctors. He was troubled by his increasing deafness, but refused to wear a hearing aid. Clementine had fallen and broken her wrist which caused her pain for many weeks. They both gained comfort from the fact that their daughter Sarah stayed with them at Hyde Park Gate for much of the winter of 1955-56.

For the rest of his life Churchill spent his time between Chartwell and Hyde Park Gate interspersed with regular holidays abroad and cruises on Aristotle Onassis's yacht. Inevitably the years took their toll and he became increasingly frail. He came back from Chartwell to Hyde Park Gate for what was to be the last time in October 1964. He seldom ventured from the house after that, although there was a constant flow of visitors. On Winston's ninetieth birthday, 30 November 1964, a crowd gathered to sing *'Happy Birthday'* and were rewarded by his appearance at a window with hand raised in the V-sign.

On 10 January 1965 he suffered a massive stroke and lapsed into a coma. When the news was made public a few days later a small constantly changing group of well-wishers kept vigil outside the house until, shortly after eight o'clock on the morning of Sunday 24 January 1965, Winston Churchill died. It was seventy years to the day since the death of his father. Being too large for Clementine alone, the two houses were sold by auction by Knight, Frank and Rutley on 28 October 1965. On a wall high up on the front of the house is one of those ubiquitous London County Council blue plaques stating with simply that *'Winston Churchill lived here: 1945 –1965.'*

Inn signs

All over England there are public houses proudly honouring the name of Winston Churchill. Two of the most prominent hostelries are opposite Churchill College, Cambridge and in Kensington Church Street, London. Most have a traditional inn sign, some of which are good whilst others are downright awful.

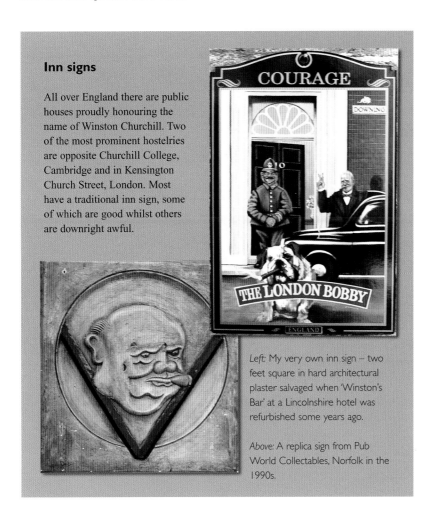

Left: My very own inn sign – two feet square in hard architectural plaster salvaged when 'Winston's Bar' at a Lincolnshire hotel was refurbished some years ago.

Above: A replica sign from Pub World Collectables, Norfolk in the 1990s.

Jigsaw puzzles

In 1937 John Waddington produced a series of four puzzles illustrating famous battles – Blenheim, The Nile, Rorke's Drift and Jutland. The *Chartwell Trust* papers at Churchill College, Cambridge reveal that Churchill wrote an account of each battle for the boxes which contained the puzzles. From 1940 onwards Churchill became the subject of many jigsaws. Those made during the war years and printed on paper conforming to economy standards are now faded, browned and foxed.

Below: A jigsaw puzzle featuring one of the most famous wartime posters.

Right: This jigsaw puzzle marking Churchill's funeral included a print of a photograph by Karsh of Ottawa.

Left: Marking the 50th anniversary of VE Day.

Below: This patriotic and colourful puzzle printed in the USA.

Knight of the Garter

St George's Chapel at Windsor Castle, was founded by King Edward IV (1461-83) as the collegiate church of the Knights of the Order of the Garter. Incumbent knights have their own stall in the chapel and their individual and distinctive banners hang from the vaulted ceiling. On the death of a knight, his (or her) banner is removed but a heraldic plaque remains for posterity. The current assemblage of plaques antedates the chapel itself and provides a roll-call of the great and the good of British history.

Churchill had refused a peerage when he was defeated in the 1945 general election because he wished to remain a member of his beloved House of Commons and, although almost seventy-one years of age, he cherished the thought of serving again as Prime Minister. In 1953 the new Queen Elizabeth II appointed him as a Knight of the Most Noble Order of the Garter, the highest Order of Chivalry which had been founded by King Edward III in 1348. The number of knights at any one time is normally restricted to twenty-six plus the Sovereign and the Prince of Wales. The motto of the Order is *Honi soit qui mal y pense* (Shame on him who thinks evil of it).

See also pages 63 and 71 for Knights of the Garter modelled by Peggy Nisbet and Karin Churchill respectively.

A hand-made reduced-scale replica of the banner of Sir Winston Churchill which hung in the chapel from 1954-65. The replica is on display at the Churchill Rooms, Bletchley Park.

The 10½-inch tall figurine, also available as a toby jug, was modelled by Ray Noble for Bairstow Manor Pottery in 1999 in an edition limited to 750. It is well modelled but with some inaccurate paint detailing. At Churchill's back is the Round Tower of Windsor Castle and a representation of his Knight's banner.

Lapel badges

'Pin' has twenty-five meanings, so says the *Oxford Dictionary*. One meaning, notably in the United States is, *'A badge fastened to the clothing by a straight piece of wire pointed at one end.'* The heyday of the 'pin' was World War II when, to compete with the insignia worn by servicemen on their uniforms, civilians adorned their lapels with suitable badges. If to wear one's heart on one's sleeve is to show one's feelings openly, then to wear a portrait of Prime Minister Winston Churchill on one's lapel during the war was an open display of patriotism.

This selection of Churchill 'pins' or lapel badges is not exhaustive, but illustrates the wide choice available.

Six badges dating from World War II. They have no great value in the UK, but may fetch up to $40 each in the USA.

Silver badge dating from World War II.

Enamel badge of locomotive *Winston Churchill* from the Railway Museum, York.

Ceramic badge dating from World War II, 2¼ inches high.

Modern badge, cut from plywood in fretwork.

V-sign-shaped Union Jack celebrates the 50th anniversary of VE Day.

Two 'Send for Churchill' badges dating from the 1951 general election.

The badge of the International Churchill Society.

Longleat

Longleat is situated four miles southwest of Warminster, Wiltshire. The magnificent Renaissance house, built between 1568 and 1580 for Sir John Thynne in a park which was designed by Capability Brown, is an attraction in its own right with its rich architecture, fine furniture, tapestries, silverware and old-master paintings.

The poster for Lord Bath's collection of Churchill memorabilia

The 6th Marquess of Bath was a fanatical collector of Churchilliana. He began by collecting Churchill's books shortly after World War II then, as he put it: *'the mania grew and with the years I went on to collect everything to do with him.'* The collection became one of the greatest accumulations of Churchill-related items in the world. Not maybe the rarest, nor the most valuable, when compared with the virtually priceless collection at Chartwell, but surely the most complete in terms of its range of popular tributes to Churchill. It included almost every commemorative medal issued featuring the great man; the memorial and centenary postage stamps from all foreign and Commonwealth countries; first editions of every one of Churchill's books and a great deal more besides. There was one of Churchill's own paintings – a full-length reclining portrait of Viscountess Castlerose painted c1930. (Another study of the same subject is in the studio at Chartwell).

In his foreword to J Eric Engstrom's book *The Medallic Portraits of Sir Winston Churchill* (Spink & Son 1972), Lord Bath wrote: *'To my mind there is only one true sign of greatness, and that is someone who can inspire. To me, Sir Winston was not only the greatest Englishman of our time, but the greatest Englishman of all time.'*

The best part of the 6th Marquess of Bath's remarkable collection of Churchilliana was on display to visitors to Longleat, to mark the Churchill Centenary in 1974, in a series of cabinets lining the Lower East Corridor leading to the State Rooms.

Unfortunately the 7th Marquess of Bath did not share his father's enthusiasm and after the 6th Marquess of Bath died in 1992 his son began to disassemble his father's Longleat Churchilliana collection. Much of the Churchilliana collection has since been sold to help offset the cost of maintaining the house. In November 1997 a modest 1938 Austin 10 saloon, EYH 409, which had belonged to Churchill between 1938 and 1950 and was acquired by Lord Bath, was sold by Sotheby's for £66,400. Originally, the car had cost £350 and Lord Bath bought it for £1,350, although he claimed to have spent £6,335 on restoration. The collection at Longleat included a pair of Churchill's blue velvet slippers which were embroidered 'WSC' in gold thread – a similar pair to that sold for £6,325 at Sotheby's, London in July 1998.

Jack Darrah from Bletchley Park stands alongside the Austin 10 Saloon, EYH 409, at the Sotheby's sale held at the Royal Air Force Museum, Hendon on 24 November 1997. The hammer price of the car he wanted to purchase for his collection was beyond his means on the day!

Long-playing records

In 1964 the Decca Record Company issued a boxed set of twelve LPs – *Winston S Churchill: his Memoirs and his Speeches* – on which Churchill read excerpts from his book *The Second World War* and re-read his notable wartime speeches. (Those made in the House of Commons were not recorded at the time).

After Churchill's funeral EMI Records issued an LP in collaboration with the BBC – *The State Funeral of Sir Winston Churchill KG OM CH*.

The musical play *Winnie*, with Robert Hardy and Virginia McKenna, opened in Manchester on 21 April 1988 but closed shortly after its transfer to the Victoria Palace, London.

Lord Randolph Churchill

Churchill's father lived to only half the age of his more illustrious son and, in an era when the production of commemorative pieces of political icons had not reached the giddy heights of the 20th century, was not nearly so often immortalized in clay.

This fairly rare parian ware bust, sculptor unknown, was produced during the 1880s when Lord Randolph was briefly Chancellor of the Exchequer. Probably made by WH Goss or Robinson & Leadbeater.

Staffordshire Pottery octagonal plate dated 1886. One of the very few commemorative pieces featuring Lord Randolph, one time Chancellor of the Exchequer, who died at the age of forty-five. The 10-inch plate with its octagonal shape, and foliate and thistle border design, in black and white is typical of plates commemorating royalty, statesmen, politicians, military and religious leaders during the late Victorian period. Value £160.

Winston Churchill's favourite
portrait of his father, painted by
Edwin Ward in 1888.

Lottery ticket

Churchill was featured on this ticket for the Spanish national lottery issued in Barcelona in February 1947. Sadly it was not a winner.

Loving cups

A loving cup is a two-handled vessel, from which people drink in turn, as it is passed hand-to-hand around the table at a banquet. By tradition whilst one guest drinks, his neighbour stands and acts as his protector. The custom arose from an age when one whose head was immersed in the wassail bowl could have been treacherously stabbed.

The Spode *Battle of Britain Loving Cup* was commissioned by the RAF Museum in 1990 to mark the 50th anniversary of the battle. Designed by Roy Trigg, in a limited edition of 500, the cup bears Churchill's tribute to the Royal Air Force: *'Never in the field of human conflict has so much*

Spode *Battle of Britain Loving Cup*

been owed by so many to so few.' The RAF badge is on the obverse and the Fighter Command badge is on the reverse. The cup is inscribed *'1940'* beneath each handle.

A superb loving cup with gilded lion rampant handles was made by Paragon China during World War II for export only. Under wartime restrictions British potteries could not make decorated china for the home market but exports were encouraged, particularly to the USA, to help pay the lend-lease debt. Note that the elaborate and colourful design incorporates the ubiquitous sepia portrait transfer of Churchill as was then being used on 'Utility' china for the British market. Otherwise, the design resembles that of Paragon's renowned royal commemoratives. Bought for $450 in Florida in 1995 by a British dealer, whereupon in England it quickly changed hands several times and was last seen in Brighton wearing a £1,500 ticket!

Paragon China Loving Cup

A loving cup was made by Shelley Pottery, now part of the Royal Doulton Group, in 1941 to commemorate the Atlantic Charter. The reverse side portrays Churchill and Roosevelt on board *HMS Prince of Wales* in Placentia Bay.

Loving Cup by Shelley Pottery

Machin, Arnold

Arnold Machin was Master of Sculpture at the Royal Academy School between 1958 and 1967. He is best known for his design of the Queen's portrait used on British coinage and postage stamps during the 1960s and 1970s. Whilst undertaking a Travelling Scholarship in Sculpture from the Royal College of Art in 1940-41 he created a number of studies of Churchill for Wedgwood. Only one of the sculptures was issued, on a tankard, during the war years, because Machin declared himself a pacifist and Wedgwood considered this would have a negative effect on sales. A second Machin design, a limited edition Windsor Grey bust, was released, primarily for export, in 1953. It was not until 1964, when Machin's stamp designs had restored public confidence, that Wedgwood strongly promoted his 1940 Churchill sculptures.

Magnets

I can't imagine a fridge magnet being stuck to refrigerator doors at Chartwell, Chequers or 10 Downing Street. Yet, the Cabinet War Rooms will sell anything that makes a profit to the collector who must have everything. Wooden fretwork £2.

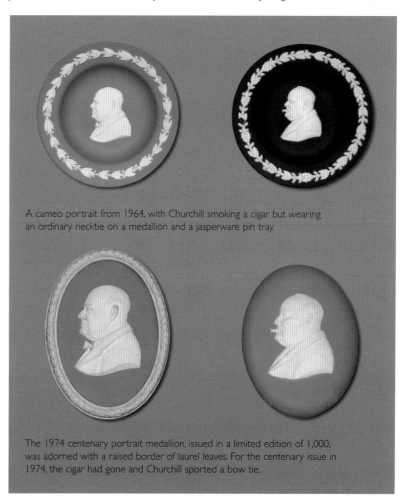

A cameo portrait from 1964, with Churchill smoking a cigar but wearing an ordinary necktie on a medallion and a jasperware pin tray.

The 1974 centenary portrait medallion, issued in a limited edition of 1,000, was adorned with a raised border of laurel leaves. For the centenary issue in 1974, the cigar had gone and Churchill sported a bow tie.

Magnifying glass

A magnifying glass and matching paperknife, crafted in pewter with a nicely detailed figure of Churchill forming the handle. Part of the wide choice of Churchilliana commemorating the 50th anniversary of VE Day in 1995.

Marquetry

AH McIntosh & Co of Kirkcaldy, Scotland were high-class furniture makers who used marquetry to good effect when decorating wall panels in the staterooms of ocean-going liners and company boardrooms.

During the nineteen-fifties pictures were classified as luxury goods and attracted purchase tax. So, to avoid tax, McIntoshs produced a range of pictures, which they marketed as trays, so they could be used to carry crockery or as wall hangings. This particular tray has spent the past 50 years hanging on the wall.

Matchbox covers

During World War II paper and cardboard were strictly rationed. Tobacconists sold cigarettes and matches loose, so to preserve the matchbox for reuse until the striking surface wore out, prudent smokers acquired a matchbox cover. It was made from thin sheet steel covered with celluloid, a highly inflammable material which really was the most inappropriate substance to have close to the sudden flare of a newly struck match! These covers often bore patriotic slogans and/or portraits of the Prime Minister.

The matchbox bears Churchill's message of 9 February 1941 to President Roosevelt – *'Give us the tools and we will finish the job.'*

The matchbox bears the message, *'Our deepest gratitude and admiration to the Allies who stood united in defeating the greatest tyrant in history.'*

Matches

Smokers who couldn't afford a lighter – or couldn't be bothered to refuel with petrol, renewing flints, replacing cotton wool and rethreading wicks – relied on matches. Matchboxes or match booklets have been a vehicle for Churchilliana.

An Australian brand of matches portrayed celebrated redheads. Churchill was in the company of the likes of Queen Elizabeth I, Danny Kaye and Maureen O'Hara. This took many by surprise, especially those who thought of Churchill as a man with a largely bald scalp surrounded by a sparse grey fringe!

The cheapest memento on sale in the Chartwell souvenir shop.

Medallic portraits of Sir Winston Churchill

Medallic Portraits of Sir Winston Churchill by J Eric Engstrom, published by Spink & Son in 1972 is described as the definitive catalogue of the medallic portraits of the great man. The book set out ninety-three coins and medals depicting Churchill. Since publication of the book, at least forty-eight more commemorative medallions have been issued between 1971 and 1995. Apart from the United Kingdom, the other countries that have issued Churchill coins or medals include Australia, Austria, Canada, Denmark, France, Germany, Italy, The Netherlands, South Africa, Switzerland, United States, Venezuela and Yemen. One of the most handsome medals was the Allied Victory Commemorative Medal

Four medals designed by David Cornell and struck by John Pinches (Medallists) Ltd of London in 1970 to mark the 25th anniversary of VE Day. Presented in numbered sets in leatherette cases the medals are 44mm in diameter and were struck in platinum (4 sets), silver gilt (300 sets), silver (250 sets) and bronze (300 sets). The reverse of each medal has a quotation from one of Churchill's wartime speeches.

The Allied Victory Commemorative Medal issued in 1945 and re-issued after Churchill's death in 1965.

A pair of medals issued to mark the 25th anniversary of the Atlantic Charter.

The Churchill Memorial Medal. 1965.

Variation of the Churchill Memorial Medal. 1965.

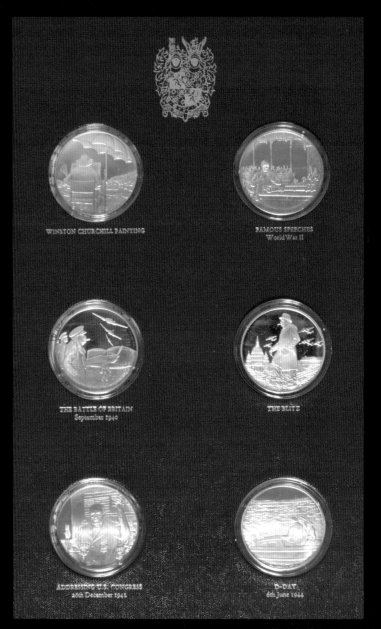

WINSTON CHURCHILL PAINTING

FAMOUS SPEECHES
World War II

THE BATTLE OF BRITAIN
September 1940

THE BLITZ

ADDRESSING U.S. CONGRESS
26th December 1941

D-DAY
6th June 1944

Churchill Centenary, 1974. Leather-bound album containing twenty-four silver medals.

issued in 1945, designed by A Lowental. 1,000 of the 63mm diameter medals were struck in bronze by John Pinches Ltd of London. On the reverse is a hand rising from a cloud holding a victory torch and inscribed: *'Unflinching, indomitable his spirit saved Britain. We will fight on land, on sea and in the air until victory is won.'* When Churchill died in 1965 this piece was re-issued as a Churchill Memorial Medal. It was in a reduced size of 50mm diameter but was otherwise identical to the Victory Medal except that it had the date of Churchill's death – 24 Jan 1965 – added to the obverse. 500 medals were issued in 22ct gold; 200 in 900ct gold; 736 in silver and 1421 in bronze. After the edition had been struck the dies were presented to the British Museum.

The pair of medals, opposite, marks the 25th anniversary of the Atlantic Charter. 60mm in diameter they were designed by Michael Rizzello and struck in 1966 by John Pinches in platinum, gold or silver. Numbered in pairs, a total of 2,420 pairs were struck. The reverse of both medals depicts the battleship *HMS Prince of Wales* on which Churchill and Roosevelt met and signed the Atlantic Charter.

The Churchill Memorial Medal, 1965, opposite, was designed by Wieslaw Peter and Edgar Kohler and struck by WJ Dingley of Birmingham. Two sizes – 57mm and 38mm – gold, silver gilt, silver and bronze.

A variation of the Wieslaw Peter and Edgar Kohler 1965 Churchill Memorial medal, opposite, struck in rather smaller quantities. The reverse side simply has Churchill's name, titles and honours above a laurel branch. The earliest strikings of this medal had a hyphen between Spencer and Churchill – a style Churchill detested – but this was removed on later examples.

One of the best of the plethora of items celebrating the Churchill Centenary in 1974 was a leather-bound album containing twenty-four silver medals portraying scenes from Churchill's life. The medals, struck by London medallists John Pinches, were encapsulated in perspex and mounted in heavy claret boards embossed with the Churchill coat-of-arms. A 'Certificate of Authenticity', signed by Churchill's former secretary Sir John Colville, was tipped into the front of each album. 4,408 sets in silver gilt were sold at £144 per set and 3,035 sets in sterling silver were sold at £192 per set. £192 in 1974 would be the equivalent of more than £900 today and there was some criticism that the Churchill Centenary Trust was profiteering but, as always, the choice was with the collector and it was one of the best of good causes.

Leather-bound album containing twenty-four medals portraying scenes from Churchill's life, to mark the Churchill Centenary in 1974.

Money box

When Churchill became Prime Minister in 1940 schoolchildren were issued with a dark green papier mâché *Save for Victory* money box in which to save their pocket money in order to buy National Savings Certificates for the war effort. Fill your box three times and you could buy your very own National Savings Certificate.

This money box would hold about five shillings (25 pence) worth of the old style penny and halfpenny coins.

Mystery package

In a broadcast on 1 October 1939 Churchill said: *'I cannot forecast to you the action of Russia. It is a riddle wrapped in a mystery inside an enigma.'*

This little china figure, 3½ inches high, is similarly wrapped riddle. Churchill appears as a lavishly gowned rather demonic-looking spectre emerging from a broken eggshell above the caption: *'Franatic Scena – Mr Churchill – It's your money I want!'* Unmarked and provenance unknown but thought to date from 1924-29 when Churchill was Chancellor of the Exchequer.

The slot for the money can be seen at the top of Churchill's head, while the slogan *'Save for Victory'* is inscribed in a confident script across his shoulders.

Nobel Prize

On 16 October 1953 Churchill learned that he had been awarded the Nobel Prize for Literature. He had coveted the Peace Prize and deeply wished to be remembered as a peacemaker and not as a warmonger – as he had been described earlier in his career. His Private Secretary, Anthony Montague Browne, wrote that his early joy turned to indifference when he learned that the award was for Literature and not for Peace. Albert Schweitzer was awarded the Peace Prize and Churchill, rather testily, remarked that he was *'not going to stand up there with that catch-' em alive.'* Churchill could not attend the presentation ceremony, as he was attending the Bermuda Conference, so Clementine and Mary, went to Stockholm on 10 December 1953 in his place and Clementine delivered her husband's prepared speech: *'I am proud, but also I must admit, awestruck at your decision to (honour) me. I do hope you are right. I feel we are both running a considerable risk and that I do not deserve it. But I shall have no misgivings if you have none.'*

The Prize was awarded in recognition of Churchill's overall literary achievements, but the citation made particular mention of *The World Crisis* and *The Second World War*.

The photograph above is a postcard publicity mailshot for a twelve-volume de luxe edition of *The Second World War* issued to celebrate the Churchill Centenary in 1974.

Oldham

Oldham, 7 miles NE of Manchester, was an important cotton-spinning centre at the end of the 19th century.

In February 1899 the twenty-four-year-old Churchill was invited to stand as one of the two Conservative candidates in a snap by-election at Oldham. He accepted, but at the poll in July, he and his Tory running mate were narrowly defeated by the two Liberal candidates. In October he sailed for Cape Town with a four-month contract to report on the Boer War for the *Morning Post* for a fee of £1,000 – (£50,000 in today's money). Churchill's well-publicised exploits in the war – the ambush of the armoured train, his capture by the Boers, the price on his head and his escape – made him a national hero and in the general election at Oldham in October 1900 he was successful, coming second in the poll only sixteen votes behind the leading Liberal.

Before taking his seat in the House of Commons, Churchill went on a three-month lecture tour of England, the USA and Canada, to speak about his experiences in the Boer War. He earned well over £5,000 – more than seven years' salary for a young professional man. Whilst he was in Canada he learned that Queen Victoria had died, so he sailed for England on the day of the Queen's funeral and took his seat in Parliament for the first time on 14 February 1901. With only a two-year break, from November 1922 to October 1924, he was to remain a Member of Parliament until October 1964. During that time he was almost continuously in the public eye, with every speech he made in Parliament, or outside it, reported in newspapers and commented on by the press and public alike. He made his maiden speech on 28 February 1901. The *Daily Telegraph* reported that he was, *'... perfectly at home, with lively gestures that pointed his sparkling sentences, he instantly caught the tone and the ear of a House crowded in every part.' 'Spell-binding,'* commented the *Daily Express.*

Churchill represented Oldham until January 1906 but, although he was fast making a name for himself on the national scene, he infuriated the local electorate by 'crossing the floor' of the House of Commons on 31 May 1904 to sit on the Liberal benches. His 'Free Trader' stance, which advocated the abolition of duties on cheap foreign textiles did not endear him to the voters of Oldham or the local Conservative Association, who passed a resolution that he, *'... had forfeited their confidence in him.'* Following his deselection at Oldham, Churchill switched to nearby Northwest Manchester, which he won in the 1906 general election and represented until April 1908. While he was MP for Northwest Manchester, Churchill became a junior minister for the first time – Under-Secretary of State at the Colonial Office.

In the Oldham Art Gallery in Union Street is a bronze portrait bust of Churchill by Jacob Epstein. It is one of a number cast by the sculptor officially commissioned by the British Government in 1946. American-born Epstein was living close to Churchill in Hyde Park Gate at that time.

However, after a few sittings, Churchill objected to the craggy appearance of the sculpture and walked out of the studio! Epstein finished the commission using photographs but, because of Churchill's aversion, the bust was not placed on public display until after his death. As well as the bust in Oldham there are seven others in semi-public locations in England and at least three others in private ownership in the USA. One of the latter was sold for $25,500 in 1991.

Orkney: The Churchill Barriers

When Churchill was appointed First Lord of the Admiralty on 3 September 1939 he realised that because of pre-war cuts in expenditure, defences at the naval base at Scapa Flow in the Orkney Islands were far from satisfactory. His fears were confirmed when in mid-October, a German U-boat entered Scapa Flow and sank the battleship *HMS Royal Oak*, then at anchor, causing the loss of more than 800 lives. Churchill paid a second visit to Scapa Flow on 31 October 1939 and commissioned the work on the defences to be carried out without delay. The Churchill Barriers, consisting of impenetrable walls of reinforced concrete blocks forming a causeway, topped by a road, continues to provide the Orcadians with an improved means of travelling between Burray, South Ronaldsay and mainland Orkney to the present day .

Much of the construction work was carried out by Italian POWs who converted a pair of Nissen huts into a Catholic Chapel, decorated by Domenico Chiocchetti, in the style of the Sistine Chapel in Rome. The chapel has been preserved and, along with the Churchill Barriers themselves, forms a permanent monument. Churchill often visited Orkney after he became Prime Minister. It was from there that he sailed on 4 August 1941 on *HMS Prince of Wales* to Placentia Bay, Newfoundland for his meeting with President Roosevelt.

Wiiistons. Churchill.

Painting as a pastime

When Churchill resigned as First Lord of the Admiralty in May 1915, because of the costly failure of his Dardanelles campaign, he became deeply depressed. In his despair and frustration, he wrote later, *'The Muse of Painting'* came to his rescue.

Having successfully experimented with the children's paintbox one Sunday in the country, he went out and bought a complete outfit for painting in oils. He told of his conversion to leisure painting in two essays in his book *Thoughts and Adventures*, subsequently re-published in a slim volume *Painting as a Pastime* (Odhams 1948).

The passion gripped him and he became a dedicated amateur painter for most of the rest of his life. David Coombs catalogued over 500 of his paintings in *Churchill: His Paintings*. David Coombs' compilation remains the standard reference and in her foreword, Clementine Churchill wrote: *'For over forty years my husband pursued the art of painting with all his customary energy and zeal. This publication will, I hope, enable many people to share something of the immense pleasure and stimulation that my husband so often found in art.'*

In 1990 Churchill's daughter Mary, Lady Soames, published *Winston Churchill: His Life as a Painter*, which, whilst not as comprehensive in its listings as David Coombs' book, benefited enormously from the technical advances in colour printing as well as its unique filial perspective.

In 1947 Churchill achieved the distinction of having two of his paintings selected for the Royal Academy's Summer Exhibition. When invited by the President of the Royal Academy, Sir Alfred Munnings, to enter some of his paintings, Winston at first refused, concerned that his reputation as a politician might influence the selection committee. He was eventually persuaded on the understanding that his paintings would be submitted under a pseudonym. In the following year Churchill's pictures were submitted in his own name and three were accepted. Shortly afterwards, he was accorded an honour he prized – Honorary Academician Extraordinary. In 1958 a

A View of Torcello, Italy. Painted in 1949. Size: 20 × 24 inches. Exhibited in the travelling exhibition in 1958, at the Royal Academy in 1959 and the New York World's Fair in 1965. (Photo courtesy Soho Gallery, London).

Bottlescape. c1932. Hangs in the house at Chartwell. (Photo courtesy The National Trust).

Still Life: Fruit. 1930s
*(Photo courtesy Soho
Gallery, London).*

Blue Grass, La Capponcina.
Oil on canvas. 24³/₄ × 30
inches. Painted in 1954 at
Lord Beaverbrook's villa
on the Côte d'Azur.
Sold at Sotheby's, London
in July 1998 for £84,000.
(Photo courtesy Sotheby's)

Garden Scene at Breccles.
c1925. Breccles was the
Norfolk country home of
Clementine's cousin
Venetia Montagu. A very
good gardener herself,
Venetia had helped
Winston and Clementine
with the design of the
gardens at Chartwell and
was later to let them
have use of her London
home when Winston
suffered a significant
financial loss in the Wall
Street crash of 1929.
18 × 24 inches, signed
'WSC'. This painting was
sold at Sotheby's in July
1998 for £45,500.
(Photo courtesy Sotheby's)

Right: Churchill's easel
and an unfinished canvas
stands behind the chair, a
gift from Sir Ian Hamilton.
He always used it when
painting. The bronze head
in the centre is Churchill's
sculpture of Oscar Nemon.

travelling exhibition of forty of Churchill's paintings was shown at the Metropolitan Museum in New York and other venues in USA, Australia, Canada and New Zealand.

Several of Churchill's paintings hang in the house at Chartwell. Many more line the walls of his studio in an outbuilding there.

Although he was approached many times, Churchill is not recorded as having sold any of his paintings, although he gave them generously to members of his family and friends. Most remain in the possession of the original recipients or their descendants including Lord Beaverbrook; the Marquess of Bath; HM the Queen; Churchill College, Cambridge; the Earl of Avon; the House of Commons; Lord Ismay; Wendy Reves; former President Truman; former President Eisenhower; the Government Whips' Office; the Duke of Westminster; Grace Hamblin (Churchill's former secretary); the Duke of Norfolk; Viscount Montgomery; Lord Salisbury; and Churchill family members.

Over the years, prints have occasionally been made available to the general public. In 1979 Churchill's grandson allowed a limited edition of 850 prints of *The View from Chartwell*, painted in 1948, to be sold on behalf of the National Trust. Coinciding with the 1990 publication of *Winston Churchill: His Life as a Painter* by Lady Soames, the *Daily Telegraph*, which serialised the book, issued prints of three Churchill paintings in a limited edition of 150 of each. These prints were excellent reproductions, but at £325-£350 each, were beyond the means of many.

During the late 1970s publishers Hallmark reproduced some of Churchill's paintings as Christmas cards, which were on sale at Blenheim Palace. The National Trust offers a selection of postcard reproductions in the gift shop at Chartwell.

In 1998, two original paintings by Winston Churchill were auctioned at Sotheby's in London. *Blue Grass, La Capponcina*, which was painted at Lord Beaverbrook's villa on the Côte d'Azur in 1954, was sold for £84,000 and *Garden Scene at Breccles*, painted in 1925 at Venetia Montagu's home in Norfolk, was sold for £45,500.

Paperweights

A paperweight made of stone and lead from the bomb-damaged House of Commons, (see pages 84/86).

Designed by Swedish engraver Rune Strand for Dartington Glass for the Churchill Centenary in 1974. A limited edition of 5,000 selling originally at 15 guineas.

85th birthday portrait of Churchill by Toni Frissell, encapsulated in clear polyester resin and sold at the Blenheim Palace gift shop in the 1960s.

Arnold Machin's Churchill Centenary piece. Blue and white jasper set into hand-cut lead crystal for Wedgwood. A limited edition of 1,000 engraved, *'Give us the tools and we will finish the job.'*

Made by Baccarat, France to mark the retirement of Churchill as Prime Minister in 1955. Limited edition of 243 were made, before moulds were destroyed in 1959. Very scarce, would probably cost in excess of £200 if you could find one.

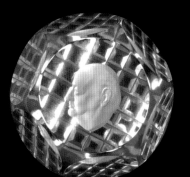

Engraved by Carol Moon for Jack Darrah's Churchill Rooms at Bletchley Park.

Pencil

Promotional pencil. c1950

A king-size pencil issued as a business promotional gift by F Chambers & Co Ltd, Nottingham, England. A much-used 1940 photograph of Churchill is accompanied by a long quotation from his celebrated 4 June speech in the House of Commons: *'... we shall not flag or fail ... we shall go on to the end ... we shall never surrender...'* The pencil had never been used and was still in its original presentation box when found on a bric-a-brac stall nearly fifty years later.

Picture medals

The Churchill Centenary Picture Medal was produced in a limited edition of 500 presented in a maroon leather case, lined with white satin and red velvet, and came complete with a pair of tweezers for handling the mezzotints. A nice portrait of Churchill, signed: *'Norris'*, on the obverse of the medal with the inscription: *'Britain's Beloved Bulldog'* and on the reverse a crisp reproduction of the Churchill coat of arms.

Made by Toye, Kenning & Spencer of London for the Churchill Centenary in 1974. This 3-inch diameter x $^1/_2$ inch thick medal is in fact a 22ct gold on sterling silver box containing 13 circular mezzotints by F Jaffe depicting scenes from Churchill's life.

13 circular mezzotints depicting scenes from Churchill's life contained in a 'pill box'. Top and bottom shown.

Plaques

1. Marcus Replicas, Bottesford. c1980
Designed by Elizabeth Sharpe for Marcus Replicas of Bottesford, Leicestershire. A well-modelled high-relief plaque in pewter-effect resin. On sale at Blenheim Palace and the Queen's Royal Lancers Museum at Belvoir Castle during the 1980s.

2. Heritage Mint, Matlock. 1995
This is another expensive looking plaque which actually cost £20. Moulded in resin on a velvet backing, it was made in 1995 by the Heritage Mint and sold in aid of the Dr Barnardo's charity.

3. John Needham & Sons. c1940s
A high-relief bust in gold-painted cast iron mounted on an oval wooden plaque 6½ x 4½ inches. Made by John Needham & Sons, Ironfounders and Engineers, Stockport, Cheshire, probably during World War II.

4. Maker unknown. 1940s
This 14-inch diameter plaque, pressed in high-quality sheet brass is a mystery. The caption, *'V for Victory'*, suggests a wartime issue but brass was placed under statutory control as soon as World War II began and its use in the making of decorative items was prohibited. A few small decorative plaques were manufactured during the war years from poor-quality scrap metal, and it showed. It seems unlikely that this plaque was manufactured post-1951 as a *'V for Victory'* retrospective.

5. Maker and date unknown
A finely sculpted bust of Churchill, which appears to be made from ebony and ivory, but is probably fashioned from a high-grade plastic material.

6. Maker unknown. 1942
In 1997, a manufacturer discovered a small cache of plaques made in 1942, tucked away in a stock room and preserved in original wrappers. The picture (right) shows him presenting one one of these plaques to Alexander, son of Celia Sandys, Churchill's granddaughter, at the Churchill Rooms, Bletchley Park. Since the Churchilliana exhibition opened in 1994, proprietor, Jack Darrah, has enlarged his display with the help of generous donations from visitors.

1. Marcus Replicas. c1980

Plastered !
This high-relief plaster casting, dating from 1940-45, has suffered the fate of so many of the well-meant wartime icons of Churchill. A combination of soft plaster and brittle paint has, after sixty years, resulted in a somewhat worse-for-wear appearance.

2. Heritage Mint. 1995

4. Maker unknown. 1940s

5. Maker and date unknown

3. John Needham. c1940s

6. Alexander, son of Celia Sandys, receiving a 'V for Victory' plaque on behalf of Jack Darrah.

Playing cards

Churchill was an inveterate gambler. He enjoyed playing chemin de fer, baccarat and roulette for high stakes in the casinos of the south of France. At home, bezique played with two packs of cards was his favourite game. One of Churchill's former secretaries has related how he was invited to make up a foursome and told that the stakes would be matchsticks. It was only at the end of the session when the matchsticks were counted and the losing participants produced cheque books to settle their accounts at £5 per matchstick, that he realised that but for a late run of beginner's luck he might have lost more than two month's salary! Appropriately Churchill featured on many packs of playing cards.

Portrait medallions

Wedgwood have had a near monopoly in the production of portrait medallions of Churchill, all of which were modelled by Arnold Machin in 1940, though some were not issued until the Churchill Centenary in 1974. The 1964 issue was commissioned by Thomas Goode & Co of South Audley Street, London to mark Churchill's 90th birthday and his award of the Honorary Citizenship of the United States but he died within two months and the medallion came to be regarded as a memorial piece.

The 1964 issue had Churchill smoking a cigar and wearing a tie. The 1974 issue replaced the necktie with a bow tie and the cigar had gone. Mounted and framed this medallion was sold by Goode's for six guineas, but is likely to cost you around £100 today.

Churchill's award of the Freedom of the City of London was marked by the Worshipful Company of Makers of Playing Cards on their pack for 1943.

A World War II issue from the Universal Playing Card Company of Leeds.

The Worshipful Company of Makers of Playing Cards commemorate Churchill's retirement as Prime Minister in 1955.

From Intercol, London in 1990 commemorating the 50th anniversary of the Battle of Britain.

Another wartime issue from the Universal Playing Card Co.

A smart black and gold pack sold during the 1990s in the Imperial War Museum's souvenir shop.

An ace from a Spanish pack.

An eight of clubs from Italy.

A joker from Belgium.

Portraits

Prints of this fine portrait by John Berrie, were distributed to schoolchildren on Empire Day 1943 in exchange for their contributions to a fund to provide gift cigarettes to '... *the Sailors, Soldiers and Airmen of the British Commonwealth who are fighting to safeguard Freedom, Justice and Security.*' The appeal was administered by the Overseas League Tobacco Fund which had provided over 50,000,000 cigarettes to the Fighting Services in 1940-42.

Below: A portrait by Sir John Lavery (1856-1941), Churchill's neighbour and friend. It was painted in 1916 when he commanded the 6th Battalion of the Royal Scots Fusiliers in Flanders. Churchill wears a French poilu's steel helmet, which now hangs below the portrait at Chartwell. The painting was presented to Churchill by the officers of the Armoured Car Squadrons in recognition of his role in the development of the tank.

" Britain's future belongs to you.
God bless you all. " Winston S. Churchill 1943

The original of this portrait, by Frank Salisbury, hangs in the Library at Chartwell. It is Lady Soames' favourite picture of her father – 'It gets him rather well, I think.' It was commissioned by the now defunct Devonshire Club and given to Churchill after the artist had made a copy to hang there. In 1991 the National Trust allowed a limited number of replicas to be painted in aid of the Churchill Memorial Trust.

Another version of the Frank Salisbury portrait of Churchill (below), which hangs in the library at Chartwell, once belonged to Lord Duncan Sandys, Churchill's son-in-law. It was auctioned by Tennants of Leyburn 1995. The pre-sale estimate was £200,000, but it failed to reach the reserve price and was later sold privately. There are other very similar versions at Harrow School and the East India Club, London, the main differences being in background and foreground detail.

A version of the portrait by Salisbury, painted in 1950, hangs in the Jockey Club at Newmarket, with Churchill depicted in formal dress. Churchill was proud to be elected a member of the Jockey Club after he took an interest in racing quite late in life. His best known horse was Colonist II who won 13 races, with prize money amounting to £13,000 in 1949-51. Other winners included Pol Roger, Loving Cup, Gibraltar III and Prince Arthur.

Two portraits of Churchill by Frank Salisbury,

London. Prints of the portrait were sold in aid of Mrs Churchill's Aid to Russia Fund.

Frank Salisbury was commissioned by the Constitutional Club to paint this portrait of Churchill in 1943. He titled it *Blood, Sweat and Tears*. When Margaret Thatcher became Prime Minister in 1979 she 'borrowed' the picture to hang in 10 Downing Street where it remained on loan until 1996. As if in anticipation of a Labour victory at the next general election the Constitutional Club, now the St Stephen's Constitutional Club, reclaimed the picture and offered it for sale at Sotheby's in 1996, where it made £139,000.

Reproduced by kind permission of DACS.

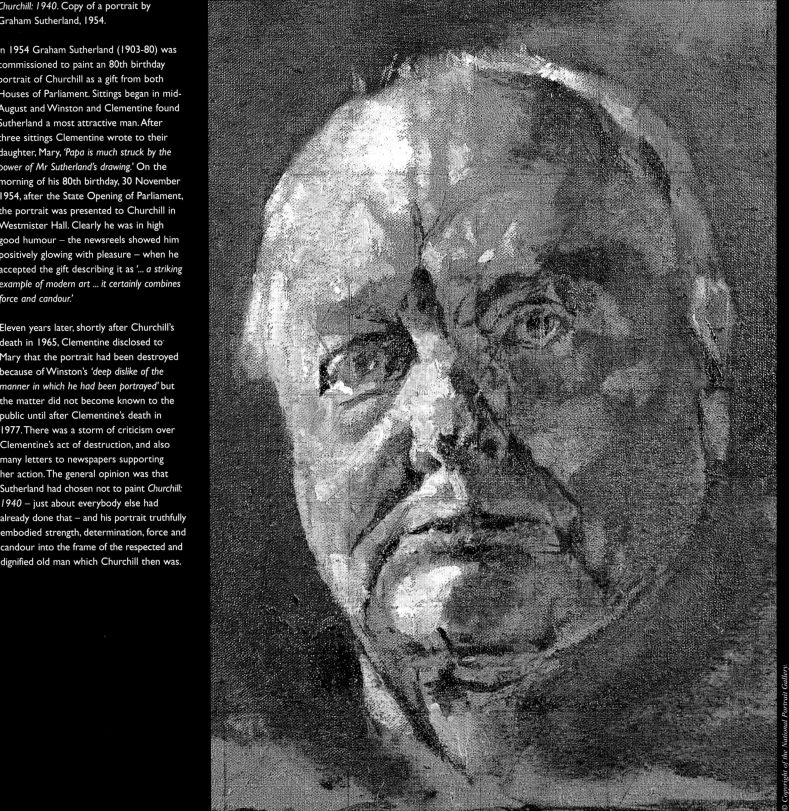

Churchill: 1940. Copy of a portrait by
Graham Sutherland, 1954.

In 1954 Graham Sutherland (1903-80) was
commissioned to paint an 80th birthday
portrait of Churchill as a gift from both
Houses of Parliament. Sittings began in mid-
August and Winston and Clementine found
Sutherland a most attractive man. After
three sittings Clementine wrote to their
daughter, Mary, *'Papa is much struck by the
power of Mr Sutherland's drawing.'* On the
morning of his 80th birthday, 30 November
1954, after the State Opening of Parliament,
the portrait was presented to Churchill in
Westmister Hall. Clearly he was in high
good humour – the newsreels showed him
positively glowing with pleasure – when he
accepted the gift describing it as *'... a striking
example of modern art ... it certainly combines
force and candour.'*

Eleven years later, shortly after Churchill's
death in 1965, Clementine disclosed to
Mary that the portrait had been destroyed
because of Winston's *'deep dislike of the
manner in which he had been portrayed'* but
the matter did not become known to the
public until after Clementine's death in
1977. There was a storm of criticism over
Clementine's act of destruction, and also
many letters to newspapers supporting
her action. The general opinion was that
Sutherland had chosen not to paint *Churchill:
1940* – just about everybody else had
already done that – and his portrait truthfully
embodied strength, determination, force and
candour into the frame of the respected and
dignified old man which Churchill then was.

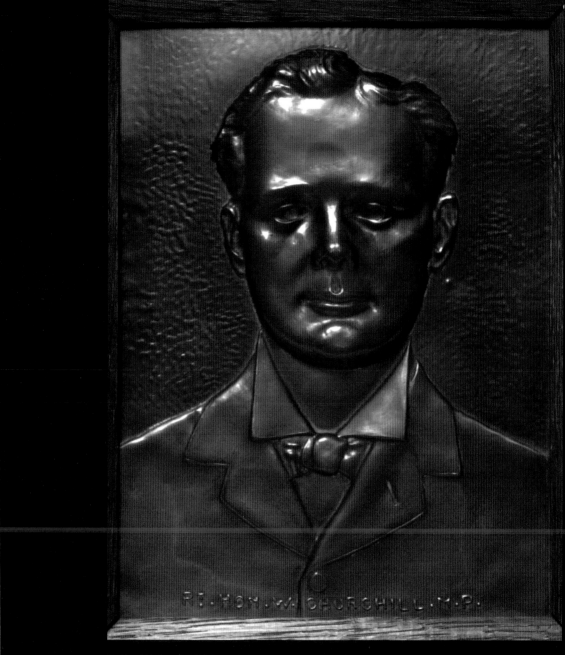

Rt Hon W Churchill MP. Bas-relief on
copper, in a 10$^{1}/_{2}$ x 9 inch oak frame. c1907.
Unsigned. Artist unknown.

Churchill was appointed Under-Secretary
of State for the Colonies in 1906 and in
1907 became a Privy Councillor. The picture
cannot pre-date 1907, but is clearly based
on a photograph of a younger Churchill –
probably around 1900 when he still had a
full head of hair. Value £150-200.

Postage stamps

Because the name of Winston Churchill is such an inspiration to so many, countries all over the world have issued stamps featuring the great man. The stamps shown on these pages are just a selection.

Nicaragua 1974

Ascension Island 1974

Anguilla 1974

USA 1965

Uruguay 1966

Paraguay 1965

British Antarctic Territory 1974

Liberia 1966

Yemen 1965

Uruguay 1966

Pitcairn Islands 1974

Ecuador 1966

Antigua 1974

The Gambia 1966

Haiti 1968

Australia 1965

Malta 1966

Canada 1965

Maldive Islands 1974

Cook Islands 1974

The Gambia 1966

Panama 1966

Pitcairn Islands 1974

Gibraltar. Centenary of the birth of Churchill. 1974.

Tristan da Cunha. Centenary of the birth of Churchill. 1974.

Grenada. Centenary of the birth of Churchill. 1974.

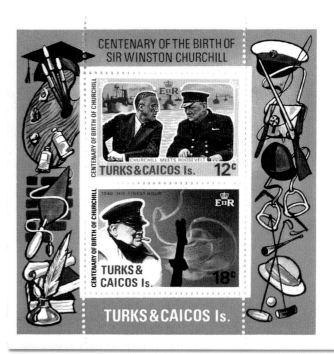

Turks & Caicos Islands. Centenary of the birth of Churchill. 1974.

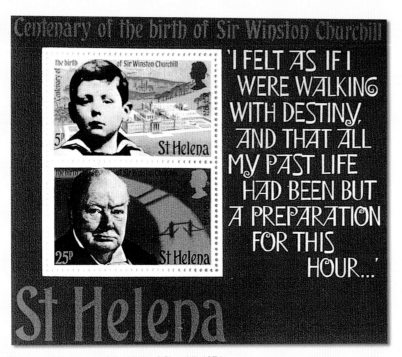

St Helena. Centenary of the birth of Churchill. 1974.

Falkland Islands. Centenary of the birth of Churchill. 1974.

Montserrat. Centenary of the birth of Churchill. 1974.

Togoland. Centenary of the birth of Churchill. 1974.

As well as Great Britain, Commonwealth countries and colonies, many other nations around the world issued memorial postage stamps when Churchill died in 1965, including Brazil, Dubai, Ecuador, Haiti, Liberia, Nicaragua, Paraguay, Panama, the USA, Uruguay, Venezuela and Yemen.

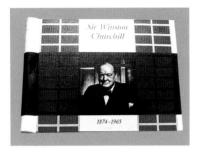

Stanley Gibbons produced a souvenir album containing all the memorial stamps.

The two UK Churchill Memorial postage stamps, 4d and 1/3, issued on 8 July 1965 were printed in sombre black & brown and dark olive green. No doubt this befitted the solemnity of the occasion although it did contrast with Churchill's request that at his funeral procession there should be *'plenty of bands'*.

The Metalimport Group attempted to brighten the scene by issuing 18ct gold replicas of the stamps, each stamp 41 x 25mm and weighing 0.643 troy ounces. 5,000 numbered and cased sets were issued and afterwards the dies were presented to the Post Office Museum.

Gold replica cased postage stamps by the Metalimport Group. 1965.

Postcards

Picture postcards first appeared in Great Britain in 1894. Around the turn of the twentieth century, the cost of postage was a halfpenny and in those early days postal regulations dictated that the address *only* could be written on the reverse with a message or greeting of up to five words written below the picture. But by 1902 these strictures were relaxed.

The craze for postcards was just part of an enormous change in society. Following the death of Queen Victoria in 1901, the Edwardians abandoned Victorian formality to indulge their taste for the splendid and extravagant. Mass travel, foreign holidays, greater mobility and the emergence of large department stores, meant that people had less time for social graces and letter-writing and welcomed this informal way of keeping in touch at half the postage cost of a letter.

Postcards catered for all tastes. The range of themes available to today's collector is boundless. Anyone who collects postcards which record Churchill's activities realise why this new medium was so popular. Faster communications, faster news and the need for politicians to react faster to world events, provided postcard publishers with a never-ending supply of material to pass on to the public – and how they loved it!

La Guerre Anglo-Boer. 1900
A Belgian card, printed in Brussels and postmarked at La Louvière, 17 May 1900. The card is captioned: *'La Guerre Anglo-Boer. Arrivée à Pretoria des prisonniers du train blindé d'Estcourt (Lord Churchill [sic] à gauche en casquette).'*

The Siege of Sidney Street. 1911
Churchill's appearance as Home Secretary at the siege of Sidney Street in 1911 received massive publicity in the press, on the newsreels and on postcards. He was strongly criticised by the Opposition in the House of Commons for interfering with the police and military direction of the affair. The Leader of the Opposition, Arthur Balfour, said: *'I understand what the photographer was doing, but what was the right honourable gentleman doing?'*

La Guerre Anglo-Boer, 1900

The Siege of Sidney Street, 1911

Engagement to Clementine, 1908

Outbreak of World War I, 1914

Electioneering 1899/1900

Engagement to Clementine. 1908
Churchill's engagement to Clementine Hozier was a newsworthy event and popular with postcard publishers. Seldom can the press announce the engagement of a Cabinet Minister.

Outbreak of World War 1. 1914
The outbreak of World War I, with Churchill as First Lord of the Admiralty, saw the postcard industry go into overdrive. The array of flags flanking Churchill's portrait on this card includes Great Britain, France, Belgium, Russia, Serbia and Montenegro.

Electioneering 1899/1900
Perhaps this is the oldest postcard in my collection. Churchill issued the same postcard portrait when he was defeated at the Oldham by-election in 1899 as when he was victorious in the election of the following year. Published by Wrench. Lightly tinted. A rare portrait of the young Churchill. My heart missed a beat when I saw this card in a dealer's oddments box for 75p, as politician's election hand-outs sometimes bear a *real* autograph, but this one is clearly silk-screen printed. Even so, it was still a bargain. Current value £20+.

Men of the Moment Series. 1914
Posted in Nairn, Scotland on 3 May 1915. Uses the photograph by Reg Haines which is very common on a range of postcards published between 1908 and 1915. *The Men of the Moment*, political and military leaders of 1914, were all given the same colourful patriotic backdrop. Within two weeks of this card being posted Churchill had resigned as First Lord of the Admiralty in the wake of the Dardanelles fiasco for which he was judged responsible.

President of the Board of Trade. 1908
A card published by FW Woolworth & Co in 1908 when Churchill was President of the Board of Trade. A rare early card.

Keepers of the Empire Series. c1914
An unusual World War I card with Churchill as First Lord of the Admiralty in a series entitled *Keepers of the Empire* published by WN Sharpe Ltd of Bradford. Real photographs were then very much a selling point for postcards and this is one of only two Churchill portrait cards known, pre-dating 1940, which uses a drawing.

Men of the Moment, 1914

President of the Board of Trade, 1908

Keepers of the Empire, c1914

Première of City Lights, 1931

Six of the world's greatest stories, 1933

Propaganda postcard, 1939

Première of *City Lights*. 1931

Churchill was a big fan of Charlie Chaplin. He dined with him in Hollywood in 1929, when he promised he would write the film-script of *Young Napoleon* if Chaplin promised to play the lead! The photograph on this postcard was taken on 27 February 1931, at the Dominion Theatre, Tottenham Court Road, when Churchill attended the première of *City Lights*. Chaplin's co-star, Virginia Cherrill, is on his left. I do not know who the lady is on Churchill's left, but she is clearly earnestly attentive.

Six of the world's greatest stories. 1933

Postmarked 4 January 1933 (postage still only a halfpenny!) This card, also with a facsimile signature, was mailed to readers of the *News of the World* to announce the forthcoming serialisation of six of the World's greatest stories re-told by Winston Churchill. It is understood that Churchill dictated the stories from his sick bed in Salzburg whilst recuperating from the paratyphoid fever he had contracted when visiting Germany in 1932.

Propaganda postcard. 1939

This fascinating photo-montage is a very early piece of World War II propaganda, probably dating from 1939. The baby is clearly Hitler, the Mother Superior is clearly Churchill and the other three nuns are possibly Eden, Chamberlain and Halifax. I have another card which has the same picture, but printed from a reversed negative, which has the caption: '*Adolph's future being decided by the Big Four.*'

The Big Four. 1944

Photochrom Ltd of Tunbridge Wells, a postcard publisher, commissioned Morris Kelham to draw a fine portrait of Churchill, based on Yousuf Karsh's 1941 photograph. This featured on an individual portrait card as well as on one depicting the Three Great Leaders. This version includes Chiang Kai Shek and is entitled *The Big Four*. It bears a 22 August 1944 postmark.

'And now little boy...'. 1945

An amusing Belgian postcard, published in 1945 after the liberation of the Low Countries, captioned in French, Flemish and English: '*And now little boy, it is time to pay!*'

The Big Four, 1944

'And now little boy...', 1945

Patriotic poems, 1944

Naval inspection, Chatham, c1946

'Working for Winston' Series. c1944

Agnes Richardson was a prolific and popular children's illustrator, whose repertoire included picture postcards. Her speciality was winsome, cherubic, children and her cards, which spanned more than four decades from the 1920s are now collectable in their own right. Through World War II Agnes drew her '*Working for Winston*' series. Each card had a smiling real photographic portrait of Churchill and a Union Jack, worked into a patriotic design. This card was postmarked 13 August 1944.

'Helpful Thoughts' Series. c1941

A Valentine's '*Helpful Thoughts*' card in a highly coloured and extremely patriotic series, published from 1941 onwards. It carried either a quotation from one of Churchill's speeches or a specially composed caption by their resident poet/lyricist Allan Junior.

'Working for Winston' series, c1944

'Helpful Thoughts' series, c1941

'Churchill, saviour of Belgium', 1945

Patriotic poems, 1944

Postage has now increased to one penny providing that only the sender's name and address and not more than five words of conventional greeting are included. Write a long message and you'll have to pay two pence! Churchill must have been too busy prosecuting the war to have noticed the Postmaster General sneak in that little bit of petty bureaucracy! I am afraid that those dreadful Allan Junior patriotic poems were a regular feature of Valentine's World War II postcards.

Naval inspection Chatham, c1946

An early post-war card published by the Royal Navy, for sailor's and their families only, showing Churchill, resplendent in one of his favourite dressing-up uniforms, Lord Warden of the Cinque Ports, inspecting a guard of honour at the Royal Naval Barracks, Chatham. Churchill considered himself a *Man of Kent,* so perhaps it was appropriate that he should wear the uniform of an ancient Kentish maritime officer to inspect the sailors at a naval base in Kent.

'Churchill, saviour of Belgium', 1945

Another evocative Belgian card from 1945. The lady, her shackles broken, draped in a tattered Belgian flag kneels and exclaims: '*À W Churchill, la Belgique reconnaissante.*' (To W Churchill, saviour of Belgium.) This postcard was sent to relatives and friends in the UK by British soldiers.

Maarschalk Stalin, President Roosevelt en de Heer Churchill op de conferentie van

Tehran Conference, 1943

THE PRIME MINISTER AT THE NORMANDY FRONT, WITH FIELD
MARSHAL SIR ALAN BROOKE, GENERAL MONTGOMERY AND
GENERAL SMUTS.

Churchill with Montgomery and Smuts, 1944

"WE SHALL DEFEND EVERY VILLAGE,
EVERY TOWN and EVERY CITY."   4

Churchill and a machine gun, 1940

VE Day. 1945

'Mobilize', Tel Aviv. 1948

Tehran Conference. 1943
This Dutch postcard shows Churchill in the
uniform of Air Commodore of the Royal
Air Force, with Roosevelt and Stalin at the
Teheran Conference in December 1943.

With Montgomery and Smuts. 1944
Churchill in his workaday naval uniform
poses with Field Marshal Sir Alan Brooke,
General Montgomery and General Smuts
at 21 Army Group HQ in Normandy on
12 June 1944. This card is stamped on the
back: *'Passed by Censor'* and carries the
Churchillian quote: *'Let us all strive
without failing in faith or in duty.'*

VE Day celebrations. 1945
Churchill, flanked by Princess Elizabeth,
Queen Elizabeth, King George VI and
Princess Margaret, acknowledges the
cheers of the crowd on the balcony at
Buckingham Palace. This card, issued by
the Imperial War Museum to celebrate the
40th anniversary of VE Day, reproduces
the Keystone Press Agency picture to a
high standard.

Churchill and a machine gun. c1940
A postcard published by EH Wilkinson &
Co of Toronto shows Churchill holding a
light machine gun. This picture appeared
in many newspapers in the UK and the
Commonwealth in July 1940 and thereafter
on postcards and ephemera for the duration
of World War II. It was used by the enemy
on propaganda material, on the British 1974
Churchill centenary issue $5^{1}/_{2}$p postage
stamp, and the dust wrapper of *Blood,
Tears & Folly* by Len Deighton.

'Mobilize', Tel Aviv. 1948
Published by the M Shoham Press, Tel-
Aviv, Palestine, during World War II.
Palestine (now Israel) was under British
mandate following the Balfour Declaration
of 1917 which undertook to establish a
national home for the Jews. Twenty years
of discussion eventually led to a solution
approved by the British Government and
the League of Nations, but not by the
Arabs or the Jews. The matter was laid
aside for the duration of World War II, but
the eventual 'settlement' in 1948 brought a
continuation of the strife which continues
to this day. The Hebrew caption on the
card, I am told, translates as *'Mobilize'*.

Posters

Let Us Go Forward Together. 1940

Replicas of this famous poster, 30 x 20 inches, can be purchased for £3 from the souvenir shops at all the Imperial War Museum sites. Remarkably an original, 22¹/₂ x 14¹/₂ inches, made £1,840 at a Sotheby's sale in July 1998.

£25 Reward. 1899

A facsimile of the poster, included in Churchill's book *My Early Life*. It was issued in Pretoria after his escape in December 1899. The Boer official, Lodk de Haas, offered a reward of £25 *'to anyone who brings the escaped prisoner of war, Churchill, dead or alive to this office.'*

Deserve Victory. 1941.
30 x 20 inches poster.
Modern replicas available at £3.

**Better Pot Luck With
Churchill Today... 1941.**
25 x 19 inches.
This poster was also issued as a postcard.

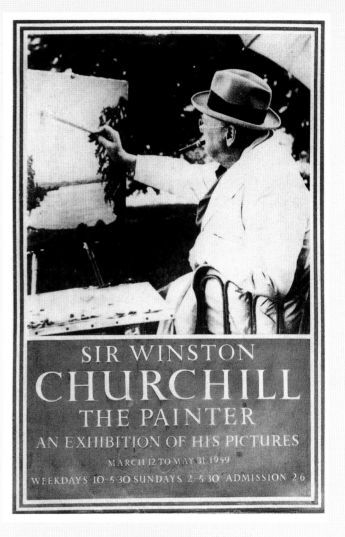

German poster. 1940

Above: Poster seen in occupied Belgium depicting a battered and tattered Churchill claiming that, '*All is going very well*', whilst all around him is in ruins. Madame la Marquise was a popular song of the time.

Poster by Henri Guignon. 1940

Right: American poster drawn by Henri Guignon, issued after Roosevelt's re-election as President in 1940, to remind isolationist Americans that Great Britain and Winston Churchill represented the last bulwark against totalitarianism.

Royal Academy. 1959

Top right: Poster advertising Churchill's pictures at the Royal Academy in 1959. Sixty-two paintings were on show and the exhibition had to be extended from two months to five months, and rehung into three galleries instead of the original two, because of the huge number of visitors. The exhibition attracted 141,000 visitors and The President of the Royal Academy, Sir Charles Wheeler, told Churchill: '*I can't think how you have found time in your life to do anything else but paint.*' Note that the price of admission to the exhibition was half-a-crown.

La triste histoire de Winston Churchill. 1944

A poster in comic strip style issued in Vichy France. It begins with Churchill's ancestor, the first Duke of Marlborough, marching into battle. Then Churchill is bombed out and almost drowns in Norway before becoming a hero *'by the skin of others'*. He sprints in retreat from Dunkirk, betrays France at Mers el Kebir and Dakar, invades the Balkans, double crosses the Serbs, leaves the Greeks stranded and marches backwards through Cyrenaica. Having incurred the displeasure of everybody around him he leaves the scene, dies and is buried with the epitaph, *'Churchill wages war, his allies in front, himself behind, you have fought his war – don't ever forget it!'*

Left:
Poster by Leslie Illingworth. 1940
1940 design for a poster by Leslie Illingworth deposited in the Public Records Office, Kew

Publicity leaflets

The by-election had been caused by Churchill's appointment as President of the Board of Trade and, under the rules of the day, MPs appointed to the Cabinet were required to seek the endorsement of their electorate. Churchill lost the election by a margin of 429 votes; catholic voters in NW Manchester were angry over his support of the Home Rule for Ireland Bill and a large contingent of Jewish voters were incensed by the Liberals' Aliens Act. Churchill was forced to find another constituency and within just over two weeks was elected as MP for Dundee.

Right: 'Free trade for ever and Churchill now.' Churchill's leaflet for the by-election in North West Manchester on 24 April 1908.

A propaganda leaflet dropped by the Luftwaffe over southern England in July 1940, a few days after Churchill was pictured in newspapers trying out a tommy gun while inspecting troops. The soldier and officials accompanying Churchill were cropped out of the picture, so that he looked like a gangster!

Handbill for Churchill's 1945 election campaign at Woodford.

Punch cartoons

His outspoken views made Churchill a regular subject for the cartoonists of *Punch*. He deliberately courted publicity to get his ideas across to as many people as possible and was always in the news. This is just a tiny selection from hundreds of cartoons that appeared in *Punch* spanning a fifty-year period.

UNPAYING GUESTS.

British Lion. "I'M AFRAID, WINSTON, THEY'LL BE VERY EXPENSIVE TO REAR."

Above: A cartoon from *Punch* by Leonard Ravenhill dates from April 1921, when Churchill as Colonial Secretary was visiting Middle East hot spots.

Below: A reassuring image from *Punch* in October 1941, showing Churchill looking across the Channel towards France from the White Cliffs of Dover.

LORD WARDEN OF THE EMPIRE

Four cartoons from 1912 issues of *Punch*, when Winston Churchill was First Lord of the Admiralty.

A SEA-CHANGE
("INTO SOMETHING RICH AND STRANGE").

First Lord of the Admiralty (at *Deal's Coast*). "WELL, THINGS HAVE CHANGED SINCE YOUR TIME; BUT OUR LOWER DECK'S AS GOOD AS EVER."
Shade of Sir Richard Grenville (of the "*Revenge*"). "YES; AND I HEAR THEY'RE UNDERPAID AS WELL AS EVER."
First Lord. "AH! THAT'S ANOTHER CHANGE WE HOPE TO MAKE."

THE PLAIN DEALER.

[The Navy Estimates just issued are expressly stated by Mr. Churchill to be conditional upon the naval programmes of other nations.]

THE TAXABLE ELEMENT.

First Lord. "THE SEA FOR ME!"
Chancellor of the Exchequer. "WELL, YOU CAN HAVE IT. GIVE ME THE LAND!"

WELL-EARNED INCREMENT.

(Design for an Admiralty Christmas-Card.)

Quotations

If I were your wife I would put poison in your coffee.

If I were your husband I would drink it.

NANCY ASTOR

WINSTON CHURCHILL

Cartoon form the cover of the *Oxford Dictionary of Insulting Quotations* published by Cassell

1 October 1939
'I cannot forecast to you the action of Russia. It is a riddle wrapped in a mystery inside an enigma.'

13 May 1940
'I have nothing to offer but blood, toil, tears and sweat.'

4 June 1940
'We shall defend our island, whatever the cost may be, we shall fight on the beaches we shall fight in the fields, we shall fight in the hills, we shall never surrender.'

18 June 1940
'Let us therefore brace ourselves to our duties and so bear ourselves that if the British Empire and its Commonwealth last for a thousand years men will still say, "This was their finest hour."'

9 February 1941
Give us the tools, and we will finish the job.

30 December 1941
'French Generals told their Prime Minister that in three weeks England will have her neck wrung like a chicken. Some chicken! Some neck!'

21 March 1943
'There is no finer investment than putting milk into babies.'

16 November 1943
'You may take the most gallant sailor, the most intrepid airman or the most audacious soldier, put them at a table together – and what do you get? The sum of their fears.'

5 March 1946
'An iron curtain has descended across the Continent.'

30 November 1954
'It was the nation that had the lion's heart. I had the luck to be called upon to give the roar'. Churchill's 80th birthday.

Winston Churchill was a master of the quip or one-liner, particularly during more than fifty years of exchanges in the House of Commons:

1903
'Mr Chamberlain loves the working man, he loves to see him work.'

1903
On a Conservative MP who left to join the Liberal Party: *'The only instance of a rat swimming towards a sinking ship.'*

1903
'If you wanted nothing done Arthur Balfour was the best man for the task, there was no one to equal him.'

1907
'We are all worms but I do believe that I am a glow worm.'

1907
'The Times is speechless and takes three columns to express its speechlessness.'

1909
'I am not usually accused, even by my friends, of being of a modest or retiring disposition.'

1909
'I like the martial and commanding air with which the Rt Hon Gentleman treats facts. He stands no nonsense from them.'

1913
'If I valued the Hon.Gentleman's opinion I might get angry.'

1914
'Perhaps it is better to be irresponsible and right than responsible and wrong.'

1918
On the award of the American Distinguished Service Cross: *'The award designates gallantry in the face of the enemy. The latter qualification was waived in my case.'*

1919
Lady Astor: *'Winston, if I were your wife I'd put poison in your coffee.'* Churchill: *'If I were your husband, Nancy, I'd drink it.'*

1922
On farming at Chartwell: *'I'm going to make it pay whatever it costs.'*

1922
The Postmaster General: *'I see my Rt Hon friend shakes his head but I am only expressing my own opinion.'* Churchill: *'And I am only shaking my own head.'*

1924
'History will deal severely with the Prime Minister (Baldwin). I know, because I shall write it.'

1926
'I decline utterly to be impartial as between the fire brigade and the fire.'

1927
Of Lloyd George's criticism of him: *'It contained a certain vein of amiable malice.'*

1930

'I can well understand the Hon Member speaking for practice, which he badly needs.'

1931

'We have all heard how Dr Guillotine was executed by the instrument he invented.' (Interjection: *'He was not.'*) *'Well, he ought to have been.'*

1931

On a Labour member: *'He spoke without a note and almost without a point.'*

1932

Referring to Alfred Blossom MP: *'Blossom, that's an odd name. Neither one thing nor the other.'*

1933

Speaking of Ramsay MacDonald: *'The Prime Minister has the gift of compressing the largest number of words into the smallest amount of thought.'*

1935

'All the years I have been in the House I've always said to myself: "Do not interrupt" and I've never been able to keep that resolution.'

1936

Of Stanley Baldwin: *'Occasionally he stumbled over the truth, but picked himself up and hurried on as if nothing had happened.'*

1938

'Look at the Swiss! They have enjoyed peace for centuries. And what have they produced? The cuckoo clock!'

1938

My Rt Hon Friend the Air Minister has not been long enough in office to grow a guilty conscience.

1940

In a speech in Paris: *'I am going to give you a warning. Be on your guard because I am going to speak in French, a formidable undertaking which will put great demands on your friendship with Great Britain.'*

1940

'In war you do not have to be nice – you only have to be right.'

1940

'There is only one thing worse than fighting with allies and that is fighting without them.'

1940

'In those days (the 1920s) *the Lord President was wiser than he is now; he used frequently to take my advice.'*

1940

To Anthony Eden: *'Will you please stop translating my French into French!'*

1940

To his Chief of Staff, General Ismay: *'Pug, this is a world of vice and woe. I'll take the vice and you can have the woe!'*

1941

'If Hitler invaded Hell, I would make at least a favourable mention of the Devil in the House of Commons.'

1941

An Eisenhower aide introduced Churchill to John D Rockefeller II *'Hm! You number your Rockefellers. We number our Georges!'*

1942

'When I was called upon to be Prime Minister nearly two years ago there were not many applicants for the job. Since then perhaps the market has improved.'

1942

'I entreat Members of the House to remember that God in his infinite wisdom did not make Frenchmen in the image of Englishmen.'

1942

'I am certainly not one of those who need to be prodded. In fact, if anything, I am the prod.'

1942

Speaking in Edinburgh: *'I have some ties with Scotland ... I was born on St Andrew's Day ... I went to Scotland to find my wife! I commanded a Scottish battalion in France in the last war. I sat for fifteen years as the representative of 'Bonnie Dundee' and I might be sitting for it still if the matter had rested entirely with me.'*

1943

Anthony Eden, on a mission to bring Turkey into the war cabled Churchill: *'Progress slow. What more can I tell Turkey?'* Churchill: *'Tell them Christmas is coming!'*

1943

'In wartime truth is so precious that she should always be attended by a bodyguard of lies.'

1944

Churchill was not pleased when his daughter Sarah married Vic Oliver the Music Hall artist. Oliver asked Churchill who he considered to be the world's greatest man. *'Mussolini,'* replied Churchill, *'he had the courage to have his son-in-law shot!'*

1944

An aide at the White House asked Churchill what he thought of the United States: *'Toilet paper too thin, newspapers too fat.'*

1944

Responding to Aneurin Bevan: *'I should think it was hardly possible to state the opposite of the truth with more precision ... He need not get so angry because the House laughs at him; he ought to be pleased when they only laugh at him.'*

(Exclusive Copyright.) MR. WINSTON CHURCHILL

(London General Press.)

A striking cartoon postcard by Underwood for the London General Press. c1970

1944

'If I am accused of this mistake I can only say that I have made a number of other mistakes of which you have not heard.'

1944

Responding to Emanuel Shinwell: *'I do not challenge the Hon. Gentleman when the truth leaks out of him by accident from time to time.'*

1944

'This is rather like sending a rude letter and being there when it arrives.'

1945

'Nobody pretends that democracy is perfect. Indeed, it has been said that democracy is the worst form of Government except all those other forms that have been tried from time to time.'

1945

'I deem it highly important that we should shake hands with the Russians as far to the east as possible.'

1945

Message to President Roosevelt when trying to conclude arrangements for the Yalta Conference: *'We shall be delighted if you will come to Malta. No more let us falter! From Malta to Yalta! Let nobody alter!'*

1945

Roosevelt urged that the Yalta Conference should take no more than six days. Churchill replied: *'I do not see any way of realizing our hopes about world organisation in five or six days. Even the Almighty took seven.'*

1945

Before a state dinner for King Ibn Saud of Saudi Arabia Churchill heard that the King's religion allowed neither smoking nor the drinking of alcohol. Churchill replied that his rule of life prescribed as an absolutely sacred rite the smoking of cigars and the drinking of alcohol before, after, and if need be during all meals and the intervals between them.

1945

Of Lord Winterton: *'I must warn the Hon Gentleman that he will run a very grave risk of falling into senilty before he is overtaken by old age.'*

1945

'I know of no case where a man added to his dignity by standing on it.'

1945

'How can I tell that my temper would have been as sweet or my companionship as agreeable if I had abjured from my youth the goddess Nicotine?'

Churchill, who always loved a joke, enjoying a quip with newly elected President S Truman and Joseph Stalin at the Potsdam Conference in 1945.

1945

After his general election defeat in 1945: *'Although always prepared for martyrdom I prefer that it should be postponed.'*

1945

'Some people tell me it (the election defeat) *is a blessing in disguise. I must say the blessing is very well disguised.'*

1945

'I could not accept the Order of the Garter from my Sovereign when I had received the order of the boot from his people.'

1946

On receiving an honorary degree from the University of Miami: *'No one ever passed so few examinations and received so many degrees.'*

1946

'My idea of a good dinner is, first to have good food, then discuss good food, and then discuss a good topic – with myself as chief conversationalist.'

1947

On the Labour Government: *'A Government of the duds, by the duds and for the duds.'*

1948

Wilfred Paling (Postmaster General 1947-50) accused Churchill of being a dirty dog. Churchill retorted: *'Well, look at what dirty dogs do to palings.'*

1948

'Hanging, if properly conducted, is I believe, an absolutely painless death.' Labour interjection: *'Why not try it?'* Churchill: *'Well, it may come to that.'*

1949

Posing for photographers on his 75th birthday. One of them said: *'I hope, sir, that I can take your picture on your 100th birthday.'* Churchill: *'I don't see why not, young man. You look reasonably fit and healthy to me.'*

1950

John Strachey was transferred from Minister of Food to Minister of War. *'As Minister of Food he couldn't produce food – now surely he won't be able to produce any war.'*

1951

To a youthful heckler during the election campaign: *'I have always admired a manly man and I rejoice in a womanly woman but I cannot abide a boily boy.'*

1951

'I am informed from many quarters that a rumour has been put about that I died this morning. This is quite untrue.'

1951

'Tobacco is bad for love but old age is worse.'

1952

To King George VI: *'When I was younger I made it a rule never to take strong drink before lunch. It is now my rule never to do so before breakfast.'*

1952

A Labour MP: *'Must you fall asleep when I'm speaking?'* Churchill: *'No, it's purely voluntary.'*

1952

Interviewed on American TV: *'Television is a wonderful thing to think that every expression on my face at this moment may be viewed by millions of people throughout the United States. I hope that the raw material is as good as the methods of distribution.'*

1952

'I always remember that if instead of making a political speech I was being hanged, the crowd would be twice as big.'

1952

'My views are a harmonious process which keeps them in relation to the current movement of events.'

1954

Referring to American Secretary of State, John Foster Dulles: *'He is the only case I know of a bull who carries his china closet with him.'*

1954

Labour proposed separating the Ministry of Agriculture from the Ministry of Fisheries: *'It would not be a good arrangement. These two industries have been long associated departmentally and, after all, there are many ancient links between fish and chips.'*

Railway Locomotive:
Winston Churchill

In 1937 Oliver Bulleid, Chief Mechanical Engineer of the Southern Railway, started designing a Pacific-type express steam locomotive with the capability to attain a speed of 100mph. World War II intervened so the first of his new designs was not unveiled until June 1941. Subsequently, it was found that a scaled-down version would be required to work certain of the SR routes and the *Battle of Britain* class locomotives resulted.

In December 1946 the fifty-first example of the *Battle of Britain* class entered service with the serial number 21C151. On 11 September 1947 it was named *Winston Churchill*. The ceremony was carried out at Waterloo Station by Marshal of the Royal Air Force Lord Dowding, who also named *Fighter Command* and *Lord Dowding* on the same occasion. It was a grand affair with a RAF guard of honour and the RAF band. Lord Dowding remarked that he wished that his great wartime leader could have been there in person.

The nameplate, fitted on either side of the boiler, was a fraction under 6 feet long and 9 inches wide with *Winston Churchill* in raised letters four inches high and *Battle of Britain Class* in 1-inch letters beneath. Under the nameplate an oval plaque $27^{1}/_{2}$

inches x $21^{1}/_{2}$ inches bore the Churchill family coat of arms in full colour on a light blue background. After the formation of British Railways in 1948, *Winston Churchill* was re-numbered 34051.

By 1965 BR was moving swiftly into its dieselisation and electrification programme and many of Bulleid's Pacific steam locomotives had already been scrapped. Fortuitously 34051 had survived and was available to haul the funeral train carrying the body of Sir Winston Churchill from Waterloo to Handborough, near Bladon, on 30 January 1965. *Winston Churchill* was finally withdrawn in September 1965 and placed in the collection of the National Railway Museum at York.

A model of *Winston Churchill* made by former Welsh miners using a mixture of fine coal dust and resin.

Winston Churchill in British Railways livery as it hauled Churchill's funeral train from Waterloo to Handborough in 1965.

Revolver

The revolver that was lent to Winston Churchill by South African homesteader John Howard during the Boer War was sold at auction at Wallis & Wallis in Lewes, East Sussex in May 2002 for £32,000.

Rota: Churchill's lion

In 1938 Mr George Thomson of Pinner won an African lion cub in a wager. He called it Rota and for three years kept the growing beast in his back garden. But by 1941, due to a lack of sufficient meat to feed the ravenous animal, he decided to present it to the Prime Minister. Churchill was amused and accepted the offer providing Rota would be securely housed at London Zoo and placed on its ration strength without any charge falling upon His Majesty's Government. In 1943 Churchill visited the zoo to inspect his lion and the event was broadcast by the BBC, featured in the press and the subject of a cartoon by David Low. Harmony Kingdom, producers of whimsical animal caricatures, featured Rota and Churchill in their 'Circus' range in the mid 1990s.

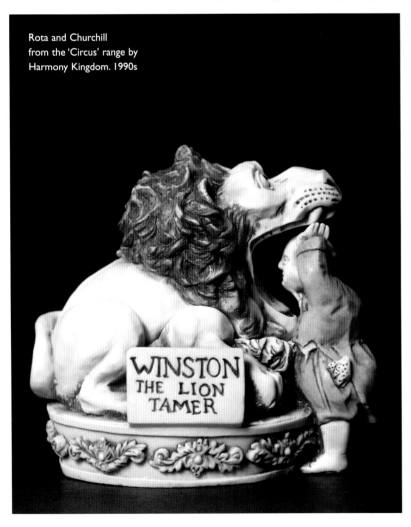

Rota and Churchill
from the 'Circus' range by
Harmony Kingdom. 1990s

WINSTON THE LION TAMER

Royal Academy

Winston Churchill took up painting in 1915, at the age of forty, when he was forced to resign as First Lord of the Admiralty in the aftermath of the Dardanelles disaster. One day in the garden at Hoe Farm, seeking a palliative to his deep depression, he watched his sister-in-law sketching in watercolours and taking up a brush began tentatively to paint a picture. He soon became absorbed in his new interest and Clementine, anxious to encourage anything which would improve her husband's mood, went to Godalming and purchased a supply of oil paints.

It so happened that the painter Sir John Lavery and his artist wife, Hazel, were near neighbours of the Churchills in London. The Laverys provided a great deal of practical help and advice regarding the purchase of painting equipment, as Churchill became totally smitten by his new hobby, so much so that he was later moved to write in *Painting as a Pastime* how *'painting came to my rescue in a most trying time.'* It remain his great passion throughout life, during which time he completed more than 500 pictures.

In 1947 Sir Alfred Munnings, President of the Royal Academy, suggested to Churchill that he should enter some paintings for the Summer Exhibition, but Churchill was reluctant. He was concerned that his work might be favoured because of his political position, rather than its intrinsic merit. Eventually, he was persuaded to enter two canvases under the pseudonym of David Winter and was delighted when both were accepted. In 1948, he entered three more paintings – this time under his own name – and all three were accepted. Churchill, who as a journalist, had reviewed the Royal Academy Exhibitions of 1932 and 1934 for the *Daily Mail*, was elected an Honorary Academician Extraordinary. His daughter, Lady Soames, once told me how well she remembered his unaffected delight at receiving this unique accolade and how thereafter he would always submit his entries 'as of right' to every Summer Exhibition. His paintings hung in every Summer Exhibition until 1964 and, after his death, there was a memorial display held at the Royal Academy in 1965. In 1958 President Eisenhower of the USA suggested that an exhibition of Churchill's paintings would *'strengthen the friendship between our two countries ... and create a wave of good will that would be both exciting and valuable.'* After opening in Kansas City, the exhibition of thirty-five pictures visited seven other American cities, four in Canada, seven in Australia and four in New Zealand, attracting over half a million visitors. In his foreword to the US exhibition catalogue President Eisenhower wrote: *'A very well-known and great friend of his and mine, the late Sir Oswald Birley, recognised as one of the most distinguished of 20th painters, once remarked to me, "If Sir Winston had given the time to art that he has given to politics, he would have been by all odds the world's greatest painter."'*

In 1959 the Royal Academy put on a one-man show of 62 of Churchill's paintings including the 35 which had been in the touring exhibition around the world the previous year. During a five-month run the exhibition, which had to be rehung in three galleries because of overcrowding in the original two, attracted 141,000 visitors. Reviewing the exhibition, John Russell wrote in The Sunday Times: *'In all of the paintings, without exception, the tone is one of such infectious enjoyment... This headlong quality runs through all his work.'*

Royal Air Force

Fascinated by the achievements of the Wright Brothers, Churchill was among the first to foresee the future importance of aircraft as both offensive and defensive weapons. As First Lord of the Admiralty in 1911 he was perturbed that the Royal Flying Corps, a recently formed division of the army, was considered to have only a reconnaissance role so he formed the Royal Naval Air Service and included bomb-dropping techniques and machine-gunnery in its training schedules.

In 1918 the RFC and the RNAS were merged to form the Royal Air Force. Appointed Secretary of State for War and Air in 1919 Churchill founded the Royal Air Force College at Cranwell. From the back benches of the House of Commons during the 1930s Churchill fought an almost single-handed crusade for funds to increase the strength of the RAF:

'I ask the Government to consider profoundly and urgently the whole position of our air defence.' (14 March 1933)

'I cannot see how we can delay in establishing the principle of having an air force at least as strong as that of any power that can get at us.' (7 February 1934)

'There is no doubt that the Germans are superior to us in the air at the present time.' (22 May 1935)

'Air armaments are not expressed merely by the air squadrons in existence, they cannot be considered apart from the capacity to manufacture.' (31 May 1935)

'The sole method ... for us to regain our old island independence [is] by acquiring that supremacy in the air.' (5 October 1938)

In April 1939 Churchill was appointed Honorary Air Commodore of 615 Squadron, Royal Auxiliary Air Force, which was then based at Kenley near his home at Chartwell. He cherished the appointment and proudly wore his RAF uniform on any suitable occasion – one of his uniforms is now preserved at Chartwell and another is on display in the Personalities Gallery at the Royal Air Force Museum, Hendon. He recognised and immortalised the role of the RAF in the Battle of Britain with his tribute: *'Never in the field of human conflict was so much owed by so many to so few.'*

(See also figurine on page 67 of Chuchill in RAF uniform, and the bone china loving cup on page 91 commissioned by the Royal Air Force in 1990 to mark the 50th anniversary of the *Battle of Britain*.)

Royal Air Force Battle of Britain Memorial Flight

'... I look forward confidently to the exploits of our fighter pilots – these splendid men, this brilliant youth – who will have the glory of saving their native land, their island home, and all they love, from the most deadly of all attacks... The Battle of France is over. I expect that the Battle of Britain is about to begin... Let us therefore brace ourselves to our duties, and so bear ourselves that, if the British Empire and its Commonwealth last for a thousand years, men will still say, "This was their finest hour."'
Winston S Churchill
House of Commons
18 June 1940

'Never in the field of human conflict was so much owed by so many to so few.'
Winston S Churchill
House of Commons
20 August 1940

The Battle of Britain took place in the skies over southeast England between July and October 1940. The Roll of Honour in Westminster Abbey lists the names of

1,503 Royal Air Force and Fleet Air Arm personnel killed in the battle. German records are far from complete but reliable estimates put the number of Luftwaffe airmen killed at in excess of 2,600. The RAF lost 1,017 aircraft. Luftwaffe losses have been estimated at 1,882 aircraft.

After the end of World War II, the 15 September 1945 was designated as the first Battle of Britain Day. Three hundred RAF fighter aircraft took part in a fly-past over central London. Thereafter the fly-past – always led by the immortal Spitfire and Hurricane – became an annual event although the numbers of participating aircraft was gradually reduced. After the 1961 fly-past the regular ceremonial flight over central London was discontinued and the RAF withdrew its then only remaining airworthy Spitfire (PM 631) and Hurricane

(LF 363) to form a Historic Aircraft Flight based at Horsham St Faith in Norfolk. The two aircraft continued to make a limited number of appearances at RAF open days around the country but by 1963 the number of these had dropped to just fifteen. Aware that it was custodian of priceless pieces of national heritage – and also aware that a single example of each aircraft type provided no cover at all against any kind of mishap – the RAF set about increasing its stock of airworthy examples. The cost of restoring historic aircraft featured high on the political agenda during a period when defence expenditure was constantly under scrutiny and the RAF was able to make only very slow and limited progress towards its objective.

Nevertheless by 1965 the Historic Aircraft

Flight had been boosted to four Spitfires – but still only the single Hurricane – and was able to increase its participation in air displays throughout the summer months. A huge bonus arrived in 1965 when Harry Saltzmann and Ben Fisz decided to make their epic feature film *Battle of Britain*. The film company paid handsomely to hire the RAF's five airworthy aircraft and also to restore several gate-guardian and museum examples to flying condition. As a result the Flight secured an additional Spitfire and the much-needed second Hurricane.

Hurricane PZ 865, *The Last of the Many!* was the last of 14,533 Hurricanes built by Hawker. Completed in 1944, she was retained by the manufacturers and used for communications and testing before being presented to the Battle of Britain Memorial Flight in 1972.

At around the same time a Lancaster (PA 474) was withdrawn from service and earmarked for static exhibition at the Royal Air Force Museum at Hendon. The RAF argued that one of the more historic airframes then doing gate guardian duty would be more appropriate for the RAF Museum and that PA 474 should be maintained in flying condition within the Historic Aircraft Flight.

Historic Aircraft Flight was renamed the Battle of Britain Memorial Flight in 1973 and in 1976 moved into a purpose-built hangar at its current base, RAF Coningsby in Lincolnshire. Its public esteem is now surely such that it must be considered untouchable by any politician seeking to further reduce defence expenditure for at least *'a thousand years'*. The present aircraft strength is the Lancaster, four Spitfires, two Hurricanes and a Dakota. Aircrew doing a tour of duty with the Battle of Britain Memorial Flight are all volunteers – and there is a long waiting list of aspirants. A twenty-strong support and maintenance ground crew, also volunteers, keeps the aircraft in immaculate order. The Flight's hangar at Coningsby is open to the public on every weekday – usually, more aircraft can be seen during the winter months. The Visitor Centre, operated jointly by Lincolnshire County Council and the RAF, has a small but interesting exhibition and well-stocked souvenir shop dominated by a portrait of Sir Winston Churchill inscribed with his words: *'Never in the field of human conflict was so much owed by so many to so few'*.

Royal Air Force College Cranwell

In the Founders' Gallery in College Hall at the Royal Air Force College, Cranwell, Lincolnshire hangs a fine portrait of Churchill painted by Cuthbert Orde. It was presented to the RAF College in 1952 by Rolls-Royce Limited. What is Churchill's portrait doing in the Royal Air Force College? What is the Cranwell connection? Churchill was one of the earliest advocates of the importance of air power as a decisive factor in any future war. As early as 1909, when he was President of the

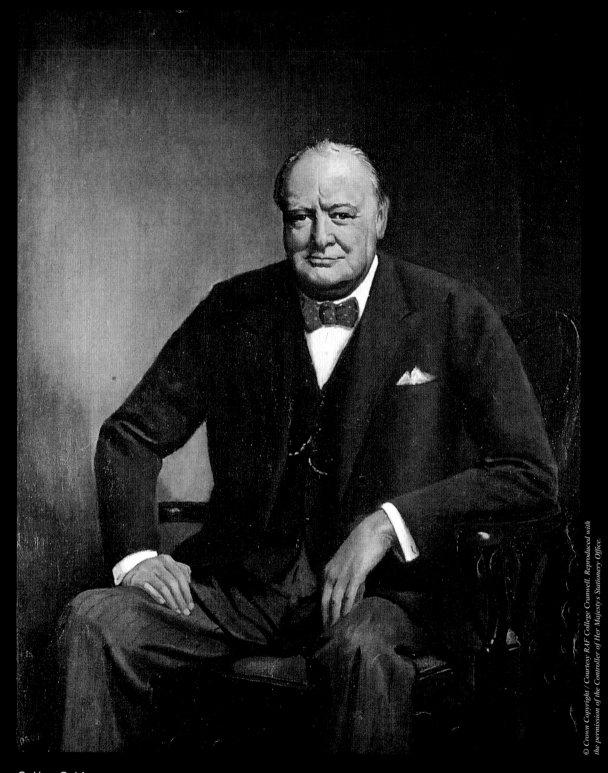

Cuthbert Orde's portrait of Winston Churchill, hanging in the Founders' Gallery.

Board of Trade, he was urging Asquith's government to make direct contact with the Wright brothers in order to be aware of the most up-to-date developments in aviation. As First Lord of the Admiralty between 1911 and 1915 Churchill authorised the requisitioning of land to the west of Cranwell village for the construction of an airfield for his newly formed Royal Naval Air Service. The new base was to be used to train pilots to fly aircraft, observation balloons and airships. It was named, navy fashion, as a ship – *HMS Daedalus*. The expansion of Cranwell was rapid during World War I. Huge airship hangars were erected, a private railway line was constructed linking the airfield to the main line at Sleaford and the base became totally self-contained with its own hospital, laundry, bakery and slaughter-house. The airmen joked that even their beef had to march to the camp! Many of the original World War I buildings remain nestling incongruously among the more modern and grander constructions on the vast and sprawling airfield. The railway line has long since gone but the railway station remains in use – as the guard room!

The Royal Air Force took over Cranwell from the Royal Navy on its formation on 1 April 1918. Later that year, after the end of World War I, Lloyd George invited Churchill to join his new government. *'Make up your mind whether you would like to go to the War Office or the Admiralty. You can take the Air with you in either case. I am not going to keep it as a separate department'.* However Churchill and Lord Trenchard, the 'Father of the Royal Air Force', were eventually able to prevail upon Lloyd George to give the RAF a continued independent existence and Churchill remained as Secretary of State for Air until 1921 during which time Cranwell became the Royal Air Force College. Churchill's name tops the Roll of Honour at the college as its very first Reviewing and Inspecting Officer in December 1920.

Throughout his 'Wilderness Years' in the 1930s Churchill almost alone amongst the politicians argued for increased rather than reduced expenditure on the Royal Air Force. In 1933, just one week after Ramsay

MacDonald had put forward Britain's proposals at the Disarmament Conference in Geneva, the German Reichstag passed an Enabling Bill giving Adolf Hitler full dictatorial powers. Churchill bitterly criticised MacDonald in the House of Commons and was depressed when he received little or no support, but as the decade progressed Churchill kept up his theme and slowly began to gain backing. In the event, the Royal Air Force got enough, but barely enough, resources to fight and win the Battle of Britain. Thus it was largely through his own relentless campaigning over more than thirty years that Churchill was able to say to the House of Commons on 20 August 1940, *'Never in the field of human conflict was so much owed by so many to so few.'* The Royal Air Force is proud to count Churchill himself as one of the few.

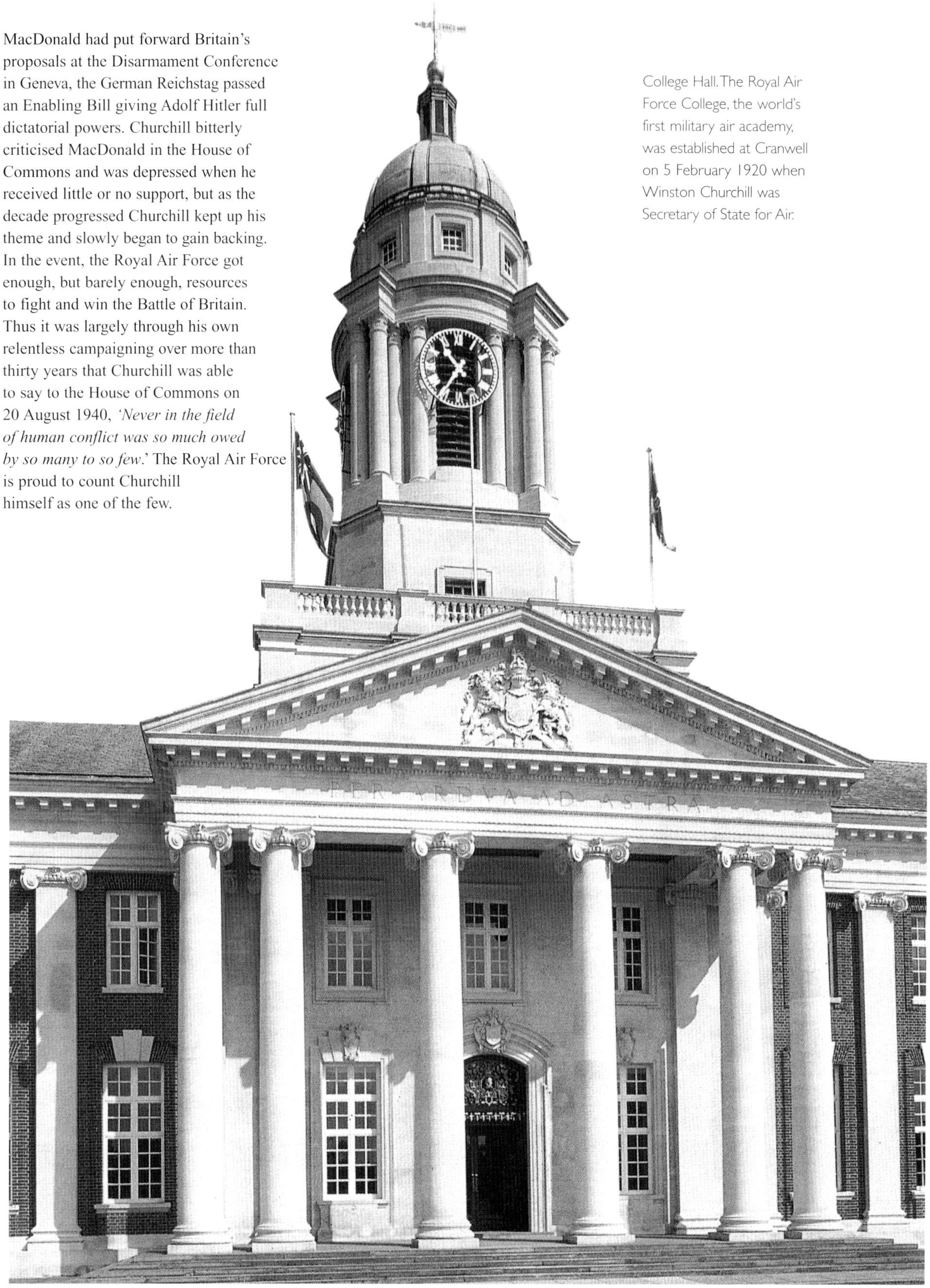

College Hall. The Royal Air Force College, the world's first military air academy, was established at Cranwell on 5 February 1920 when Winston Churchill was Secretary of State for Air.

Royal Doulton

Founded in 1815 by John Doulton, who was joined by his son Henry in 1835, this small pottery in Lambeth, south London rapidly expanded its original product range of earthenware beer bottles and roofing tiles. Soon the factory was turning out vast quantities of water and sewage pipes and ceramic sanitary wares to meet the Victorian craze for newfangled fitted bathrooms. In 1862 Doulton produced its first piece of art pottery, a reproduction of a 16th century German saltcellar, and in 1877 acquired a second pottery in Burslem, Stoke-on-Trent. In 1887 Henry Doulton was knighted by Queen Victoria – the first potter to be so honoured, so his flourishing business took the title Royal Doulton. Today Royal Doulton claims to be Britain's premier pottery – although that claim is hotly contested by the likes of Wedgwood, Royal Crown Derby, Spode, Minton and others. It has to be said, though, that Doulton's multifarious output tends to be of inconsistent quality – perhaps they try too hard to be all things to all men. Their best pieces give them world dominance in decorative pottery. Certainly Doulton have been a major producer of Churchilliana for more than sixty years but it, like the rest of their range, has been of mixed distinction.

Above: Regulations during World War II limited pottery manufacture to undecorated crockery for domestic use. Decorative wares were reserved for export, mainly to the USA, where pottery made a valuable contribution towards the lend-lease debt. Potteries applied a standard sepia transfer of Churchill to their 'Utility' pieces, but Doulton used a superior three-colour transfer.

Left: Designed by Harry Fenton, these toby jugs remained in production for fifty-one years and become one of Doulton's all-time best-sellers. Because they were made in such vast quantities Harry Fenton's tobies do not have a great secondary market value although the very earliest jugs backstamped '*Winston Churchill Prime Minister of Great Britain 1940*' can fetch up to three times more than later versions which were stamped '*Winston Churchill*'.

A china box, 3 x 3½ x 2 inches, with four insert trays dating from 1941. The front of the box and each of the trays is decorated with a design of oak leaves and acorns surrounding different quotes from Churchill's wartime speeches.

Decorative within the 'Utility' regulations, but of little practical use. Scarce. Has been seen priced at up to £200 in the UK and $350 in the USA.

Royal Military Academy Sandhurst

On the northern fringe of Camberley in Surrey, but just across the county boundary into Berkshire, the Royal Military Academy, Sandhurst is set in attractive countryside. The original buildings date from 1807 when it was decided to consolidate the Army's then dispersed officer training facilities onto a single site. The land had formed part of the estate of William Pitt (the Younger). When Prime Minister, Pitt had encountered strong parliamentary opposition against his attempts to increase the Army vote to counter the threat of Napoleon. Pitt died before work on the Academy commenced, but its first graduates were available to participate in Napoleon's eventual defeat.

Churchill's entry to Sandhurst in 1893 was hardly due to youthful ambition. His demanding and irascible father decided that Winston did not have the brains to contemplate a university career or enter the legal profession or the church. Winston appeared to do his best to prove his father right, needing three attempts to pass the entrance examination and then only qualifying for the cavalry class which was deemed inferior to the infantry class. Lord Randolph, by then terminally ill with syphilis, castigated his son: *'There are two ways of winning in an examination, one creditable, the other the reverse. You have unfortunately chosen the latter...'* Churchill's own account of his eighteen months at Sandhurst occupies the whole of Chapter 4 of *My Early Life*. He confesses that he spent several months in the 'awkward squad' – a category still in use for those cadets failing to ascend the learning curve at the required rate! He enjoyed the riding-school and considered himself well-trained to sit and manage a horse.

However, most of Churchill's chapter on his time at Sandhurst was clearly written tongue-in-cheek and is devoted to those extra-curricular activities which tended to display his youthful propensity towards his combative political life to come. He tells how he led a charge of fellow cadets to 'liberate' the bar at the *Empire Theatre*, Leicester Square – then a favourite haunt

Churchill Hall, Sandhurst

of prostitutes – and of his subsequent campaign in support of the *Anti-prudery Society*. Shortly after he left Sandhurst the father of a fellow cadet accused Churchill of committing a homosexual act whilst at the Academy. Churchill immediately sued and the action was settled out-of-court with an award of damages to him of £400 (around £25,000 in 2002 terms).

As a young MP in 1902, Churchill took up the case of twenty-nine Sandhurst cadets who had been sent down, without charge, following a spate of arson attacks. He attempted to raise the matter in the House of Commons without success, but was able to use his contacts with the aristocracy to get it tabled in the House of Lords, with the result that all but two of the cadets were reinstated and the Commandant was replaced. Thereafter, Churchill's further direct connections with his *alma mater* tended to be fairly rare. The development of his political career resulted in his becoming very much a Royal Navy man

by the outbreak of World War I. By the end of that conflict he was taking a keen interest in promoting the infant Royal Air Force. His role in the development of the tank in World War I had its roots in his training as a cavalry officer, but was incongruously performed from his position as First Lord of the Admiralty. As Minister of Defence in World War II he presided directly over the Army Chiefs of Staff but, according to 'Pug' Ismay: *'not once during the whole war did he overrule his military advisers on any purely military question.'*

Since it was first decided that the Royal Military College and the Royal Military Academy should be consolidated on a single site at Sandhurst, there has rarely been a period when some sort of expansion has not been taking place. 'Temporary' buildings have become 'permanent' and 'permanent' buildings have been adapted to uses other than those originally foreseen. For example a brick building, originally built as a contractor's shed, became the

terminus for a light horse tramway connecting the site to Blackwater railway station. A drill shed became temporary sleeping accommodation, a bicycle store was a rifle range, a cinema was a lecture room, a model room was a book store and a 'temporary' extension to the library. The latter was originally the gymnasium!

A great fire in 1873 was a disaster. The central block, the library and most of the classrooms were completely burnt out. The military, history and reference libraries, valuable manuscripts and records were entirely destroyed. The cost of rebuilding delayed for many years expansion and increased accommodation for cadets, through a shortage of funds. As a result Sandhurst has become something of a hotchpotch of architectural styles. This is nowhere more apparent than in Churchill Hall which was opened by Lady Soames, Churchill's youngest daughter, in 1970. It has, say the critics: *'...all the appearance of the back view of a grandstand'.*

Rug

This woven cotton rug, 60 x 30 inches, hung behind the bar of a public house on the Isle of Wight for many years. Very finely woven to an intricate design, it incorporates the flags of Nationalist China (pre-1949), the USA, Great Britain and the USSR; the caption *'1939 – Victory – 1945'* and an unmistakable caricature of Winston Churchill. Experts considered that the design and style of weave suggested that the rug was of Russian origin and typical of the cotton weaving industry of Estonia. The portrait of Churchill, the Union Flag and the incorporation of a lion and a unicorn in the design, suggest that the rug was made for export – possibly a one-off private commission. The provenance theory was given further credence when the rug was bought by the US Ambassador to Estonia in 1995.

Russian dolls and figurines

Those gaily painted wooden dolls which are successively taken apart to reveal ever smaller dolls have long been a feature of Russian folk art. This up-to-date version depicts British Prime Ministers Tony Blair encapsulating in turn John Major, Margaret Thatcher, Harold Wilson and – at the heart of the matter – Winston Churchill.

This accurately modelled and skilfully painted figurine is moulded in pewter or a similar metal. It portrays Churchill in the uniform of an Air Commodore at the Yalta conference in February 1945 and is part of a set of three figurines – the other two representing Roosevelt and Stalin. Thought to be of Russian origin. Rarely seen in Western Europe or the United States.

St Martin's Church, Bladon
Oxfordshire

St Martin's is the parish church of Bladon-with-Woodstock. The present building dates from 1804 although a church has existed on the same site since the 11th century. By the end of the 18th century the building had become a ruin, and was completely demolished and rebuilt. Only one piece of stone from the original building remains, apparently the lid of a child's coffin, in a corner near the font. There are several memorials inside the church, but only one, on the south side of the nave, near the pulpit, is connected with the Churchill family. It is a stained glass window, depicting St Michael and St George and inscribed to the son of Winston's cousin, the 9th Duke of Marlborough: *'In loving memory of Ivor Charles Spencer-Churchill 1898-1956'*.

In the churchyard, on the north side of the tower, are six Churchill family graves.

Furthest from the path, left to right, Lord Randolph Churchill 1849-1895, Winston's father: Lady Randolph 'Jennie' Churchill 1854-1921, Winston's mother: John Strange Spencer Churchill 1880-1947, Winston's brother: Consuelo Balsan 1877-1964, first wife of 9th Duke of Marlborough: Ivor Charles Spencer Churchill 1898-1956, Winston's cousin: Winston Leonard Spencer Churchill 1874-1965 and the ashes of Clementine Ogilvy Spencer Churchill 1885-1977.

In 1998 the Churchill graves were restored and the ground around them protected from their 20,000 annual visitors. The Churchill Grave Trust set up by Churchill's family and admirers raised $350,000 to fund restoration and ongoing maintenance.

Right: The grave of Sir Winston (1874-1965) and Lady Clementine Spencer Churchill (1885-1977).

JENNIE RA
CHURCHIL

WINSTON
LEONARD
SPENCER
CHURCHILL
1874 · 1965

CLEMENTINE
OGILVY
SPENCER
CHURCHILL
1885 · 1977

CHURCHILL

St Paul's Cathedral

A modest plaque, set in the floor below the Dome of St Paul's Cathedral, marks the spot on which Churchill's coffin rested during his State Funeral Service on 30 January 1965. Following his death at his London home, 28 Hyde Park Gate, on 24 January Churchill's body had lein in State in Westminster Hall for three days whilst long queues of people waited in sleet and snow, often for up to three hours, to pay their last respects. It was reported that more than 320,000 people filed past the coffin. For a while, on the eve of the funeral, the Prime Minister (Harold Wilson), the leader of the Opposition (Sir Alec Douglas-Home), the leader of the Liberal Party (Jo Grimond) and the Speaker (Sir Harry Hylton-Foster) took a turn in mounting guard at the four corners of the catafalque.

After Big Ben had struck 9.45 on the morning of 30 January it was silenced for the rest of the day. Churchill's coffin, covered with a Union Jack and with his Order of the Garter resting on it, was placed on a gun carriage by a bearer party of Grenadier Guards. Escorted by a Royal Air Force contingent the gun carriage was pulled by a detachment of 98 Royal Navy ratings and the procession went by way of Parliament Street, Whitehall, Trafalgar Square, the Strand, Fleet Street and Ludgate Hill to St Paul's. Hundreds of thousands of people lined the route and it was estimated

that tens of millions watched on television or listened over the radio.

As Churchill had approached his ninetieth year the inevitability of his eventual death prompted the Prime Minister to set up a committee, under the chairmanship of the Duke of Norfolk, to plan for a State Funeral. The planning operation, given the code name *Operation Hope Not*, resulted in superbly efficient organisation on the day. It has been suggested that Churchill himself had played a substantial part in organising his funeral, but Anthony Montague Browne, his Private Secretary from 1952-65, says that is untrue. The only injunction he gave was: *'Remember, I want lots of marching bands at my funeral.'* He got nine.

A congregation of three thousand gathered in St Paul's Cathedral for the thirty-minute service. It included the Queen, the Duke of Edinburgh and members of the Royal Family; foreign Heads of State – there were four Kings, a Queen, fifteen Presidents and Marshal Koniev of the USSR; members of the Churchill family; Sir Winston's secretary; family servants and gardeners; boys from Harrow School; representatives of the armed forces and civilian services. The pall bearers were all men who had served with Churchill during his World War II Premiership and the officiating clergy included the Archbishop of Canterbury and the Bishop of London. To conclude the service, trumpeters high

The scene inside St Paul's Cathedral at Sir Winston Churchill's funeral.

up in the Whispering Gallery sounded the Last Post and Reveille. Then the procession reformed and marched through the City of London to Tower Pier. There the coffin was piped aboard the PLA launch *Havengore* and, to the strains of *Rule Britannia* and the roar of a fly-past by sixteen Lightning fighters of the Royal Air Force, taken upstream to Festival Pier and on to Waterloo Station. From Waterloo the funeral train, drawn by *Winston Churchill,* the *Battle of Britain* class locomotive, was taken to Long Handborough, the railway station nearest to the churchyard at Bladon, close by Blenheim Palace, where after a short private service Sir Winston Churchill was buried.

Salisbury Hall

Salisbury Hall, five miles south of St Albans in Hertfordshire, displays a rich mixture of Roman, Norman, Medieval and Renaissance architectural features. According to legend it was one of the meeting places of Nell Gwynn and Charles II. In 1905 Salisbury Hall became the home of Winston Churchill's mother after her marriage to her second husband, George Cornwallis-West. She had never before had a home with enough land for a proper garden and Winston helped her to decide which plants she should grow and where to plant them. Winston often stayed with his mother at Salisbury Hall and it was there that he began writing his biography of his father. In the spring of 1908 Winston became President of the Board of Trade in Asquith's government and, on the following weekend, attended a party to celebrate the event given by his mother at Salisbury Hall. One of the guests took Winston's eye. His mother introduced them. It was Clementine Hozier.

By 1939 the Design Department of the de Havilland Aircraft Company had outgrown its space at the Hatfield headquarters. Salisbury Hall was nearby and standing vacant and semi-derelict, so the Department moved in. Many of the fittings and furnishings had not been removed and in a glass case on the wall of a lavatory was a stuffed pike. There is a legend that the shape of the fish had some influence on the designers as they attended to calls of nature whilst working on the design of the fuselage of the Mosquito aircraft. Whether or not one cares to believe the legend, it is an authenticated fact that the pike had been caught in the moat by Winston Churchill on a visit to see his mother.

The Mosquito, the *Wooden Wonder*, was designed on a private enterprise basis by de Havilland after they had initially encountered scepticism and disinterest at the Air Ministry. The company was very aware that metal was in short supply and that, in any event, the nation's metal-bashing capacity was already fully stretched by current aircraft production.

Eleven of the pall bearers leaving St Paul's Cathedral. *Near side, left to right:* Harold Macmillan, Field Marshal Sir Gerald Templar, Lord Bridges, Field Marshal Viscount Slim, Lord Avon, Field Marshal Earl Alexander of Tunis. *Far side, left to right:* Sir Robert Menzies, Lord Normanbrook, Lord Ismay, Lord Portal, Earl Attlee.

Earl Mountbatten of Burma was the twelfth pall bearer but is out of shot. Lord Montgomery was ill and could not attend.

Mosquito 1 Mk 3 RR299, built at Leavesden in 1945, which after service with the RAF was transferred to British Aerospace and based at Hawarden. The aircraft was on the civil register as G-ASKH but was repainted in service markings for its part in the film *633 Squadron*.

It had experience of the extensive use of wood in aircraft construction – the famous Comet Racer of the 1930s had been built largely of wood – and were cognisant of the fact that the woodworking skills of the furniture industry could be employed in the war effort. This unique aircraft played an important role in the prosecution of 'Churchill's War' and the eventual allied victory. There is an interesting direct connection between Churchill and the Mosquito. When he went to Russia in October 1944 to meet Stalin, a Mosquito of 544 Squadron was given the daily task of flying the diplomatic bag to Moscow. The Russians were somewhat awestruck by the unique aircraft and, in spite of wartime difficulties, provided VIP treatment for the crew in the form of caviare, vodka and seats at the Bolshoi Ballet.

Today, Salisbury Hall is the Mosquito Museum. The original prototype is back where it began and is the centrepiece of a fascinating exhibition which includes examples of other famous de Havilland aircraft.

Saltcellar

This little china bust has a large hole in its base, closed by a rubber bung and a small hole in the top of the hat. It is intended to be a receptacle for dispensing salt. This type of saltcellar is usually paired with a pepper pot. Did this Churchill saltcellar have a mate? If so, who? It is post-1953 since it has Sir Winston embossed across the back of the shoulders. Even the cruet specialist, who attends the major antiques fairs, was unable to provide an answer.

Savoy Hotel

In 1884 Richard D'Oyly Carte, who had already built the Savoy Theatre to stage Gilbert and Sullivan's comic operas, decided to build the most luxurious hotel in London. He specified that the hotel, which would incorporate the theatre, should compete with the best in America. Built on the site of the 13th century Savoy Palace, between the Strand and the River Thames, D'Oyly Carte's new hotel became the subject of much conjecture and exaggerated gossip. Londoners who could never aspire to enter its portals could marvel at tales of its seventy bathrooms – a quite unheard-of number in those days.

It was to the Pinafore Room at the Savoy Hotel in 1911 that Winston Churchill came, with his friend Frederick ('FE') Smith (later Lord Birkenhead) to found the Other Club. The pair had been invited to join The Club, an old established and very exclusive gentlemen's dining club which was seeking some spirited new blood. In the event, when their names were put up for election, they were blackballed. Churchill remarked: *'It was rather like asking a man to dinner and kicking him down the steps before he entered your house.'* Affronted, Churchill and Smith formed the Other Club, *'to meet once a month when Parliament is sitting.'* The object of the Other Club is to dine.

The rules of the club included:

The Club shall consist of no more than fifty Members, and not more than twenty-four Members of the House of Commons. The Executive Committee shall have plenary powers. There shall be no appeal from the decision of the Executive Committee. The names of the Executive Committee shall be wrapped in impenetrable mystery. Nothing in the Rules or intercourse of the Club shall interfere with the rancour or asperity of party politics.

The cocoon of impenetrable mystery has made it impossible to establish the identity of its founder members other than Churchill and Smith. However after the latter died in 1930, at the age of fifty-seven, it appeared to leave Churchill with autocratic power! There was no pecking order at table. The food was of remarkable quality, the wine was too – and also in quantity. The social atmosphere was affable, in spite of full compliance with the rule not to interfere with rancour or asperity. The standard of after-dinner speaking and repartee was of the highest order. One regular after-dinner activity of the Other Club was a contest whereby a member, drawn by lot, chalked a subject on a blackboard. A second member, also drawn by lot, was then shown the subject and required to make an immediate and impromptu speech about it. On one evening a member chalked *'sex'* on the blackboard. Churchill, who had drawn the short straw, rose and said, *'It gives me great pleasure,'* and then sat down again!

A roll call of the Other Club over the years reads something like a directory of the great and the good, although some of Churchill's nominees did not always find universal favour with the other members – Aristotle Onassis, for example. There is no doubt that the club was Churchill's great joy. From its foundation he attended regularly – in war and peace, in office and out – for fifty-four years. He attended his last Other Club dinner on 10 December 1964 and exactly a month later suffered the massive stroke from which he died. The final forward entry in his engagement diary, the only entry for February 1965, was the next fortnightly meeting of the Other Club – 4 February.

Schooner: *Sir Winston Churchill*

The Sail Training Association, based at The Hard, Portsmouth, is a charitable organisation founded in 1956 with the objective of developing the character of young people through providing opportunities for them to experience sea-going training.

The Association's courses enable young men and women normally aged between 16 and 24, of all nationalities, to undertake two-week adventure voyages facing together, in friendship and competition, the challenge presented by racing at sea under sail.

Although the majority of expeditions are carried out in the coastal waters of the British Isles the Association regularly enters its ships in the biennial *Cutty Sark Tall Ships Race* and in recent years has operated winter voyages based on the Canary Islands. The ship's officers are highly experienced seamen but all crew duties are carried out by the young volunteers who are normally nominated by schools, all kinds of youth organisations or employers. The STA operates two ships, both topsail schooners, the *Malcolm Miller* and the *Sir Winston Churchill*, the latter having been launched on 7 February 1966.

The *Sir Winston Churchill* is almost 46 metres long and displaces 281 tons. She is of all timber construction, carries a square topsail on the foremast and is fore-and-aft rigged with three jibs and a fore-topmast staysail. She can accommodate 34 boys or girls and 9 adult officers. Life aboard is deliberately spartan and rigorous and designed to test young people to the limit of their ability. Nevertheless the majority thoroughly enjoy their two-week voyage, many seek a second opportunity and the sailings are invariably over-subscribed.

Right: A model in brass of the schooner *Sir Winston Churchill*, is sold as a fund-raiser. Another popular souvenir is an all-glass model made in the form of a ship in a bottle.

Far right: There is a small but busy souvenir stall on *Sir Winston Churchill* set up to raise money for the *Sail Training Association.* This little plate, *'Help build a schooner for Britain's youth,'* is just one of the items on sale.

Above: The Sail Training Association's schooner Sir Winston Churchill .

Silhouettes

Etienne de Silhouette, Minister of Finance to Louis XV, was the man who gave his name to profile portraits cut out of black paper and then mounted on a light ground. They became popular as an inexpensive alternative to a painted portrait. Winston Churchill's distinctive profile made him a popular subject for silhouette artists.

Widely used silhouette by Elizabeth Baverstock. Often used as a headline symbol or logo.

The logo for a London chain trading in popular souvenirs of London. The proprietor happens to be a Mr Churchill. He is not, so far as I know, any relation to his famous namesake, but he evidently finds the association a benefit to trade. This large silhouette can be seen on the fascia of one of his shops.

By Silhouette Designs of Bexleyheath, Kent. Sold for many years in the Chartwell souvenir shop.

Silverware

Asprey Cigarette Box. 1974
Asprey & Co of New Bond Street, London produced a five-piece Churchill Centenary range. This rosewood, cedar lined, cigarette box has a relief bust of Churchill by Oscar Nemon on the lid. Original cost £95. This example bought at auction in 1994 for £95.

Garrard Bonbon Sweet Dish. 1974
Part of Garrard's Churchill Centenary range. Designed by John Spencer-Churchill, Winston's nephew, and Garrard's Chief Designer, Alex Styles in a limited edition of 100. It had sold out by the end of 1974. Garrard's Centenary Collection consisted of a punchbowl and eight cups; a wine jug and six goblets; a cigar humidor; a pair of salvers; a cigarette box; a pair of coasters; a statuette; a bonbon dish and a paperknife. The entire collection cost £5,185.

The Churchill Centenary. 1974
Below: A silver gilt tray, decanter and six goblets made by Mappin and Webb of Regent Street. The tray and decanter were decorated with embossed and gilded replicas of the Churchill coat of arms and the goblets carried a lion couchant supporting a banner gules.

Photo courtesy Mappin & Webb

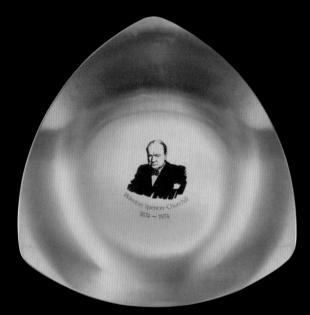

Above left:

The Churchill Annigoni Plate. 1974

Probably the most widely available piece of Churchill silverware. Produced by the Pobjoy Mint and issued in a limited edition of 2,500 by the Heritage Club for the Churchill Centenary. The Italian artist Pietro Annigoni worked in England during the 1950s and painted oil portraits of Queen Elizabeth II in 1955 and 1970 and of President John F Kennedy in 1961. This silver plate with its etched and enamel-filled line drawing was a rare medium for him but is very effective.

Above right:

John Pinches Dish, 1974

A gilt portrait adorns this silver dish, endorsed by Sir John 'Jock' Colville, Churchill's former secretary, for the Churchill Centenary Trust. It is mounted on velvet in a 10 x 10 inch oak standing frame and supplied in a blue presentation box embossed with the Churchill coat of arms. It is advertised as a limited edition but the size of the edition was not declared. An attractively designed and packaged item.

Below left:

Dish by Old Hall. 1974

An curved triangular fruit dish made by Old Hall, England in 1974.

Below right:

Dish by Joseph Hazeldine. 1965

A silver dish designed by Joseph Hazeldine for silversmiths A Edward Jones of Birmingham in 1965. The portrait medallion was also sold separately in gold, silver or bronze.

Slippers

A pair of leather-lined, leather-soled, dark blue velvet slippers embroidered *'WSC'* in raised gold thread and stamped *'N Tuczek, Clifford Street, Bond Street, London W'*. Dating from the 1950s, these slippers were auctioned by Sotheby's in July 1998 and sold for £6,325. *(Photo courtesy Sotheby's).*

Statues

Major public statues of Winston Churchill can be found in many countries including the United States (at least four), Canada, Belgium, Luxembourg, Denmark, Norway and Brunei. This survey includes only the full-size statues, accessible to the public, in the United Kingdom.

The most public UK statue of Churchill must be that in Parliament Square, London, appropriately overlooking the House of Commons. Sculpted by Ivor Roberts-Jones the bare-headed and brooding figure leaning heavily on a walking stick, in the words of Lady Soames: *'... combines a sombre likeness with considerable allegorical allusion.'* The statue, funded by public subscription, was unveiled by Lady Churchill on 1 November 1973. The ceremony was attended by HM the Queen, the Queen Mother, the Prime Minister and no less than four former Prime Ministers.

Not far away, inside the House of Commons, is Oscar Nemon's seven feet tall, one ton, bronze statue of Churchill with arms akimbo and head thrust forward as if making a speech. This was also unveiled by Lady Churchill, in December 1969, and stands beside the Churchill Arch at the entrance to the Commons Chamber. When the chamber was rebuilt after World War II, the arch, at Churchill's suggestion, was left bearing the scars of the 1941 bombing (see also page 84).

Another Oscar Nemon statue is the massive seated bronze on the Green at Westerham just two miles from Chartwell. The marble plinth bears the inscription: *'This plinth was presented by Marshal Tito and the people of Yugoslavia as a symbol of Yugoslavian soil in homage to Sir Winston Churchill's leadership in the War. 23 July 1969.'*

A third Nemon statue is in the Guildhall, London. This was the first major statue of Churchill, having been commissioned by the Corporation of the City of London to mark his 80th birthday in 1954. It was unveiled on 21 June 1955. At the ceremony Churchill said: *'I greatly admire the art of Mr Oscar Nemon ... I also admire this particular example, which you, my Lord*

Smokers' requisites

A pipe tamper replicating Churchill's V-sign but with the facility to be used in the reverse mode in appropriate circumstances. Heavy solid brass with the vestiges of its original silver plating.

A hand-carved tobacco jar. Originates from the Bavaria in 1945.

Meerschaum (hydrated magnesium silicate), a fine white clay, has been used for making the bowls of tobacco pipes for generations. Since it can be moulded as well as carved, fine detail can be achieved. This pipe was made to order in 1988 for its original owner by a Turkish pipe maker.

A hand-carved briar pipe. Several variations exist – carved by individual craftsmen so that no two are exactly alike.

Below: The statue of Churchill in Parliament Square.
Right: The statue of Churchill in Westerham, Kent
Below right: The statue of Churchill in the Houses of Parliament

*Mayor, have just unveiled, because it seems
to be such a very good likeness ... but on
this point I cannot claim to be either
impersonal or impartial.'*

Churchill was reported to be very pleased
with the result in contrast to his reaction to
the Graham Sutherland portrait painted in
the same year.

Churchill was MP for Epping/Woodford
from 1924. His constituents were rightly
proud of their association and to express
their appreciation commissioned a statue
by David McFall. Larger than life, this
statue, eight feet tall excluding the plinth,
was unveiled in October 1959 by Field
Marshal Lord Montgomery with Churchill
himself in attendance. Lady Churchill took
an intense dislike to the statue and tried to
have it taken down.

The St Margaret's Bay Trust, near Dover
in Kent, commissioned Oscar Nemon to
execute the statue now to be seen in the
Pine Gardens. This nine feet tall striding
giant on a massive black granite plinth
inscribed with the, *'We shall fight on the
beaches...'* quotation, was unveiled by
Churchill's grandson, Winston Churchill
MP, on what would have been his 98th
birthday, 30 November 1972.

Oscar Nemon created another statue,
which was unveiled by Queen Elizabeth
the Queen Mother and witnessed by Lady
Soames, in the grounds at Chartwell. The
life size bronze of Winston and Clementine,
seated and casually attired, is a replica of
a statue sited in Kansas City, USA, which
was completed by Nemon just before his
death in 1985 (see also page 42).

At the junction of New Bond Street and
Old Bond Street in London is a double
statue of Churchill and Roosevelt. By
American sculptor Laurence Holotcener,
the statue, entitled *The Allies*, was unveiled
by HRH Princess Margaret on 2 May 1995
to mark 50 years of peace. The sculture
was a gift from the Bond Street Association
to the City of Westminster and the people
of London. The two figures are seated at
either end of an ordinary park bench and
the space between them is a well used
photo opportunity spot.

Above: The sculpture of
Churchill and Roosevelt
by Laurence Holotcener
which stands at the
junction of New and Old
Bond Street, London.

Right: A signed maquette,
206 inches long × 12
inches high, of Holotcener's
Bond Street statue.
The maquettes had been
offered by the Catto
Gallery, Hampstead in
1997 in a limited edition
of 50 at £7,050. The art
world was surprised in
July 1998 when the third
signed proof of the
maquette was sold at
Sotheby's, London for
£14,950.

Tableware

Tableware, usually called crockery, must first and foremost be functional. Most tableware is surprisingly strong. A china plate may not survive being dropped from a great height onto a hard floor, but its protective glaze will resist scratching by cutlery and the most robust application of abrasive cleaners. Whilst retaining its functional properties, tableware may also be decorative. The tradition of superbly decorated wares inaugurated by the Bow, Chelsea, Derby and Worcester factories in the 18th century has been continued to the present day by such as Coalport, Spode, Royal Doulton, Wedgwood and many others.

1. Pottery unknown. 1886
Winston Churchill's father, Lord Randolph Churchill, was featured on a Staffordshire Pottery china plate in 1886 when he was Chancellor of the Exchequer.

2. WH Goss. 1880s
A tiny bud vase by WH Goss, the leading source of crested china from 1858 to 1939. This piece dates from the 1880s and carries the Churchill family coat of arms,

3. CT Maling & Sons, Newcastle-upon-Tyne, (Cetemware). 1914
Amusing little caricature of Churchill by C Miguel. This plate was part of a series depicting leading politicians. Although produced before Maling's earned their reputation for gold register printing this is a finely detailed and high quality earthenware plate. Maling's pottery closed down in 1963 but its archives and many examples of its products since 1853 are held by Tyne & Wear Museums Service. Very rare. I have never seen an example at auction in the UK but understand that one was sold in the USA in 1991 for $1,000.

4. Pottery unknown. 1914-15
Churchill's tenure as First Lord of the Admiralty lasted for the first ten months of World War I. After the Dardanelles debacle he spent five frustrated months in the sinecure office of Chancellor of the Duchy of Lancaster before resigning to serve with the Royal Scots Fusiliers on the Western Front. After a further five months

he returned to political life to spend over a year as a backbencher before regaining office as Minister of Munitions. Thus Churchill's portrait is missing from much of the patriotic china issued during the war years. This rare oval dish portrays him in First Lord's uniform.

5. Pottery unknown. 1940-45
Marked only *'AV – REG No 805205'*. The widely used wartime sepia portrait transfer of Churchill has been applied to an Art Deco shape jug from the 1930s.

6. Copeland/Spode. 1941
White earthenware with either black or sepia transfers. This large jug, $7\frac{1}{2}$ inches tall, was produced under wartime restrictions. It has a good portrait of Churchill surrounded by a warship, an aircraft and a tank with quotations from his speeches above and below. Several different transfers appeared on the reverse of other versions of this jug. Examples have made $120-£180 in UK auctions; $340-$400 in the USA.

7. Elijah Cotton. BCM Nelsonware. 1940-45
A large four-colour transfer captioned *'There'll always be an England'* adorns this two-pint milk jug. Much of the surviving wartime tableware from the Elijah Cotton Pottery has suffered degradation due to a fault in the original clay or glaze.

8. Lancasters, Hanley and Gray's Pottery, Stoke-on-Trent 1940-45
These two potteries used the same body moulds but affixed different handle shapes. The rim, foot and handle gilding is much more elaborate on the Gray's Pottery mug. All's fair in love and war and if the potteries were obliged to produce standard 'Utility' ware they could at least compete on the embellishments.

9. Wedgwood. 1941-45
A white bas-relief portrait of Churchill by Arnold Machin with a heraldic lion on the reverse captioned *'Give us the tools and we will finish the job.'* Pale blue glazed earthenware. Paired with a similar tankard depicting Roosevelt and an American eagle and the caption *'This can be done'.*

1. Pottery unknown. 1886

2. WH Goss. 1880s

3. CT Maling & Sons. 1914

4. Pottery unknown. 1914-15

5. Pottery unknown. 1940-45

6. Copeland/Spode. 1941

7. Elijah Cotton 1940-45

11. Skerretts, Hanley. 1940-45

12. Royal Doulton. 1941

13. Wade Heath & Co, Burslem. c1941

8. Gray's Pottery. 1940-45

9. Wedgwood. 1941-45

10. Ascot White. 1941-45

14. Wartime 'Utility' Bone China. 1940-45

10. Ascot White. 1941-45

The reverse of this mug has a matching line drawing transfer of President Roosevelt smoking a cigarette in a long holder and between the portraits of the two leaders is a large 'V'.

11. Skerretts, Hanley. 1940-45

Unusually this large mug, as well as the ubiquitous sepia portrait transfer of Churchill, has on the reverse in full colour a bulldog squatting on a Union flag with the caption *'Come on!!'*

12. Royal Doulton. 1941

A one-pint earthenware tankard with an unusual full-colour transfer incorporating 'RAF' and 'V' symbols and the Morse code '...–' cypher. On the reverse of the tankard the inscription *'Victory not only for ourselves but for all – Churchill'*. Scarce.

13. Wade Heath & Co Burslem. c1941

A two-handled loving cupand tankard, both in earthenware. Nicely modelled figures of Roosevelt and Churchill form the handles of the loving cup and convoys of ships and aircraft are streaming across the Atlantic. Captioned around the foot *'Let's drink to victory, let's drink to peace'*. The tankard, in two-tone green, uses the same mould of Churchill for its handle and is captioned *'Roll out the Barrel'* – from a popular wartime song.

14. Wartime 'Utility' Bone China. 1940-45

'Utility' bone china from major potteries, like Sutherland (left) and Paragon (right), could be of the highest quality in spite of the restrictions placed on decorating. Shape, style and limited colouring enhanced the standard sepia portrait transfer of Churchill.

The Paragon set is unusual in having the transfer placed inside the cup (so that the Prime Minister surfaced as one drank one's tea!) and the well of the saucer is inscribed *'Never was so much owed by so many to so few'*. These better pieces are now much-sought-after collectors items – I have seen the Paragon set priced at £225 in London W1 and the Sutherlands set at $150-$200 in the USA.

15. J&G Meakin 'Sunshine' design 1940-45

A pale cream body colour, a gently curved shape, embossed fronds in the corners and a bold gilt rim line enhance this otherwise plain wartime 'Utility' plate. Meakin's for some reason backstamped this plate with two different registered design numbers – 561073 and 351413.

16. AG Richardson (Crown Ducal) 1940-45

Arthur Richardson's Cobridge pottery employed Charlotte Rhead from 1931 to 1942. It is not known whether she created the deep relief Florentine border design of this plate. The *Fighting Premier* transfer is from a photograph by Cecil Beaton.

17. Alfred Meakin. c1941

Alfred Meakin's tableware designs usually copied those of leading manufacturers, but this *Champions of Democracy* plate was an exception. A large full-colour transfer of Roosevelt and Churchill facing the Statue of Liberty, with the furled flags of the US and GB repeated around the rim, gave the plate a bright appearance uncommon at the time. It is interesting to note that the portrait of Churchill is the regular sepia transfer printed in reverse.

18. Elijah Cotton (BCM/Nelsonware). 1940-45

Serrated shape with a deep relief border and four-colour transfer of Churchill, with warships and an aircraft in the background, captioned *'There'll always be an England'*.

19. AJ Wilkinson Newport Pottery. 1941

Superb full-colour relief caricature portrait captioned *'Let us go forward together'* from Churchill's first speech in the House of Commons as Prime Minister. Signed on the back by Clarice Cliff. This decorated version, produced for export only, is rarely seen in the UK. A plain cream version, produced in limited quantities for the home market, is also very scarce. The plain cream Honeyglaze plates do not carry Clarice Cliff's signature, adding weight to the belief that she was essentially a colourist and not a modeller.

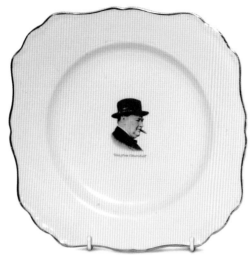

15. J&G Meakin 'Sunshine'. 1940-45

18. Elijah Cotton. 1940-45

16. AG Richardson. 1940-45

19. AJ Wilkinson, Newport Pottery. 1941

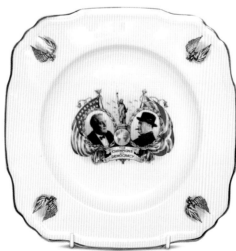

17. Alfred Meakin. c1941

20. AJ Wilkinson, Royal Staffordshire Pottery. 1942

21. Grimwade Royal Winton. 1941

22. Royal Doulton. 1940-45

23. James Kent Limited, Longton. 1941-45

27. Grimwades
Royal Winton. c1945

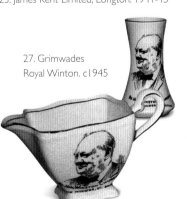

24. Pottery unknown. 1940-45

25. Pottery unknown. 1940-45

26. Taylor & Kent of Longton. 1940-45

28. Pottery unknown. c1945
29. Royal Doulton. c1945

20. AJ Wilkinson. Royal Staffordshire Pottery. 1942

Ties with the United States were getting stronger. The Lend-Lease Bill was passed by the US House of Representatives. On 9 February 1941 Churchill made a broadcast to the USA, *'Deeds not words... Put your confidence in us... Give us the tools and we'll finish the job.'*

The Royal Staffordshire Pottery responded by adding an informal portrait transfer of President Roosevelt beside the customary wartime image of the Prime Minister. A border of stars between ochre rim lines give this 'Utility' plate a more than usually decorative finish. Scarce.

21. Grimwade Royal Winton. 1941

The Churchill-Roosevelt theme is extended to this pleasant little trinket dish. Grimwades also made an unusually shaped ashtray with a matching design. Fully captioned, *'Franklin D Roosevelt, President, USA'* and *'Rt Hon Winston Churchill, Prime Minister, Gt Britain'* with bouquets of flowers and the two national flags, it seems likely that the dish was principally intended for export.

A smaller version, described as *'one of the prettier small ceramics'*, was spotted a few years ago in a US catalogue priced at $150.

22. Royal Doulton. 1940-45

Pin dish, sometimes called a sweet dish, with its simple shape enhanced by crimping around the rim and Doulton's usual superior 'Utility' transfer.

23. James Kent Limited Longton. 1941-45

This decorative plate from Kent's marked the Churchill-Roosevelt connection from the signing of the Atlantic Charter in 1941 right up until Roosevelt's death in 1945.

24. Pottery unknown. 1940-45

One of the many unmarked 'Utility' pieces, this pin dish achieves added interest from its gently curved eight-sided shape. The dish as the vestiges of a silver rim line. Silver was rarely used for rim lining, since it is less hard wearing than the gold and even the gold lustre paint normally used on cheaper tableware.

25. Pottery unknown. 1940-45

A pleasing use of shape to enhance the wartime table was offered by this little bone china pin, or sweet, dish with its 'Utility' portrait transfer of the Prime Minister.

26. Taylor & Kent of Longton. 1940-45

Ashtray with an RAF pilot's badge and a quotation from Churchill's famous tribute to the *'Few'*.

27. Grimwades Royal Winton. c1945

Cream jug and bud vase.

28. Pottery unknown. c1945

Wartime 'Utility' cream jug.

29. Royal Doulton. c1945

Trinket box, with speech quotations on the back and sides, containing four 3 x 2 inch china trays each with a further different quotation from one of Churchill's speeches.

30. TG Green & Co. 1941

Coffee mugs made by TG Green & Co of Church Gresley, Derbyshire in 1941 to mark the Atlantic Charter, with caricature portraits of Churchill on one side and Roosevelt on the other. Green's also made a matching plate. Roosevelt was not depicted smoking a cigarette as often as Churchill was portrayed smoking his cigar and the hazards of smoking were not widely appreciated in the 1940s, but Roosevelt's death in 1945 was attributed to lung cancer while Churchill went on happily smoking cigars for another twenty years without their having apparently any injurious effect.

31. Grimwade Royal Winton. 1941

Grimwades was founded in 1886 and operated potteries in Stoke-on-Trent and Hanley during World War II. The company employed Mabel Leigh as a designer, but it is not known whether she had a hand in the design of this plate. Grimwades used the same portrait transfer of Churchill – *'Rt. Hon Winston Churchill, Prime Minister, Great Britain'* – on a wide range of 'Utility' tableware and also paired it with a portrait transfer of President Roosevelt on a similar range for export to the USA.

32. John Tams, Longton. 1951

When Churchill returned as Prime Minister in 1951 many wartime restrictions were

30. TG Green & Co
1941

still in force. The new government made it a priority to get rid of food rationing, but restraints on the manufacture of decorated china for the home market remained whilst preference continued to be given to exports. This portrait transfer of the Prime Minister appeared on 'Utility' tableware throughout Churchill's second term and beyond. The Harleigh bone china plate with its intricate gilt over black border is typical of the many pieces which went on sale early in 1965.

33. Coalport. 1969
Chartwell had opened to the public in 1966. This Coalport pin tray, a companion to the Westerham statue tray, was on sale to tourists for many years. The pair were available gift-boxed, if memory serves me, for 62 pence.

34. Coalport. 1969
Nemon's statue of Churchill was erected on the Green at Westerham in 1969. This little bone-china pin tray went on sale in nearby souvenir shops, an indication that Coalport are just as ready to produce simple, inexpensive items for the many as they are to create grand designs for the few.

35. Pottery unknown. 1965-90
This bone-china pin dish, with a portrait transfer based on the 1941 photograph of Churchill by Karsh, was on sale at Blenheim Palace for over twenty five years – five shillings in 1965, rising to £2.29 by 1990.

36. Ridgway China. 1965
When Churchill died in 1965 many potteries resused the 1951-55 transfer for their memorial issues. This enabled them to get products to market ahead of the major potteries who needed time to produce their original designs.

31. Grimwade Royal Winton. 1941

36. Harleigh China. 1965

32. John Tams, Longton. 1951

37. 'CN', Western Germany. 1965

33/34. Coalport. 1969
35. Pottery unknown. 1965-90

38. Wedgwood. 1964

39. Spode. 1965-67

37. 'CN', Western Germany. 1965

A rare tribute to Churchill from his former adversary. A nice coloured portrait transfer on a large, 10-inches diameter plate.

38. Wedgwood. 1964

Commissioned by Thomas Goode & Co, South Audley Street, London to mark Churchill's 90th birthday. Black and white jasper. Note that Arnold Machin's portrait has Churchill smoking a cigar and wearing an ordinary necktie. Border of oak leaves. Issue price was £1.05. A blue and white jasper version was also available at 92½ p. The black jasper edition remained on sale as a memorial piece after Churchill's death.

39. Spode. 1965-67

Probably the nicest of all the Churchill commemorative plates. Commissioned from Spode by Thomas Goode & Co, in a limited edition of 5,000, the Churchill Plate in crimson, royal blue, green and gold, matched the superb Churchill Vase. Likely to be $100-£180 in the UK now and $500 upwards in the USA.

40. John Tams, Longton. 1965

Portrait transfer based on the Yousef Karsh photograph with a quotation from Churchill's *Never in the field of human conflict...* speech on the reverse. A long-running design used by many different potteries and sold at Blenheim Palace, Chartwell and the Imperial War Museum, other such outlets.

41. Denby Tableware, Derbyshire 1960s

Joseph Bourne's pottery northeast of Derby has long been famous for its stoneware. It produced a popular series of coffee mugs featuring places and personalities representing various regions of Britain. The Thames & Chilterns mug depicted King Alfred, Shipton-on-Cherwell, Windsor Castle, Uffington White Horse and Winston Churchill.

42. Wedgwood. 1974

The centenary issue in blue and white jasper had a different Arnold Machin portrait – the cigar has gone and Churchill wears a bow tie. Border of laurel leaves. Inflation had increased the issue price to £2. The 1974 dish is common around the

40. John Tams, Longton. 1965

41. Denby Tableware, Derbyshire. 1960s

44. Crown Staffordshire. 1966

46. Coalport. 1974

45. Crown Staffordshire. 1977

42. Wedgwood. 1974

47. Wilson's of Paignton. 1974

43. Highland Arts Studios, Ceil Island. 1974

48. Wedgwood. 1974

49. Pottery unknown. 1974

53. Dunoon Ceramics. 1980s

50. McLaggan Smith. 1980s

54. Paragon China. 1974

55. Coalport. 1990

51. Highland Arts Studios. 1980

52. Caverswall China. 1990

56. Caverswall China. 1985

secondary market at £5-£8 although I once saw an example, described as 'now scarce', offered by a London dealer at £49. Seen priced at $50 in a 1991 US catalogue.

43. Highland Arts Studios Ceil Island. 1974
A simple but unique centenary design from one of the smallest potteries. The unusually lengthy obverse inscription explains that the portrait of Churchill was drawn by local artist C John Taylor in 1943 – '... when the battle of the Atlantic was at its height'.

44. Crown Staffordshire. 1966
Small bone-china pin tray, commissioned by the National Trust, with its gilt rendering of the Churchill crown. It was available for many years in the Chartwell gift shop at around five shillings when first offered but had increased to £1.50 twenty years later.

45. Crown Staffordshire. 1977
A royal commemorative piece celebrating the Queen's Silver Jubilee, but featuring the seven Prime Ministers who had served her during her reign. The omnipresent Karsh portrait of Churchill makes another appearance on china.

46. Coalport. 1974
This centenary goblet in bone china by D Brindley was produced as a limited edition of 1,000. A heraldic design in purple and black with extensive intricate gilding. Now around £80 in the UK and up to $250 in the USA.

47. Wilson's of Paignton. 1974
Bone china. Many smaller potteries were licensed to use this design by the Churchill Centenary Trust. The backstamp indicates that Wilson's produced it in a limited edition but does not give the edition size. The plate is numbered 87.

48. Wedgwood. 1974
Black basalt plate issued in quantity for the Churchill centenary with a bas-relief bust by Arnold Machin as the centrepiece. The backstamp includes a quotation from HM the Queen '... enthusiastic in debate, imperturbable in adversity and generous in triumph'. Up to £30 now in the UK; $130-$150 in the USA.

49. Pottery unknown. 1974
The Woodford Division of the Conservative Association sponsored this plate for the Churchill Centenary and David McFall's controversial statue of Churchill 'among the glades of Epping Forest' forms the centrepiece. At the 1959 unveiling of the statue, Churchill remarked that its feet were too big. When the sculptor told Churchill's bodyguard that it was 'best viewed from some distance', he muttered, 'the greater the distance the better!' The *New York Daily News* reported that it 'looks like the statue of a moronic.'

50. McLaggan Smith Mugs Alexandria. 1980s
A caricature portrait sketch and a facsimile of Churchill's signature with a rare 'Made in Scotland' impressed mark give this little earthenware mug a certain uniqueness.

51. Highland Arts Studios. 1980
C John Taylor's portrait of Churchill is featured on this calendar plate for 1980 commemorating the 40th anniversary of the Battle of Britain.

52. Caverswall China. 1990
Miniature cup and saucer made to mark the 50th anniversary of Churchill's appointment as Prime Minister. The saucer is 2 inches in diameter and the cup is less than 1 inch high. Caverswall are a leading producer of miniaturised ceramics for the collectors market.

53. Dunoon Ceramics. 1980s
Black glazed stoneware beaker with gilt silhouette portrait of Churchill produced exclusively for the Imperial War Museum and sold at Lambeth, the Cabinet War Rooms, *HMS Belfast* and Duxford airfield.

54. Paragon China. 1974
This plate, in a limited edition of 1,000, complements the magnificent Paragon cigar casket (see page 51). The Churchill coat of arms is enclosed by a heavily chased and gilded rim.

55. Coalport. 1990
A Peter Jones commission. Limited edition of 5,000 designed by John Ball marking the 50th anniversary of the Battle of Britain. £20 in the UK.

57. Oakley Fine China. 1983

58/59 Caverswall China. 1990

60. Royal Doulton. 1994

60a. *Their finest hour*

60b. *Give us the tools*

60c. *Blood, toil, tears and sweat*

60d. *This is your victory*

56. Caverswall China. 1985
The 40th anniversary of VE Day. Crowd scene in front of Buckingham Palace on 8 May 1945, cameos of the King and Queen on the balcony and the Prime Minister. A royal commemorative and a piece of Churchilliana all in one – double the number of collectors. £20 in the UK but reported at $125 in the USA.

57. Oakley Fine China. 1983
Commissioned by the National Trust, John Holder's colourful plate proved a best-seller in the Chartwell gift shop.

58. Caverswall China. 1990
Celebrating the 50th anniversary of Churchill's appointment as Prime Minister.

59. Caverswall China. 1990
The 50th anniversary of Churchill's appointment as Prime Minister. Matches the plate, the beaker, the cup and saucer, the thimble. Caverswall's commemoratives leave no collecting niche untouched.

60. Royal Worcester. 1990
Four plates commissioned by the Hamilton Collection – a mail order collector plates firm. Designed by Malcolm Greensmith. A series of eight plates depicting World War II events, of which four featured Churchill, each in an edition of 19,500. £21 from the Hamilton Collection, but only £10 from Royal Worcester.

61. Royal Doulton. 1994
Commissioned by the Bradford Exchange to commemorate the 50th anniversary of D-Day. Backstamped *'We shall fight on the beaches...'* An edition *'limited to 75 firing days'*.

62. Thimblemania. 1995
A pottery which normally specialises in china collectors' thimbles produced its 50th anniversary of VE Day thimble (£1), a mug (£4) and this plate (£8). A glorious montage of Churchill determinedly stomping through battle scenes with a long backstamp quoting from his broadcast victory message.

63. Fenton China Co. 1995
Matching the mug and with the same backstamp.

62. Thimblemania. 1995

63. Fenton China Co. 1995

64. Royal Doulton. 1995

65. Caverswall
China. 1990

66. Sutherland China. 1990

67. Peter Jones China. 1992

68. Aynsley China. 1995

69. John Tams. 1995

70. Sovereign China. 1990

72. The D-Day Museum. 1994

73. Fenton China Co. 1995

68. Norfolk Royal, Norwich. 1995

74. Burgess, Dorling & Leich. 1999

75. Gerry Ford Design. 1990

76. Berkshire Pottery. 1996

77. 'STL', England. 1995

64. Royal Doulton. 1995

A limited edition of 2,500 designed and signed by Andrew Wheatcroft. *'Collectors' Gallery Edition'* 10$^1/_2$-inch diameter plate marking the 50th anniversary of VE Day.

65. Caverswall China. 1990

Lionhead beakers, depicting a golden lion's head on either side, are a specialist collector's item and Caverswall are a specialist supplier of such items. This one, in olive green and gold, marks the 50th anniversary of Churchill becoming Prime Minister. Designed by Stephen Barnsley in a limited edition of just fifty pieces. £40.

66. Sutherland China. 1990

Commissioned by Peter Jones China to mark the 50th anniversary of Churchill's wartime coalition. Edition of 2,000.

67. Peter Jones China. 1992

The 50th anniversary of the Battle of Alamein. Montgomery gets the portrait on this wraparound desert battle scene but Churchill gets the quote: *'It may almost be said. Before Alamein we never had a victory. After Alamein we never had a defeat.'* Backstamped with a plan of the battlefield. Limited edition of 2,500.

68. Aynsley China. 1995

A Peter Jones commission. Perhaps the best of the 50th anniversary of VE Day commemorative mugs. Churchill stands between the King and Queen on the Buckingham Palace balcony on 8 May 1945. Peter Jones offered a range of items – a plate, a vase, a pin tray and trinket box, all to the same design.

69. John Tams. 1995

Have you noticed that Churchill's V-sign is the wrong way round? He did occasionally reverse his hand but whether intentionally or inadvertently nobody can be certain. I spoke to the John Tams pottery about this one but they claimed to have supplied plain white blanks to a number of different independent decorators and did not know which was responsible for this design.

70. Sovreign China. 1990

50th anniversary of the Battle of Britain. On the reverse, transfers of a RAF Spitfire and a Luftwaffe Messerschmitt 109.

71. The D-Day Museum, Portsmouth. 1994

The wraparound design of this mug is based on a section from the *Overlord Embroidery*, a massive needlework panorama depicting Churchill and Brooke going ashore to meet Eisenhower and Montgomery a few days after the landings.

72. Fenton China Co. 1995

50th anniversary of VE Day. Bone china. A colourful wraparound design featuring Churchill acknowledging the cheers of a cosmopolitan crowd. Backstamped, *'Our gratitude to our splendid allies goes forth from all our hearts' – Winston Churchill.'* £4 with matching plate for £10.

73. Norfolk Royal, Norwich. 1995

Typical of the cheap 50th anniversary of VE Day commemorative mugs available in abundance from cut-price shops and market stalls at around £2.

74. Burgess, Dorling & Leich. 1999

A replica of the 1941 Burgess & Leigh *Champions of Democracy* coffee mug. Burgess & Leigh, founded in 1862, were notable producers of Churchilliana during World War II.

In the late 1990s the business was restructured, becoming Burgess, Dorling & Leich, and began reissuing many of the best toby jugs and other 'Burleigh Ware' products from the previous sixty years. The mug has a high relief portrait of Churchill on the front and, on the back, his 1941 message to President Roosevelt – *'Give us the tools and we'll finish the job.'*

75. Gerry Ford Design. 1990

A bone china mug marking the 50th anniversary of Churchill's appointment as wartime Prime Minister and giving the dates of his birth and his death.

76. Berkshire Pottery. 1996

For Churchill College, Cambridge. Sold to raise funds for the Churchill Archives Centre. Inscribed on the reverse: *'The Churchill Papers – Preserving a Heritage of Greatness.'*

77. 'STL', England. 1995

50th anniversary of VE Day. Earthenware.

Wartime 'Utility' tableware

During World War II British potteries were prohibited from manufacturing decorated tableware for the domestic market. Those potteries which had built up a pre-war export trade were permitted to continue producing decorated wares but only for export to the United States to help repay the lend-lease debt. Otherwise crockery for the British housewife's table had to be plain and unadorned. Just white and a few pastel shades were allowed as body colours and one embellishment – a sepia portrait transfer of the Prime Minister. The profile of Churchill, in a homburg hat and smoking a cigar, was to be found on every imaginable piece of china produced by virtually every pottery in the land. Royal Doulton were allowed to use a slightly more elaborate sepia portrait transfer of the Prime Minister encircled by a garland of oak leaves and acorns, but its potteries at Lambeth and Burslem were partly turned over to producing industrial ceramics and its engineering workshops were requisitioned to make forms and castings for the armament factories. Doulton potteries suffered more than fifty instances of bomb damage during air raids. What with bomb damage in the homes and bomb damage in the potteries it is a wonder that sufficient 'Utility' tableware was produced to keep the domestic market supplied. Many potteries made a virtue out of necessity and produced pleasing designs within the tight restrictions.

This jug from an unknown English pottery revives the pre-war art deco shape formerly used for an Ovaltine promotional piece. Resourceful potteries made a brave effort to brighten their 'Utility' tableware. Limited to a few plain body colours and a standard sepia portrait transfer of Churchill for decoration, they turned to shape to add interest.

Royal Doulton's more elaborate transfer on a 'Utility' plate.

A trinket box or cigarette box backstamped *'Newhall Pottery, Hanley, Staffs'.*

1. Park Farm Pottery, Norfolk. 1980s

4. Royal Doulton. 1940-45

5. Royal Doulton. 1999

2. Pottery and date unknown

6. Wedgwood. 1965.

3. Prince William Ware. 1975

7. Naval and Military Club. 1980

Tankards

1. Park Farm Pottery, Norfolk. 1980s

This one-pint earthenware tankard with full-colour transfer depicts the locomotive *Winston Churchill,* that hauled Churchill's funeral train from London to Bladon. It is based on a painting by Derick Bown, who committed an unfortunate error in his otherwise fine painting. He has painted *Sir Winston Churchill* on the nameplate but, unlike its namesake, the locomotive was never given the accolade!

2. Pottery and date unknown

Creamware tankard, no maker's marks, with bas-relief portrait of Churchill wearing a military cap and smoking a cigar. Relief heraldic lion on the reverse side with an all-round design of acorns and oak leaves. $4^{1}/_{2}$ inches high, one-pint capacity. Almost certainly dates from World War II.

3. Prince William Ware. 1975

Churchill gave a high priority to the abolition of food rationing, but in spite of his efforts the rationing of cheese, butter, margarine and meat did not end until the summer of 1954. Restrictions on potteries over the production of decorated tableware for the home market remained in force, although they were strongly encouraged to produce for export – notably to the United States. As soon as Churchill returned to office, the potteries were quick to begin applying a new portrait transfer to their 'Utility' tableware. It was an excellent depiction and was to endure for at least twenty-three years and long after the restrictions on decoration were removed.

This half-pint, gilded, tankard has an interesting inscription on the reverse, *'West End Conservative Club Annual Dinner 26th November 1975.'* The tankard is backstamped *'Prince William Ware, warranted 22 carat gold, Made in England.'*

4. Royal Doulton. 1940-45

One pint earthenware tankard with the 'Utility' portrait transfer of Churchill surrounded by oak leaves and acorns. On the reverse, an extract from his *'Finest hour'* speech of 18 June 1940. Seen priced at £145 in the UK and $250 in the USA.

5. Royal Doulton. 199?

A hand-decorated one-pint tankard by José Miralles for Royal Doulton. A wraparound design shows scenes from 'Churchill's War' including his meeting with Montgomery on the Normandy beaches and the joyous victory celebrations in London on VE Day. Limited edition of 2,500.

6. Wedgwood. 1965

The *Churchill Tankard* in blue, green and black in a wraparound design combines Churchill's portrait, based on the Karsh photograph, with a view of Chartwell.

7. Naval and Military Club. 1980

Five inches high, glass-bottomed polished pewter one-pint tankard, issued to mark the 40th anniversary of Churchill's appointment as Prime Minister. The high relief portrait medallion based on the Churchill crown is surrounded by engraved dates and details of his birth, military and political career.

Tea caddy

A printed tin-plate tea caddy depicting the political and military leaders at the start of World War I. On the lid a portrait of King George V and around the sides the Czar of Russia, the Grand Duke Nicholas, the King of the Belgians, General Joffre, Sir John French, Lord Kitchener, Sir John Jellicoe and plain Mr Winston Churchill. It is one of the few pieces of Churchilliana dating from World War I. All are highly sought after by collectors – up to $150 in the USA.

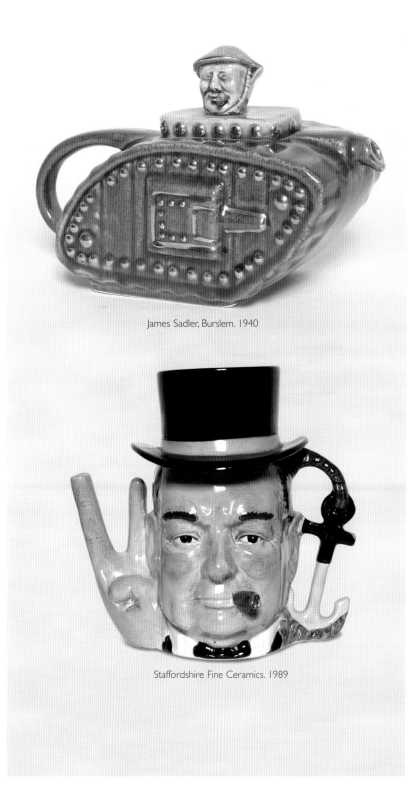

James Sadler, Burslem. 1940

Staffordshire Fine Ceramics. 1989

Teapots

Teapots are utilitarian containers with a lid, spout and handle in which tea is made. They can also be outlandishly shaped and decorated articles of little or no practical use but highly prized by collectors. They are yet another form in which Churchill has been commemorated.

James Sadler, Burslem. 1940

The Churchill tank teapot made by James Sadler & Sons of Burslem in 1940 is a revival of the body design of their World War I tank teapot made from 1918 into the 1920s. When Churchill became Prime Minister Sadler's dusted off their original moulds and cast a new cover (lid) with the unmistakable head of Churchill, smoking a cigar and wearing a golden steel helmet, peering from the turret. The teapot marked Churchill's role as *'Father of the Tank'* in 1915. Very rare.

Staffordshire Fine Ceramics. 1989

This Churchill teapot was primarily for export to the USA where there is an ardent band of collectors of 'fun' teapots – the zanier the better. The designer, Paul Singh, in fact used the body mould of the 1939 Shorter and Son character jug adding a cigar and Churchill's fingers raised in a V-sign. The tea pours out through Churchill's second finger! The undersized homburg hat looks quite ridiculous from the back where it reveals, below the brim, a pink bald pate above a fringe of red hair and inscribed: *'I have nothing to offer but blood, toil, tears and sweat.'* The backstamp reads: *'50 years anniversary of World War II. Staffordshire Fine Ceramics. Hand painted. Winston Churchill 1874-1965. 'We shall never surrender.'* I am told that the teapot originally sold for $100 in the USA.

Wileman & Co, Stoke-on-Trent. 1900

This Foley Intarsio teapot, just 5 inches high, was made by Wileman & Co, Stoke-on-Trent in 1900. It is the first ceramic representation of Churchill. He was just 25 years of age and already a household name through his Boer War exploits and as newly elected MP for Oldham. Featured on this teapot he found himself in exalted company alongside such senior politicians of the day as Joseph Chamberlain, Arthur

Patriotic teapot presented in 1939 to housewives responding to the call to hand in their aluminium pots and pans to provide material for the aircraft industry in the *'war against Hitlerism.'* However, much kitchenware handed in was of inferior quality for the manufacture of Spitfires!

Balfour, Lord Rosebery and Lloyd George. All the teapots had identical bodies with different covers (lids) depicting politicians in caricature form. To avoid any doubt, the name of each individual was printed inside the neck of each pot. All the Foley Intarsio teapots are now very rare, the Churchill version extremely so. A Lloyd George pot made £500 at a Phillips, London auction in 1991 and a Lord Rosebery was displayed in Camden Passage in 1995 at £400.

This Churchill teapot remains firmly in the hands of its proud owner but, should he ever be prevailed upon to sell it, I would be surprised if the bidding did not exceed £1,000 in the saleroom.

The Foley Intarsio teapot by Wileman & Co. Stoke-on-Trent, 1900

Fitz & Floyd. 1990s

Another modern teapot, made in Taiwan and marketed in the USA by Fitz & Floyd as part of their Collector's Teapots series *Figures from History* in the 1990s. Fitz & Floyd, predominantly manufacturers of ceramic giftware, are based in Sri Lanka, but much of their production is done in Japan and Taiwan. All the Churchill props are there – homburg hat, cigar, bow tie, bulldog and artists palette – and as for likenesses, there are far worse.

Fitz & Floyd teapot. 1990s

Teapot stand

This teapot stand with the Churchill coat of arms on a ceramic tile recessed into a block of polished oak was on sale in the souvenir shops at Chartwell and Blenheim Palace in 1974 and for some years after.

Teaspoons

Silverware from the World War II period is rare, as the use of silver was restricted to essential needs. Special dispensation allowed the manufacture of silver spoons in limited quantities to enable the moneyed classes to observe the time honoured tradition of having their babies *'born with a silver spoon in their mouth.'*

Thimbles

These little devices, originally designed to protect the tip of a lady's finger whilst she sat sewing, have been around for four thousand years or more. Examples dating from 3000BC, found in the pyramids of Egypt, suggest that they have often been highly decorative as well as utilitarian. In Roman times thimbles were cast in bronze. Steel thimbles were common in the 18th and 19th centuries and many were made of silver, although few are hallmarked.

In December 1997 Christie's devoted an entire auction sale to thimbles. The Thimble Society of London has over 800 members. Churchilliana collectors have a wide choice of thimbles. Prices in the UK range from 50 pence upwards, but in the USA thimbles can be be very expensive.

A selection of Churchill teaspoons. Many designs exist. In this case the second and third from the left are solid silver, hallmarked 1941 and 1965 respectively; the others are silver-plated. Solid silver spoons, £10-£12; silver plated ones around £3.

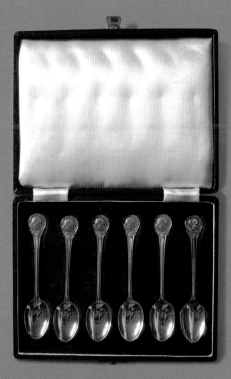

The set above is by B&J Sippel of Sheffield and hallmarked 1944. Value now about £75.

Toby jugs

The first pottery jug featuring a full-length stout and bibulous gentleman was made by Ralph Wood of Burslem around 1760. The jug depicting a Yorkshireman, one Toby Fillpot, with a reputation for consuming formidable quantities of ale, caught the public imagination and the format was soon being copied by many other potteries. 'Toby' became the generic term for any ornamental jug featuring a full-length human figure. By the end of the 18th century the production of toby jugs had become a major industry and potteries all over Britain and in France, Germany, Holland, the USA and elsewhere were busy turning out endless variations on the original theme. Politicians and leading establishment figures became popular subjects and their depictions varied from highly satirical caricatures to shamelessly patriotic icons. Early in the 20th century toby jugs featured such personages as Asquith, Gladstone, Lloyd George, Haig, French and Kitchener. By the time he reached middle age Winston Churchill was an archetypal toby jug subject. He was stout, jolly (usually), with a penchant for distinctive headgear, a partiality for alcoholic refreshment and (a little later) a highly recognisable two-fingered gesture.

H Goss, Longton. 1927
The first Churchill toby jug.

1. H Goss, Longton. 1927

6^{1}/$_{2}$ inches tall. The first Churchill toby jug. Made in two colourways – blue suit or green suit. Churchill, as Chancellor of the Exchequer, introduced a Betting Tax and is depicted with his hands clasped in prayer and wearing a white top hat inscribed: *'Any odds – bar one, that's me who kissed the Blarney Stone.'* A rather rudimentary piece of pottery with simple modelling and fairly crude paintwork. Scarce. Value: UK £250; USA $500.

2. Royal Doulton. 1940-91

Made in three sizes: 9 inches, 5^{1}/$_{2}$ inches and 4 inches high. Modelled by Harry Fenton. In production for fifty-one years and Doulton's all-time best-selling toby jug. Replaced a loving cup, designed in 1940 by Charles Noke, which Churchill did not like and which was withdrawn. Early examples of this jug, dating from 1940-41, are backstamped *'Winston Churchill, Prime Minister of Great Britain, 1940'* and serious collectors are prepared to pay 3-4 times as much for these as for the widely available later examples which are simply backstamped *'Winston Churchill'*. First edition examples are rare but later editions are in plentiful supply. UK prices (first edition prices in brackets): Large £60 (£175), Medium £40 (£125), Small £30 (£110). US prices: Set of three $300 ($1150). (See also page 134).

3. Burgess & Leigh, Burslem. 1941

11 inches tall. *Bulldogs* was modelled by Ernest Bailey and was the first toby jug to associate Churchill with a bulldog. Backstamp: *'John Bull Churchill 1940. We shall defend every village, every town and every city.'* Issued in plain white for the UK market and two colourways – a brown coat or a red coat – for export. Fairly scarce. Recent auction prices: UK (coloured version) £580; US (uncoloured) $750. In the late 1990s the pottery, now known as Burgess, Dorling and Leigh, began making second-edition versions of this toby using the original moulds. These are selling at £100-150 and can be distinguished by the 'BD&L' backstamp.

4. Burgess & Leigh, Burslem. 1941

5 inches tall. Also modelled by Ernest Bailey. Titled *Victory* – the inscription on

the plinth, '...–', spells out the morse code for 'V'. Yes, it is a toby jug – Churchill's figure, though heavily truncated, is in fact full-length. *Victory* was the first toby jug to depict Churchill giving his famous V-sign. The smallest and the cheapest of the 1941 Churchill tobies, it was also the most popular. As a result it is quite easy to find on the UK secondary market, though prices have risen sharply in recent years. Value: UK £100+; USA $200. Burgess, Dorling and Leigh are also remaking this jug using the original moulds; marked 'BD&L' they can be purchased for around £50.

5. Burgess, Dorling & Leigh Burslem. 1999

The old-established pottery of Burgess & Leigh became Burgess, Dorling and Leigh in 1999 and began reissuing many of its successful pieces going back to those designed by Charlotte Rhead in the 1920s. It is remarkable that a pottery which had been as prolific as Burgess & Leigh should have retained so many of its historic moulds. Among the first 'second edition' issues over the 'BD&L' backstamp were the two Winston Churchill toby jugs designed by Ernest Bailey in 1941. Distinguishable by the new backstamp the 'second edition' pieces of *Bulldogs* were issued in both the original and a choice of colourways. Here, the blue coat is illustrated, yellow or green coats were also available.

6. John Beswick, Longton. 1941-54

9 inches high. Beswick, now part of the Royal Doulton Group, only ever produced six toby jugs and that of Churchill was their first and only truly original design. It was modelled by freelance sculptor H Watkin. Churchill holds a scroll reading: *'We shall fight on the beaches, the landing grounds, in the fields, in the streets and on the hills, we shall never surrender – Churchill 1940.'* a paraphrase of Churchill's actual words of 4 June 1940. The Prime Minister is seated on a chair draped with a Union flag. In addition to the Beswick backstamp the toby illustrated has the additional mark 'CeePeeWare' indicating that it was an early example intended for export to the USA. Some examples of this toby were fitted with either a removable bald head or a top hat. Recent UK auction, £300; USA 1993, $350.

Royal Doulton. 1940-91

Burgess & Leigh, Burslem. 1941

John Beswick, Longton. 1941-54

Burgess & Leigh, Burslem. 1941

Burgess, Dorling & Leigh Burslem. 1999

Kirklands of Etruria, Stoke-on-Trent. 1941

7. Kirklands of Etruria Stoke-on-Trent. 1941

10$\frac{1}{2}$ inches high. In 1939 Kirklands had produced a distinctive character jug of Churchill to mark his reappointment as First Lord of the Admiralty. This toby jug, unique at the time in having a removable top hat, ensured Kirkland's place amongst the foremost producers of Churchilliana during World War II. The removable hat, intended to act as a drinking cup, a feature of many 18th century tobies, introduced a hazard for those pottery enthusiasts who habitually turn everything upside down to examine the backstamp. So, sadly, many examples of the Kirklands toby are now seen hatless. Quite scarce as a complete jug. £185 in the UK; $350 in the USA.

8. CH Brannam, Barnstaple. 1941

9 inches high. This long-established, small Devonshire pottery had enjoyed some success with inexpensive tobies aimed at the popular end of the market. This toby reflects its rustic origins by depicting Churchill wearing leggings and looking rather like a bucolic farmer. Churchill's pose and oversize top hat are reminiscent of the Kirklands toby, but in this case the top hat is fixed. The modelling is crisp but the decoration and glazing is crude. The tobies had either a red or a blue coat with an orange waistcoat and Churchill's complexion varied from florid to swarthy. I would guess that the edition would not have been very large. Certainly the Brannam toby is seldom seen around the secondary market. Although it is the least attractive of the Churchill tobies its rarity has pushed the UK price up to around £100 and $250 in the USA.

9. Wilkinson's, Royal Staffordshire Pottery, Burslem. 1941

12 inches high. One of the finest of the Churchill tobies. Produced in a limited edition of 350 (although it is believed that the full edition was not completed) and signed by Clarice Cliff. It is unlikely that Clarice Cliff had more than a minor role in modelling this toby and that it was largely the work of Sir Francis Carruthers Gould who had designed a superb series of World War I leaders for Wilkinson's in 1915-17. Carruthers Gould's World War I series would surely have included Churchill had he not resigned over the Dardanelles affair and it is believed that this toby was modelled, but withheld in 1915 and then resurrected and modified by Clarice Cliff in 1941. Her modification will have included the bulldog seat and the caption: *'Going into action and may God defend the right.'* The original issue price was five guineas (£5.25). Recent auction prices have been UK £1,350, US $2,750.

10. WR White, Stoke-on-Trent. 1942

9 inches high. The toby illustrated was part of the Tristan Jones commemorative ceramics collection auctioned by Phillips in January 1991. Apart from this one, I know of only one other uncoloured example of this delightful jug. Mr White's toby was the first to portray Churchill in what was to become his workaday naval uniform of Royal Yacht Squadron cap and double-breasted reefer jacket although his thumbs-up sign had, in the previous year, been largely been superseded by the exclusive and abiding V-sign. The two known uncoloured versions of this toby are both clearly backstamped *'Stoke-on-Trent, England, Modelled by WR White, 1942'*, but a very similar unmarked coloured version also exists. The toby illustrated sold at Phillips for £242 but the owner of the only other known uncoloured version would not be persuaded to part with his example for twice that price. So far as is known both remain firmly in British hands.

11. Leonard Jarvis. 1947

7 inches high. Lord Mackintosh of Halifax, an ardent collector of early toby jugs, employed Leonard Jarvis as his restorer. Jarvis was commissioned to model a toby of his employer in the style of the 18th century jugs. Lord Mackintosh was so delighted with the result that he instructed Jarvis to produce a similar toby depicting his much admired compatriot – Winston Churchill. Mr Jarvis's toby, in muted colours and translucent glazes, faithfully followed the style of the earliest tobies. He portrayed Churchill as an artist, clutching palette and brushes, with shoulder length hair, a tricorn hat, frock coat, knee breeches and buckled shoes. An inkpot and quill pen is by his right foot and a bricklayer's trowel at his left side. Very few examples of this toby were made – I have never seen one numbered in greater than 200 – and consequently it is rarely seen at auction. In 1991 one realised £800 in the UK; in the USA in 1993 an example made $2,500.

12. Staffordshire Fine Ceramics Tunstall. 1987

9$\frac{1}{2}$ inches high. There was a forty-year gap before the second post-war Churchill toby appeared. Staffordshire Fine Ceramics exports more than 80% of its output, mainly to the USA; originally, the jug was not offered in the UK. The *Number Ten Toby*, so called because a reproduction of the door to 10 Downing Street appears on its right-hand side, was to be produced in a limited edition of 1,000. Sales in the US were disappointing and in 1995, coinciding with the 50th anniversary of VE-Day, the toby was released in the UK. Without significant promotion and very little high-street exposure, the total number sold failed to reach three figures. The *Number Ten Toby* remains available to order from the pottery in the UK at around £100 or from SFC stockists in the USA at $300.

13. WT Copeland (Spode) Stoke-on-Trent. 1941

8$\frac{1}{2}$ inches high. Designed and signed by Eric Olsen. This chunky little Churchill toby was produced as a pair with a matching jug of President Roosevelt to commemorate the Atlantic Charter. A plain white version was made for distribution in the UK whilst the earlier fully decorated examples were exported – mainly to the USA and Canada. Aside from the long-running Royal Doulton Churchill toby the Copeland/Spode jug is now the most widely available of the World War II issues. Recent UK auction prices have covered a wide range – £140-£275 – for both plain and coloured versions. In the

8. CH Brannam, Barnstaple. 1941

10. WR White, Stoke-on-Trent. 1942

11. Leonard Jarvis. 1947

'*We shall fight on,*
if necessary
for years,
if necessary alone!'

An historic addition to the
famous Toby Jug series.
This model of our Premier
is a work of art, and will be
valued down the years as a
treasured symbol of an epic
age. A limited **5** GNS
issue of 350 at

China Department, Second Floor.

——By Government Order——
THE STORE WILL CLOSE AT 4 P.M.
(SATURDAYS 1 o'c.)
from Monday November 25 to Saturday December 28

HARRODS LTD   LONDON SW1

Harrods leaflet promoting the Royal
Staffordshire Pottery Churchill Toby Jug
for Christmas 1941. Note that the store
was obliged to close '*by Government Order*'
at 4.00pm. A 'black-out' was in force, as
the Luftwaffe visited most nights.
Rationing was being progressively
extended and there was a clear need to
curtail any excess of Christmas spirit!

Wilkinson's, Royal Staffordshire Pottery, Burslem. 1941

12. Staffordshire Fine Ceramics. 1987

13. WT Copeland (Spode). 1941

16. Kevin Francis Ceramics. 1991

18. Potteries unknown. c1940-50

14. Kevin Francis Ceramics. 1989

15. Kevin Francis Ceramics. 1990

17. Kevin Francis Ceramics. 1991

19. Kevin Francis Ceramics. 1993

USA the plain toby is scarcer and has made up to $650 compared to $325-$450 for the decorated version.

14. Kevin Francis Ceramics
London. 1989

9 inches high. Modelled by Peggy Davies, the celebrated former Royal Doulton designer, after she had left the company to start her own business. *Spirit of Britain* was released in a limited edition of 5,000 to commemorate the 50th anniversary of Churchill becoming Prime Minister and captioned *'Tantum Mirabile Est'* (So much is owed) and *'Civitas habuit leonium animum'* (The nation had the lion's heart, I provided the roar). One of the best ever images of Churchill, this toby was available in three colours – black, blue or white suit. I have seen an unissued trial piece with an all-over blue flambé glaze. The official issue price in the UK was £150, but heavy discounts were available. Prices of up to £200 were seen on the secondary market whilst the toby was still available at RSP from the pottery! In the USA a 'pre-production' launch price of $205 became $250 within a year. In 1994, a four-inch-tall 'shrink' – 'Mini Churchill Lion' – appeared in a limited edition of 750 to augment the success of *Spirit of Britain.*

15. Kevin Francis Ceramics
London. 1990

9 inches high. Modelled by Douglas Tootle and produced by Peggy Davies Ceramics for Kevin Francis. *Standing Churchill* owed much to Burgess & Leigh's 1941 *Bulldogs* toby. In a limited edition of 750, with blue or grey colourways, *Standing Churchill* was a great success and the edition sold out in 16 months. Initially priced at £120, the toby soon ran to £150 on the secondary market ($250 in the USA).

16. Kevin Francis Ceramics
Stoke-on-Trent. 1994

9 inches high. *Winston Spencer Churchill D-Day Landings*, modelled by Andy Moss and potted by Peggy Davies Ceramics in a limited edition of 750, marked the 50th anniversary of D-Day. Titled *Overlord* – the code name for the invasion – the toby incorporates some delightful features. Churchill sits on a representation of the Normandy cliffs wearing a steel helmet

and blue-grey siren suit, cigar clutched in his left hand and right arm raised in a V-sign. Beneath his left foot lies a cracked bust of Hitler. The twin handles, in the shape of a 'V', are decorated with the UK and US flags and topped by cameo busts of Montgomery and Eisenhower peering over Churchill's shoulders. Launched at £140 in the UK and $245 in the USA the edition sold out in under two years.

17. Kevin Francis Ceramics
London. 1991

9 inches high. *Naval Churchill* in a limited edition of 750 was modelled by Douglas Tootle who was praised for its detailed paintwork. Churchill's Lord Warden of the Cinque Ports full-dress uniform was hand-painted to the very highest standard. The almost obligatory V-sign is retained and Churchill's left hand rests on the hilt of his sword as he straddles a map of the British Isles with the caption *'Never Despair'*. An anchor forms the handle of the jug. 630 examples were sold before the toby was withdrawn, and the moulds destroyed, on the dissolution of the Kevin Pearson/ Francis Salmon partnership. The jug was available in blue or white. Launch price in the UK was £125 later increasing to £150. After its dicontinuation the toby was being offered at £175 by a London dealer. The regular price in the USA was $290.

18. Potteries unknown. c1940-50

A toby jug is defined as: *'... a vessel in the form of a seated or standing human figure, usually having a handle and a spout or lip, designed for holding or pouring liquids but generally ornamental rather than utilitarian.'* Well' the two fairly crude little jugs illustrated opposite meet all those criteria, albeit their capacity to hold a liquid is rather limited. The jug stands $3^{1}/_{2}$ inches high and has no maker's marks. The cigar would be over two feet long in scale! Probably 1950-51. The jug is $2^{1}/_{2}$ inches high, very roughly painted, also unmarked and probably dates from the war years.

19. Kevin Francis Ceramics
London. 1993

9 inches high. Maybe a third Churchill standing toby in three years was more than the market could take and many would say *Political Churchill* was the least attractive

20. Kevin Francis Ceramics. 1994

of Douglas Tootle's designs. Whatever the reason, this toby was the least successful of the Kevin Francis Churchill tobies. Standing, hand on hip, in front of a lectern bearing a BBC microphone and behind a Union flag draped bulldog, Churchill seems uncomfortably posed in an awkward and cluttered arrangement. The toby does not look like a jug and with only a very small and inconveniently placed pouring hole, could hardly function as such. Purists were not impressed. *Political Churchill was* launched in the UK at £150, with some discounting, and at $290 in the USA. Recently, I saw an example at an antiques fair being offered at £80.

20. Kevin Francis Ceramics London. 1994

9 inches high. Shortly before the Kevin Pearson/Francis Salmon partnership was dissolved they announced plans to produce a series of modern satirical tobies, in the style of the 18th century Fiddler and Midshipmite jugs, featuring prominent politicians. A total edition of 750 with no more than 150 tobies of any one subject was proposed. John Major would be the first and customers were invited to nominate further 'victims'. I suggested Churchill. So here he is in tricorn hat, frock coat, knee breeches and buckled shoes playing on his violin any of the laments he might have expressed during the downs of his career. Price in the UK was £120 but it was potted to order only and very few were made.

21. Kevin Francis Ceramics London. 1991

6^{1}/$_{4}$ inches high. Kevin Francis Ceramics' success with its first two Churchill tobies prompted a third within three years. Peggy Davies had died shortly after modelling her *Spirit of Britain* toby and her former apprentice, Andy Moss, made adjustments to her winning formula in producing this spin-off, *Little Winston*. A bulldog replaced the lion beneath Churchill's left hand and most of the embellishments of the larger toby were omitted in order to reduce decoration costs and achieve a lower selling price. In a limited edition of 2,500, *Little Winston* was available in two colourways – black coat/striped trousers or blue suit – and cost £55 before discount in

21. Kevin Francis Ceramics. 1991

23. Kevin Francis Ceramics.

22. Kevin Francis Ceramics. 1995

24. Kevin Francis Ceramics. 1999

the UK and $110 in the USA. Remarkably examples appeared at a premium on the secondary market in the UK whilst the toby was still available from the pottery at list price.

22. Kevin Francis Ceramics Stoke-on-Trent. 1995

9^{1}/$_{2}$ inches high. *The Winston Spencer Churchill – 50th anniversary of VE Day* toby was the eighth Churchill toby made by Peggy Davies Ceramics in six years, under the Kevin Francis brand. On this occasion the edition of 750 included up to 250 examples in an exclusive colourway for members of the International Churchill Society. The ICS special edition carried a unique backstamp and a number of colour differences. Churchill is depicted on the balcony of Buckingham Palace, cigar in mouth and arm aloft in a V-sign, flanked by the British bulldog and the American

eagle. The eagle perches on a cracked swastika and the handle rises from a draped Union flag. Launch prices were £150 and $275 (ICS members £130 and $225) and the edition sold out, and the moulds were destroyed, at the beginning of 1997. Secondary market prices of up to £180 have been seen.

23. Peggy Davies Ceramics Stoke-on-Trent

9 inches high. Peggy Davies Ceramics, producers of the Kevin Francis range of hand-made and hand-coloured porcelain, was a prolific source of some of the best new pieces of Churchilliana during the last decade of the 20th century. It is apt that for its exclusive guild piece for the year 2000 Peggy Davies Ceramics should have produced *Churchill – The Great Statesman* toby jug. Its exclusive guild piece each year is a special edition limited to the

number of orders received from members of the *Kevin Francis Collectors Guild*. The toby jug, depicting Churchill seated at a BBC microphone with speech script in his right hand, was designed by Pamela Jones and modelled by top ceramic sculptor Andy Moss. £140 to KF Guild members.

24. Kevin Francis Ceramics Stoke-on-Trent. 1999

9 inches high. The *Churchill-Boer War Centenary* toby jug modelled by Andy Moss and potted by Peggy Davies Ceramics in a limited edition of 500. It depicts Churchill, at the age of twenty-four, as a correspondent for the *Morning Post*. He is seated on an ammunition box with a copy of the *Morning Post* at his feet and, at the back, another copy of the *Morning Post* together with a pen forms the handle. Not a good likeness. Issue price was £155, but this was widely discounted down to £130.

Towels

Tobies and figurines – colourways

It is a long established practice in the pottery industry to apply different colour combinations to the same basic pattern or design. This gives the collector a choice and, uniquely, appeals to that small fraternity who must have one of each!

Left: In 1995 250 examples of the Kevin Francis *50th anniversary of VE Day* toby jug were produced in a special colourway (right) exclusively for members of the International Churchill Society.

Right: Bairstow Manor Pottery provided a choice of four colourways, painted to order, of their *Winston the Bricklayer* figurine in 1996. Early orders showed a preference for the brown suited version.

Penny plain and twopence coloured

Thus wrote Robert Louis Stevenson in *Father Apollinaris*. During World War II, the British potteries were prohibited from making decorated china for the home market although they were encouraged to continue making it for export to the United States, where it made a valuable contribution towards the lend-lease debt.

Left: Burgess & Leigh's Bulldogs 1941.

Right: WT Copeland's (Spode) toby, also 1941, which was paired with a toby of President Roosevelt. The white version, much scarcer in the USA, will nowadays make up to $650 there compared to $325-$450 for the fully coloured toby.

30 x 19 inch cotton tea towel marking the 50th anniversary of D-Day. It depicts four of thirty-four panels of the *Overlord Embroidery* in the D-Day Museum at Portsmouth. The second panel from the top shows Churchill touring the Normandy beaches with George VI and the Generals, Montgomery, Brooke and Eisenhower, a few days after the landings.

Tea towel celebrating the 50th anniversary of VE Day. Flags of the allies border the scene ouside Buckingham Palace on 8 May 1945.

Tricolore

A portrait of Churchill printed on a French flag for the Paris victory parade in 1945. Speaking in Paris on Armistice Day, 1944, Churchill said: *'For more than thirty years I have defended the cause of friendship, of comradeship and alliance between France and Great Britain... It is a fundamental principle of British policy that the alliance with France should be unshakable, constant and effective.'*

Urn

In 1950, Churchill was awarded the Freedom of the City of Worcester, home of the Royal Worcester porcelain company. To mark the occasion they commissioned the superb *Churchill Urn,* depicting a fine view of Worcester Cathedral, hand-painted by Harry Davis (1885-1970) head of Royal Worcester's painting workshop and perhaps the most collectable of all the porcelain decorators in its history. It is the practice at Royal Worcester that, when completing a one-off prestigious commission, a replica is made for display in the Museum of Worcester Porcelain adjacent to the factory. In the case of the *Churchill Urn,* the replica was loaned out for exhibition in the south of England from where it was stolen and has never been seen since. Before he died Harry Davis painted this second replica and it is that which can now be seen at Worcester; the original is at Chartwell.

USS Winston S Churchill

Ten years after the Royal Navy submarine *HMS Churchill* was withdrawn from service another warship was named after Britain's former Prime Minister, First Lord of the Admiralty and Honorary Citizen of the United States of America. He would have been proud to wear his unofficial wartime naval uniform of Royal Yacht Squadron cap and reefer jacket aboard *USS Winston S Churchill.*

Left:
A commemorative cover issued by the International Churchill Society.

Right:
First day in commission, Norfolk, Virginia, 10 March 2001.

Photo courtesy the Museum of Worcester Porcelain and Henry Sandon.

USS WINSTON S. CHURCHILL
IN WAR: RESOLUTION
IN PEACE: GOOD WILL
DDG 81

The Abbeydale Vase. 1964

SIR
WINSTON
LEONARD
SPENCER-
CHURCHILL
K.G. P.C. O.M.
C.H. F.R.S. M.P.

FIEL PERO DESDICHADO

STATESMAN

SOLDIER

Vases

The Abbeydale Vase. 1964

Honorary Citizenship of the United States of America was bestowed upon Churchill in April 1963. He was too ill to attend the ceremony in Washington so Randolph, his son, stood in for him. President John F Kennedy said, in presenting the award: *'In the dark days and darker nights when Britain stood alone – and most men save Englishmen despaired of England's life – he mobilized the English language and sent it into battle.'* Thomas Goode & Co of South Audley Street, London commissioned Abbeydale China to produce the covered vase in a limited edition of 250 to mark the event. 11 inches high in a rounded octagonal shape with an eagle finial and lion head handles, richly decorated in cobalt blue, gold and raised gold, the vase carried a portrait of Churchill, his family crests and the dates of his birth, his office as Prime Minister and award of his American citizenship. Churchill died shortly after the vase was issued and it came, wrongly, to be regarded as a memorial piece. The original issue price was £75. An example made £920 at Sotheby's, London in 1998 and another sold for $3,000 in 1993 in the USA.

The Spode Churchill Vase. 1965

14 inches high in rich claret, cobalt blue and white with extensive gilding, the vase was available in a limited edition of 125 only. Churchill's portrait is contained within the royal blue and gold belt of the Order of the Garter – *'Honi Soit Qui Mal Y Pense'* – encircled by laurel leaves and surmounted by his family crests and motto. His dates of birth and death are on a scroll reading: *'In grateful remembrance.'*
A white panel on the reverse of the vase, headed: *'He expressed the unconquerable spirit of the nation'*, contains in gilt letters two long quotations from his speeches of 4 June and 18 June 1940 *'... we shall never surrender'* and *'... this was their finest hour.'* The original price of the vase was £125 in 1965, which in current terms would be the equivalent of around £1,400. In 1991 an American dealer quoted $2,750 for: *'... the largest and most beautiful of the ceramic remembrances'* but at Christie's, London in 1992 a vase sold for £935 and at Sotheby's, London in 1997, another made £850.

The Coalport 'Sir Winston Churchill' Vase. 1974

The Centenary of Churchill's birth in 1974 was marked by a fine exhibition at Somerset House in London and other exhibitions at Blenheim Palace, Chartwell and Longleat. The Post Office issued a special set of postage stamps and the Churchill Centenary Trust, presided over by Churchill's former private secretary, Sir John Colville, arranged the production of the greatest range of commemorative items celebrating a non-royal person ever offered in British history. The star piece from the ceramics industry was the *'Sir Winston Churchill'* vase, commissioned from Coalport by high-class china retailer Francis Sinclair of Doncaster in a limited edition of 200. The vase is 12 inches tall, in bone china and heavily gilded, with a golden eagle atop the cover. The obverse of the vase bore a hand-painted view of Blenheim Palace. On the reverse was the Churchill coat of arms flanked by silhouette of Sir Winston and garlands of oak leaves and acorns. The original price of the vase was £250. I have noted that a London W1 dealer displayed a vase priced at £1,000 a few years ago and an American correspondent advised that another was being offered there for $1,800.

The Coalport *Sir Winston Churchill* Vase. 1974

THANKS for the VICTORY

NEW ERA COMPANY WEMBLEY

VE Day: 50th anniversary

Peter Jones China of Wakefield, Yorkshire are a major retailer of commemorative ceramics in the UK. If any event is worthy of commemoration you can be sure that Peter Jones will mark it. They commission pieces from most of the major potteries, usually to their own design, which range from limited edition covered vases costing hundreds of pounds, right down to a humble coffee mug. This selection is from their 50th anniversary of VE Day range.

Pin tray by Royal Worcester, mug by Aynsley (see page 157) and trinket box by Sutherland China. Also available was a plate by Royal Worcester and a £595 'Celebration' covered vase in a limited edition of 100 by Aynsley.

Victory banners and bells

Peace in Europe in 1945, signalled a new beginning, and victory over Germany was celebrated wildly amid street parties, parades and the waving of multitudes of flags and banners across the world.

Left: This brightly printed banner, 3 feet × 2 feet, was made by the New Era Company of Wembley. It hung from the first-floor window of a house in Coventry in 1945 overlooking the route of the Victory Parade. It then spent fifty years neatly folded in a drawer before being hung from the same window in the same house by the daughter of the original owner to celebrate the 50th anniversary of VE Day. The story was featured on the front page of the *Coventry Evening Telegraph* and the owner received a congratulatory letter from the Lord Mayor of Coventry.

Left: This 4ft × 3ft batik printed in Indonesia celebrates VE-Day a day early. The banner was found at an antiques fair in Holland and depicts good portraits of Churchill and Roosevelt looking resplendent in their top hats. Scarce.

Bottom left: These crudely cast little bells are embossed all around with cameo relief portraits of Churchill, Roosevelt and Stalin. Their ringing tone is more of a clunk than a melodic chime but their appeal lies in the inscription around the foot – *'Cast with metal from German aircraft shot down over Britain 1939-45 – RAF Benevolent Fund.'* They caught the public imagination in 1945 and the RAF Benevolent Fund organised production at a number of different foundries to keep up with demand, hence the variations in shape. Churchill was vice-president of the RAF Benevolent Fund from its formation in 1919 until his death in 1965. At the *Battle of Britain* Dinner in 1945 a 'specially finished' bell was presented to him. The RAFBF and the RAF Museum are 'pretty sure' that this was the bell that was given back to be auctioned for the benefit of the Fund. It made £1,200, an incredible sum at the time, equivalent of around £30,000 today.

Victory medal

Designed by A Loewental of Lincoln and struck by John Pinches (Medallists) of London. 1,000 examples, 63mm diameter, in bronze were issued in 1945. On the reverse, a hand holds a victory torch around which is inscribed, *'Unflinching, indomitable, his spirit saved Britain and so the world.'* The medal was reissued when Churchill died, with the line 'OB 24 JAN 1965' added. Precious metals had then been released from wartime restriction and it was struck in gold (700) and silver (736) as well as bronze (1421). (See also page 93).

Vicky

Vicky, alias Victor Weisz (1913-1966), was a Hungarian Jew born in Berlin. He was forced to flee from the Nazis, first to Budapest and then to London. By 1941 he was a regular contributor to the *News Chronicle* where Churchill was frequently featured in his cartoons until the latter's retirement in 1955.

Here Vicky mimics Sir John Millais' famous painting *Bubbles* and has Churchill dreaming that the Labour Government will be defeated over its failure to abolish rationing.

Video and audio cassettes

It comes as no surprise that countless videos, audio tapes and books have been published about such a great statesman as Sir Winston Churchill. This spread shows a selection of video and audio tapes to whet the appetite.

Right:
Churchill – The Finest Hours
WH Smith. 1964

Below left:
Churchill – A Vivid Portrayal of Britain's Greatest Statesman.
BBC Publications. 1993

Below right:
The Voice of Winston Churchill
This England. 2000

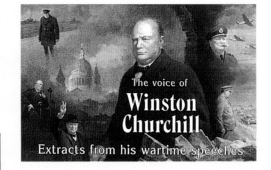

From COLUMBIA PICTURES

A FILM BY CARL FOREMAN AND RICHARD ATTENBOROUGH

ROBERT SHAW · ANNE BANCROFT
and
SIMON WARD

YOUNG WINSTON

with special appearances by
JACK HAWKINS · IAN HOLM · ANTHONY HOPKINS
PATRICK MAGEE · EDWARD WOODWARD and JOHN MILLS
Written for the screen and Produced by CARL FOREMAN
Based on 'MY EARLY LIFE' by WINSTON CHURCHILL
Directed by RICHARD ATTENBOROUGH
Musical score by ALFRED RALSTON AN OPEN ROAD-HUGH FRENCH PRESENTATION PANAVISION · COLOUR

Top left:
My Early Life
Harper Collins. 1993

Below left:
*Winston Churchill –
25 Years of His Speeches*
Argo. 1991

Top right:
*Speaking for Themselves.
The personal letters of
Winston and Clementine
Churchill*
BBC Publications. 1999

Below right:
The Island Race
Naxos. 1995

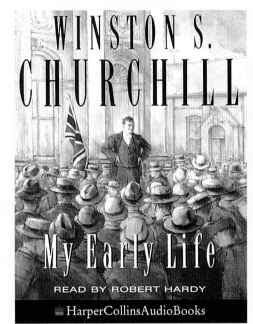

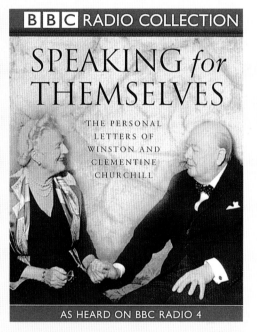

Above:
Young Winston
Columbia Pictures. 1972

Right:
*The Voice of Winston
Churchill*
Decca. 1965

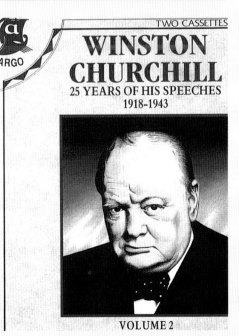

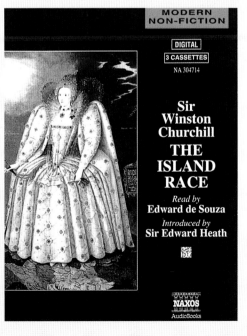

V-sign

A china V-sign which was sold as a paperweight. Can be used in reverse when occasion demands.

Churchill's V-sign became his symbol, his salute, his hallmark his talisman even. He did not invent it, he just turned it inside out and cleaned it up. As a former soldier, and indeed as a former Harrow schoolboy, Churchill knew that the original gesture, with knuckles facing out, had for more than 500 years been used around the world as a crude expression of disrespect, defiance, insolence and vulgarity.

It has been said that when wars were fought by men armed with bows and arrows, when an archer had emptied his quiver he would continue to raise his first two fingers, as if to draw back his now impotent bow string, in a gesture of contempt and provocation towards the enemy. Churchill was generally careful to give his version of the V-sign with the knuckles facing in. The gesture was to acquire a whole new meaning; defiance, yes, but also hope, determination and victory. It was to go down in history, not only as the trademark of one man, but as a symbol of the resolution of a whole nation.

When did Churchill first use the V-sign? His son, Randolph, writing in *Churchill: His Life in Photographs* captions picture No. 203: *'Shortly after his return from the United States [he meant Newfoundland] ... the Prime Minister ... gives the first of his innumerable and famous V-signs: August 1941.'* In fact two weeks earlier, before Churchill left for Placentia Bay, the *Daily Express* published a photograph captioned *'The V-sign – this novel salute made by the Prime Minister at the conclusion of his interview...'* Let us not quibble over a fortnight. Churchill was first seen to use the V-sign in August 1941. It did not gain immediate acceptance.

Churchill's Private Secretary, Jock Colville, wrote in *The Fringes of Power: Downing Street Diaries 1939-1955* of Churchill's visit to Coventry on 26 September 1941 – *'The PM will give the V-sign with two fingers in spite of the representations made to him that this gesture has quite another significance.'* But Churchill persisted and, brushing aside all objections, thereafter used it frequently and extensively. As often as not it was returned with great joy and enthusiasm. It became the symbol of the *V for Victory* campaign.

Detail from a figurine designed in 1985 by Andrew Turner for the History in Porcelain series. The figurine depicts Churchill on the doorstep of 10 Downing Street in May 1940 and the V-sign is an anachronism, or a piece of artistic licence, since it was not 'invented' until the following year.

Churchill's protégé, Brendan Bracken, the Minister of Information, was extremely well connected with all the newspaper proprietors and the campaign got off to a flying start. Publishers, large and small, potteries and souvenir makers of all kinds produced *V for Victory* merchandise. One of the first pieces on the market was an amusing little *V for Victory* toby jug designed by Ernest Bailey for Burgess and Leigh of Burslem. The fame of the gesture spread to neutral Spain and the Sureda Pottery produced a rather inaccurate figurine of Churchill recognisable only because it had an arm aloft in a V-sign.

Toby jug from Kevin Francis Ceramics marking the 50th anniversary of D-Day in 1994.

Occasionally Churchill forgot himself (or perhaps he didn't!) and delivered his V-sign with knuckles facing out. In the vast Churchillian photographic archive there are no more than a handful of examples where he has been caught with his hand inside out and, as often as not in such cases, he has the sort of expression on his face which suggests that the reversal of his hand may not have been inadvertent! The publishers of Andrew Roberts' book *Churchill: Embattled Hero* picked their cover illustration from the *Hulton Deutsch Collection*. It is of the rare 'knuckles-out' variety and, I suspect, was deliberately chosen to match the contents of the book.

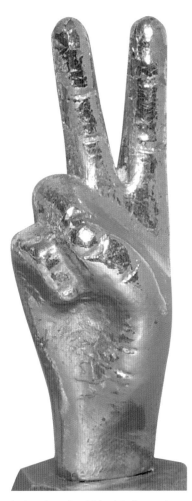

A chromium-plated 'V', originally a car bonnet mascot, has been mounted on a hardwood block as a desk ornament.

Right:
Was this deliberate or did he forget himself?

Walmer Castle: Lord Warden of the Cinque Ports

Banner of the Lord Warden of the Cinque Ports. Its heraldic description is: *'Per pale gules and azure three lions passant guardant conjoined to as many ships hulls in pale or.'*

Walmer Castle lies about $1\frac{1}{2}$ miles south of Deal on the Kent coast. It was built as one of a chain of coastal forts by Henry VII in the mid-sixteenth century as a protection against possible invasion by the French. Quatrefoil in plan, with a central tower, its walls are more than 12 feet thick and were originally surrounded by a sea-filled moat. The castle was stormed and captured by the Parliamentarians in the Civil War. In 1708 the castle was adapted for domestic use and became the official residence of the Lord Warden of the Cinque Ports, a confederation of English Channel ports, originally comprising Dover, Hastings, Hythe, Romney and Sandwich. This alliance was formed in the 11th century to provide the King with a navy. By the beginning of the 18th century much of its importance had diminished and the role of Lord Warden became purely ceremonial, remaining in the gift of the monarch.

Many prominent statesmen have held the office including William Pitt the Younger and the Duke of Wellington, who died at Walmer Castle in 1852. After Churchill's death the title of Lord Warden passed to Sir Robert Menzies, the former Prime Minister of Australia, and after Menzies death – the office is held for life – Queen Elizabeth the Queen Mother became the

Bernard Hailstone's portrait, painted in 1955, hangs in Dover town Hall. It was the last portrait of Churchill to be painted from life.

first female Lord Warden. The Lord Warden retains the right of residence at Walmer Castle, and is also Constable of Dover Castle. Reasonably comfortable, if rarely used, living accommodation remains available, but most of the castle has been given over to a museum devoted to its former residents.

Churchill was appointed Lord Warden in December 1941 but claimed that he was too busy prosecuting the war to attend the inauguration ceremony until August 1946! There was however another entirely valid reason for not holding the traditional and colourful ritual in 1941; Walmer Castle was within the range of German guns based on the French coast. The King gave Churchill special permission to fly the standard of the Lord Warden of the Cinque Ports at his house flag at Chartwell and one of those flags now hangs in the study there. Another example, torn and frayed from having been flown, was sold in the USA in 1991 for $6,000. Churchill also had some miniature editions of the flag made which he flew on the bonnet of his car and was much amused when, on numerous occasions, it was mistaken for the Royal Standard. A pair of these were sold at Sotheby's in 1998 for £10,925.

Bairstow Manor Pottery, Stoke-on-Trent. Hand-painted 10 inches high china figurine of Churchill in the uniform of Lord Warden of the Cinque Ports (see also page 67).

Churchill in his splendid Lord Warden's uniform usually upstaged every guard drawn up in his honour.

Undoubtedly Churchill, with his love of dressing up, was greatly attracted to the Wardenship of the Cinque Ports by its flamboyant ceremonial uniform. He wore it on every occasion he possibly could including, notably, for the coronation of Queen Elizabeth II. There are a number of fine portraits of Churchill wearing the full dress uniform of the Lord Warden, notably those by Dennis Ramsey, which hangs in Deal Town Hall, and by Bernard Hailstone, which hangs in Dover Town Hall. Bernard Hailstone's portrait was painted in 1955 and was the last for which Churchill gave a sitting. Whilst Hailstone was painting his study Churchill confided to him how much he detested Graham Sutherland's 80th birthday portrait for which he had sat the previous year. It was later disclosed that Sutherland's portrait had been destroyed on Lady Churchill's instructions. Another portrait of Churchill wearing the uniform of Lord Warden of the Cinque Ports hangs in the National Maritime Museum, Greenwich. It is by John Leigh Pemberton but is in fact a copy of Oswald Birley's portrait which hangs in Trinity House with Churchill's uniform altered from that of an Elder Brother of Trinity House.

Waxworks

Madame Tussaud (1761-1850) was born Marie Grosholtz in Switzerland. As a teenager she began working for her uncle who had opened an exhibition of wax figures in Paris. When Marie was thirty-four, and by then the sole owner of the Paris waxworks, she married Monsieur Tussaud who was eight years her junior. Seven years later she left her husband in charge of the business in Paris and came to England with a touring version of the exhibition. The waxworks operated on an itinerant basis for thirty-three years before settling in Baker Street, London in 1835. It moved the short distance to its present, and larger, premises in Marylebone Road in 1854. For over 160 years, except when closed after a fire in 1925 and by wartime bombing in 1940, Madame Tussaud's waxworks has consistently been one of London's top tourist attractions.

The first model of Winston Churchill was put on exhibition in 1908, the year of his marriage to Clementine Hozier, and his regularly up-dated figure has remained on display ever since. The photograph is of the model which was in the exhibition in 1961. The replica Garter robes worn by this model are now on display at Chartwell – Churchill's genuine robes having, by tradition, been returned to the Queen on his death. *(Photo courtesy Madame Tussauds').*

Wedgwood

Josiah Wedgwood & Sons Ltd was founded in Stoke-on-Trent in 1759 and grew into one of the two giants of the British ceramics industry. Between 1941 and 1974 Wedgwood were prolific producers of Churchilliana – all of it designed by Arnold Machin in 1940 when he was on a Travelling Scholarship for Sculpture from the Royal College of Art. Machin went on to become Master of Sculpture at the Royal Academy and design the Queen's portrait on the British coinage and postage stamps.

Josiah Wedgwood V retired as managing director of Wedgwood in 1964 ending the tradition of family control and the company embarked on a series of acquisitions and joint ventures. One of the latter eventually led to Wedgwood being taken over in 1986 to form the present day Waterford-Wedgwood Group.

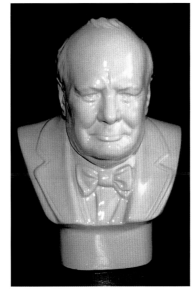

An American collector wrote to me in 1996 enclosing a photograph of this bust. It is backstamped *'Wedgwood, England'* but he had been unable to find any mention of it in specialist reference books or catalogues in the USA. I had recently written an article in *Finest Hour* warning readers that Wedgwood fakes were being circulated, notably in the USA, and he wondered if his bust was not all it should be. With the aid of the Wedgwood

Top: Two items produced for the Churchill Centenary in 1974: a blue and white jasper pin tray and a portrait medallion.

Above left: A 1974 joint venture with Waterford Glass resulted in this fine crystal paperweight inscribed all around: *'Give us the tools and we will finish the job.'*

Above right: Another 1974 collaboration, this time with Ronson, produced this blue and white jasper table lighter.

Left: Arnold Machin's 1940 bust of Churchill was issued in Windsor Grey in 1954 and 1974 with an uninscribed plinth. Black basalt versions were issued in 1964, 1965, 1974 and 1985, some with plain plinths but others with at least three different inscriptions. This one: *'I have nothing to offer but blood, toil, tears and sweat'* was made in a limited edition of 750 for the Churchill Centenary.

Museum at Barlaston, Stoke-on-Trent I was able to reassure him. The bust, 11 inches high by 8 inches across the shoulders, was designed in 1940-41 by the young Arnold Machin but not issued until 1953. It was one of the first pieces made in Wedgwood's then new Windsor Grey body which they had perfected only in the previous year. My correspondent had commented on the squat, rather top heavy appearance of the base of the bust and wondered whether it should have a separate wooden plinth like a similar Royal Doulton bust but the Research Assistant at Barlaston replied that she could discover no reference to any sort of detachable plinth in the Museum's records. The Museum has records going back to Josiah Wedgwood's first designs in 1759 and the staff are always helpful in regard to any query over the provenance of Wedgwood products.

Westminster Abbey

On 19 September 1965, eight months after Sir Winston Churchill had died and at the service marking the 25th anniversary of the Battle of Britain, HM Queen Elizabeth II unveiled a memorial stone in the floor of Westminster Abbey, attended by more than forty members of Sir Winston's family, midway between the Great West Door of the Abbey and the tomb of the Unknown Warrior. The stone bore the inscription: *'Remember Winston Churchill. In accordance with the wishes of the Queen and Parliament the Dean & Chapter placed this stone on the 25th anniversary of the Battle of Britain 15 September 1965'.*

The Churchill memorial stone in the floor of Westminster Abbey.

Every year thereafter, until her own death in 1977, Clementine returned to the Abbey on the anniversaries of Winston's birthday and death, to lay flowers at the memorial.

The basket of flowers and remembrance card which was laid on the memorial on 30 November 1999, the 125th anniversary of Churchill's birth, by his daughter Lady Mary Soames, is now displayed in the Churchilliana Collection at Bletchley Park.

Will

Winston Churchill left £304,000 gross. At current prices that would be in excess of £3 million but, it should be noted, he had salted away considerable sums from his literary earnings into trust funds in order to escape tax. In *Speaking for Themselves* Mary Soames reveals that her father wrote to her mother from the south of France in May 1957, after Clementine had complained that she was having difficulty in making ends meet in London. Churchill replied: *'Do not let the idea that I am mean tease your mind. As a matter of fact I take every lawful opportunity of passing money to you which will avoid the 67% toll which the State will almost certainly take at my death.'*

Churchill had received just over £250,000 for the British, Commonwealth and Foreign rights of *The Second World War*, $250,000 for the American book rights and $1.5 million for the American serial rights. All these earnings were placed into the Chartwell Trust which paid him an annual tax-free sum of £20,000 and escaped any liability to tax at his death. He bequeathed to Clementine all recordings of his speeches and extracts from his writings which had

not been part of the '1946 settlement' and expressed the wish that she should 'feel no reluctance or hesitation' in selling any of his pictures. His son-in-law, Christopher Soames, was given his choice of three racehorses, not exceeding £7,500 in value, with an option to purchase the remainder!

Woven silk

This looks like a line drawing based on Yousuf Karsh's famous 1941 photograph, but it is a very finely detailed portrait woven in silk by Brough, Nicholson & Hall of Leek, Staffordshire, produced as a memorial piece when Churchill died in 1965. The company had been in the silk weaving business since 1815, originally in Macclesfield, Cheshire – for long the centre of the English silk industry. The portrait, $4^{1}/_{2}$ x $3^{1}/_{2}$ inches, was sold mounted in a white folded card listing Churchill's dates and achievements. Not often seen around the secondary market; £20-£25 in the UK, $100 in the USA.

X-rated

This harmless-looking little china doll, just 4 inches high, is not what it seems. Made in Portugal during World War II for export to Germany, it is a rather unpleasant piece of pornography. A somewhat mandarin-like Churchill wears a red towelling dressing gown. Pull a cord at his back and an erect copulatory organ, three feet long in scale, flashes from beneath his robe. Well, no doubt it amused the Wehrmacht.

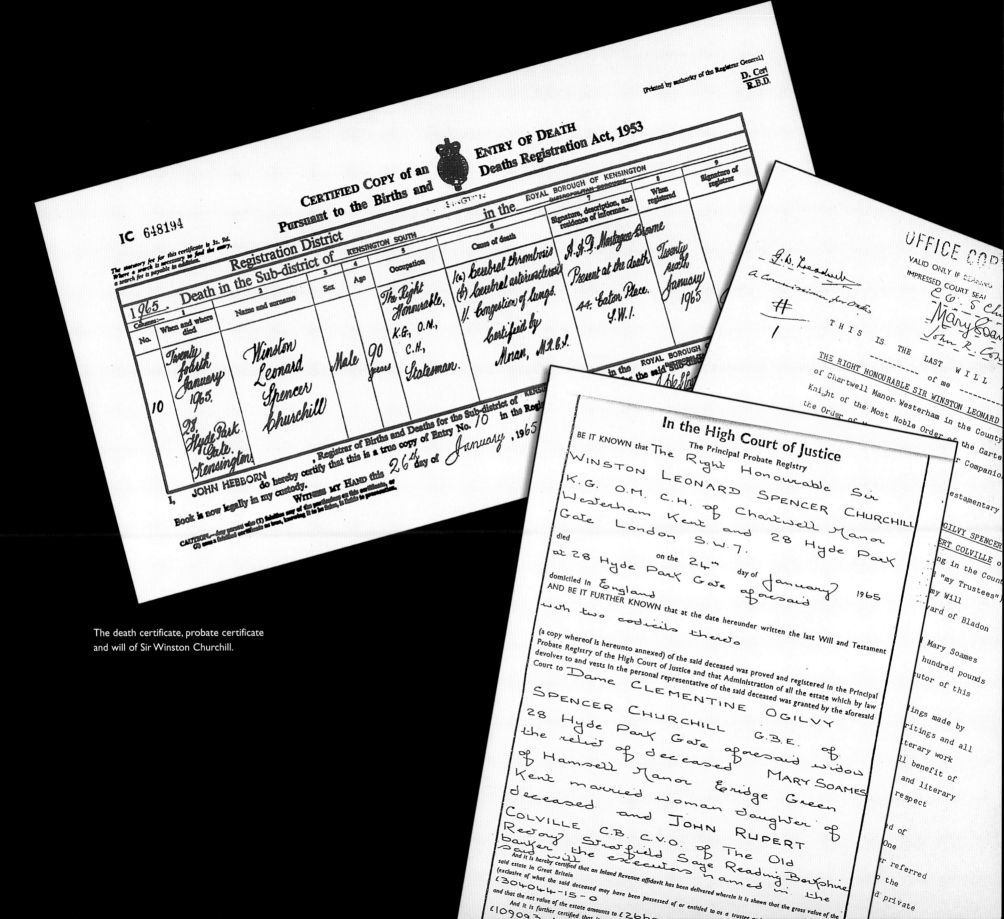

The death certificate, probate certificate
and will of Sir Winston Churchill.

Yemeni rial

Apart from Great Britain, and the Isle of Man, the only country in the world to issue a legal tender Churchill commemorative coin was the Kingdom of Yemen. The King of the Mutawakelite Kingdom of Yemen decreed in 1965 that 6,000 silver coins, each in the value of one rial, should be struck by the French Mint in Paris. At that time the Royal Yemeni army was trying to regain control of the country from the revolutionary republican government. It is hard to speculate how many of these coins went into circulation. I found this one many years ago and have yet to see another.

The UK Churchill cupro-nickel crown

The Yemeni Churchill silver one rial coin

The Isle of Man Churchill silver crown

In entirely poor taste is this Churchilliana china money box manufactured in the Third Reich, 1940-45, in which Hitler Youth were encouraged to save their pfennigs. Lavatorial humour was a feature of both British and German amusement during the generally unfunny years of the World War II and, since all is fair in love and war, we too produced our share – although I have not seen anything quite as nasty as these. Two colourways.

Yalta

Churchill met Roosevelt and Stalin at Yalta in the Crimea in February 1945. This charming little ceramic sculpture (right) depicts a jack-booted Stalin, an ailing Roosevelt wrapped in a cloak, (he died two months later) and Churchill dressed as an Air Commodore of the Royal Air Force. Origin unknown – probably Russian.

Zippo lighters

The Zippo Manufacturing Company of Bradford PA has been making cigarette lighters since 1932. It has successfully countered a decline in sales for utilitarian purposes, as smoking has diminished, by marketing a range commemorating every conceivable occasion. Zippo lighters carry a lifetime guarantee but I suspect that this has not been an onerous burden on the company. The vast majority of Zippo's decorative lighters are rarely struck and spend their lives in a display thus avoiding any wear and tear. Zippo's two Churchill lighters mark the 50th anniversary of VE Day *(right)* and the 50th anniversary of his becoming Prime Minister *(below)*.

The International Churchill Society

The International Churchill Society was founded in 1955 and has branches in the United Kingdom, Australia and Canada. It has an affiliated organisation, the Churchill Center, Washington, DC, in the United States of America. Membership of the UK branch is drawn from all around the world.

The Society publishes a quarterly journal, *Finest Hour*, in association with the Churchill Center and sponsors publications, seminars, conferences, exhibitions, memorabilia, research, scholarships and visits concerned with the life and achievements of Sir Winston Churchill.

Churchill's long political career would by itself have fully stretched most men. He was a Member of Parliament spanning sixty-four years, twice Prime Minister and holder of most of the other high offices of state. But in addition, he also found time to write nearly fifty books, win the Nobel Prize for Literature and become an accomplished painter, good enough to exhibit at the Royal Academy.

The Society, in co-operation with the National Trust, The Imperial War Museum, Churchill College Cambridge, Blenheim Palace and other like-minded institutions, aims to ensure that Sir Winston's name and deeds are imparted to succeeding generations.

Sir Winston's youngest daughter, Lady Soames, is Patron of the Society and several of his grandchildren and great grandchildren are members. Other members include the Duke of Marlborough, Baroness Thatcher, Sir Martin Gilbert (Churchill's biographer) and Anthony Montague Browne (Churchill's last Private Secretary).

The International Churchill Society
(Depts NCB)
PO Box 1257
Melksham
Wiltshire
SN2 6GQ

Books by Sir Winston Churchill

The Story of Malakand Field Force 1897
Longmans Green, 1898

The River War
Longmans Green, 1898

Savrola
Longmans Green, 1899

London to Ladysmith via Pretoria
Longmans Green, 1900

Ian Hamilton's March
Longmans Green, 1900

Mr Brodrick's Army
Humphreys, 1903

Lord Randolph Churchill
Macmillan, 1906

For Free Trade
Humphreys, 1906

My African Journey
Hodder & Stoughton, 1908

Liberalism and the Social Problem
Hodder & Stoughton, 1909

The People's Rights
Hodder & Stoughton, 1910

The World Crisis
Thornton Butterworth, 1923-31

My Early Life
Thornton Butterworth, 1930

Thoughts and Adventures
Thornton Butterworth, 1930

India
Thornton Butterworth, 1931

Marlborough: His Life and Times
Harrap, 1933-38

Great Contemporaries
Thornton Butterworth, 1937

Step by Step
Thornton Butterworth, 1937

Arms and the Covenant
Harrap, 1938

Into Battle
Cassell, 1941

The Unrelenting Struggle
Cassell, 1941

The End of the Beginning
Cassell, 1943

Onwards to Victory
Cassell, 1944

The Dawn of Liberation
Cassell, 1945

Victory
Cassell, 1946

War Speeches 1940-45
Cassell, 1946

Secret Session Speeches
Cassell, 1946

The Second World War
Cassell, 1948-54

The Sinews of Peace
Cassell, 1948

Painting as a Pastime
Odhams/Ernest Benn, 1948

Europe Unite
Cassell, 1950

In the Balance
Cassell, 1951

Stemming the Tide
Cassell, 1953

A History of the English Speaking Peoples
Cassell, 1956-58

The Unwritten Alliance
Cassell, 1961

Frontiers and Wars
Eyre & Spottiswoode, 1962

Young Winston's Wars
Cooper, 1972

If I Lived My Life Again
WH Allen, 1974

**Winston Churchill:
Complete Speeches 1897-1963**
Chelsea House/Bowker, 1974

**The Collected Essays
of Sir Winston Churchill**
Library of Imperial History, 1976

Foreign language editions of many of the books were published as well as de luxe editions, abridged editions and derivatives. *London to Ladysmith* and *Ian Hamilton's March* were later combined into a single-volume *Boer War*.

The World Crisis spawned an illustrated edition titled *The Great War* published in both 3 and 4 vol. form by George Newnes, 1933-34. *The Second World War* appeared in standard, de luxe, abridged, illustrated and foreign language editions. Spinning-off from *A History of the English Speaking Peoples* were *The American Civil War*, *The Island Race* and *Heroes of History*.

**The Official Biography:
Winston S Churchill**
In 1960 Sir Winston Churchill appointed his son, Randolph, to be his official biographer and granted him the exclusive use of the letters and papers held in the Chartwell Trust. Randolph Churchill died in 1968 after completing the first two volumes of the biography and the task was taken over by Sir Martin Gilbert. Each of the eight main volumes published by Heinemann, is accompanied by two or three additional 'Companion' or 'Document' volumes providing the full text of all quoted sources. As at May 2002, 24 volumes had been published, including 3 volumes of the *War Papers*, extending the span of supplementary narrative to 1940.

1: Youth 1874-1900 (608 pages)
2: Young Statesman 1901-14 (775 pages)
3: 1914-1916 (988 pages)
4: 1917-1922 (967 pages)
5: 1922-1939 (1167 pages)
6: Finest Hour 1939-41 (1308 pages)
7: Road to Victory 1941-45 (1417 pages)
8: Never Despair 1945-65 (1438 pages)

Bookends from the
bomb-damaged House
of Commons in 1941,
(see page 24).

Bronze busts incorporating
bookends by Jon Douglas,
(see page 24).

Select bibliography of books about Sir Winston Churchill

Churchill on the Home Front
Paul Addison, Cape, 1992

Churchill the Writer
Keith Alldritt, Hutchinson, 1992

Concerning Winston Churchill
George Arthur, Heinemann, 1940

Churchill as Historian
Maurice Ashley, Secker & Warburg, 1968

Mr Churchill in 1940
Isaiah Berlin, Murray, 1949

Churchill: Master of Courage
Princess Bibesco, Hale, 1957

Churchill as I Knew Him
Violet Bonham Carter
Eyre & Spottiswoode, 1965

Churchill: A Brief Life
Piers Brendon, Secker & Warburg, 1984

Winston Churchill
Lewis Broad
Sidgwick & Jackson, 1964

Long Sunset
Montague A Browne, Cassell, 1995

Churchill and Harrow School
EDW Chaplin, Harrow School, 1941

Churchill: The End of Glory
John Charmley
Hodder & Stoughton, 1993

Churchill's Grand Alliance
John Charmley
Hodder & Stoughton, 1995

Churchill: His Life in Pictures
Randolph S Churchill
Weidenfeld & Nicholson, 1955

Footprints in Time
John Colville, Collins, 1976

The Fringes of Power
John Colville
Hodder & Stoughton, 1985

Churchill: His Paintings
David Coombs, Hamish Hamilton, 1967

Menzies and Churchill at War
David Day, Angus & Robertson, 1986

Churchill's Secret War
Robin Denniston, Sutton 1997

Winston Churchill: Men & Movements
David Dilks, Hamish Hamilton, 1965

Military Life of Winston Churchill
Trevor Dupuy, Watts, 1970

Churchill by his Contemporaries
Charles Eade, Hutchinson, 1953

Medallic Portraits of W Churchill
J Eric Engstrom, Spink, 1972

Churchill at Chartwell
Robin Fedden, Pergamon, 1969

Churchill: Man of the Century
Neil Ferrier, Robinson, 1955

Churchill: If I Lived My Life Again
Jack Fishman, WH Allen, 1974

Churchill in His Time
Brian Gardner, Methuen, 1968

The Tragedy of Winston Churchill
Victor Germains, Hurst & Blackett, 1931

Churchill: A Photographic Portrait
Martin Gilbert, Penguin, 1974

Churchill: The Wilderness Years
Martin Gilbert, Macmillan, 1981

Churchill's Political Philosophy
Martin Gilbert, OUP, 1981

In Search of Churchill
Martin Gilbert, Harper Collins, 1994

Not Winston, Just William?
Jim Golland, Heron Press, 1988

Mr Churchill: A Portrait
Philip Guedalla, Hodder & Stoughton, 1941

The Irrepressible Churchill
Kaye Halle, World Publishing, 1966

A Churchill Anthology
FW Heath, Odhams, 1962

Churchill and the Dardanelles
Trumbull Higgins, Heinemann, 1963

Churchill's Literary Allusions
Darrell Holley, McFarland, 1987

Former Naval Person
Richard Hough
Weidenfeld & Nicholson, 1985

Simply Churchill
Roy Howells, Hale, 1965

Churchill: A Study in Failure
R Rhodes James
Weidenfeld & Nicholson, 1970

Churchill
Roy Jenkins, Macmillan, 2001

Churchill's Generals
John Keegan
Weidenfeld & Nicholson, 1991

Winston Churchill
R Crosby Kemper, Un. Missouri, 1996

Churchill & Roosevelt: Correspondence
Warren F Kimball, Collins, 1984

Churchill as War Leader
Richard Lamb, Bloomsbury, 1991

Connoisseur's Guide to Churchill Books
Richard Langworth, Brassey's, 1998

Churchill and the Politics of War
Sheila Lawlor, Cambridge, 1994

Churchill as Warlord
Ronald Lewin, Batsford, 1973

Winston Churchill
Elizabeth Longford, Book Club, 1974

The Duel: Hitler v Churchill
John Lukacs, Bodley Head, 1990

My Years with Churchill
Norman MacGowan, Souvenir Press, 1958

Winston Churchill's Toyshop
R Stuart MacRae, Kineton, 1971

The Last Lion
William Manchester, Joseph, 1983

The Caged Lion
William Manchester, Joseph, 1988

Servant of Crown & Commonwealth
James Marchant, Cassell, 1954

The Young Winston Churchill
John Marsh, Evans Bros, 1955

Battle: Life Story of W Churchill
Hugh Martin, Gollancz, 1940

Downing Street: The War Years
John Martin, Bloomsbury, 1991

The Age of Churchill
Peter de Mendelsson
Thames & Hudson, 1961

I was Churchill's Private Secretary
Phyllis Moir, Funk, 1941

The Struggle for Survival
Charles Moran, Constable, 1966

Churchill: 1874-1915
Ted Morgan, Cape, 1983

Churchill as Peacemaker
James Muller, Cambridge, 1997

I was Churchill's Bodyguard
Edmund Murray, WH Allen, 1987

Mr Churchill's Secretary
Elizabeth Nel
Hodder & Stoughton, 1958

Churchill by His Enemies & Friends
Philip Paneth, Alliance Press, 1943

Churchill: Studies in Statesmanship
RAC Parker, Brassey's, 1993

A Seat for Life
Tony Patterson, Winter, 1980

The War and Colonel Warden
Gerald Pawle, Harrap, 1963

Citadel of the Heart
John Pearson, Macmillan, 1991

Winston Churchill
Henry Pelling, Macmillan, 1974

Fisher, Churchill & Dardanelles
Geoffrey Penn, Cooper, 1999

Churchill in America
Robert H Pilpel, Harcourt, 1976

Churchill and the Generals
Barrie Pitt, Sidgwick & Jackson, 1981

Churchill
Clive Ponting, Sinclair Stevenson, 1994

The Churchill Years
Robert Reid, Pobjoy Mint, 1974

All About Winston Churchill
Quentin Reynolds, WH Allen, 1964

A Man Arose
Cecil roberts, Macmillan, 1941

Winston Churchill
Bechhofer Roberts, Mills & Boon, 1927

Churchill: An Unruly Life
Norman Rose, Simon & Schuster, 1994

Churchill and the Admirals
Stephen Roskill, Collins, 1977

From Winston with Love and Kisses
Celia Sandys, Sinclair stevenson, 1994

Wanted Dead or Alive
Celia Sandys, Harper Collins, 1999

Churchill's Indian Summer
Anthony Seldon, Hodder & Stoughton, 1981

Winston Churchill
Robert Sencourt, Faber, 1940

Clementine Churchill
Mary Soames, Cassell, 1979

A Churchill Family Album
Mary Soames, Allen Lane, 1982

Churchill: His Life as a Painter
Mary Soames, Collins, 1990

Speaking for Themselves
Mary Soames, Doubleday, 1998

Churchill and Secret Service
David Stafford, Murray, 1997

Burying Caesar
Graham Stewart
Weidenfeld & Nicholson, 1999

Churchill as Writer and Speaker
Herbert L Stewart
Sidgwick & Jackson, 1954

Churchill's Black Dog
Anthony Storr, Collins, 1989

Churchill & Hitler: Victory & Defeat
John Strawson, Constable, 1997

Churchill on Courage
Frederick Talbott, Nelson (USA), 1996

Four Faces and the Man
Alan JP Taylor, Allen Lane, 1969

In Informal Study of Greatness
Robert L Taylor, Doubleday, 1952

Churchill: Member for Woodford
David A Thomas, Cass, 1995

The Assassination of Winston Churchill
Carlos Thompson, Smythe, 1969

The Yankee Marlborough
RW Thompson, Allen & Unwin, 1963

Churchill and the Montgomery Myth
RW Thompson, Allen & Unwin, 1967

Churchill and Morton
RW Thompson
Hodder & Stoughton, 1976

Sixty Minutes with Churchill
WH Thompson, Johnson, 1964

Vote of Censure
GM Thomson, Secker & Warburg, 1968

Churchill: His Life and Times
Malcolm Thomson, Odhams, 1965

Ascalon: Churchill's Wartime Flights
Jerrard Tickell, Hodder & Stoughton, 1964

True Remembrances
Phillip Tilden, Country Life, 1954

When the Moon was High
Ronald Tree, Macmillan, 1975

Winston Churchill
VG Trukhanovsky, Rrogress, 1978

Churchill: His Life in Pictures
Ben Tucker, Sagall Press, 1945

WSC – A Cartoon Biography
Fred Urquhart, Cassell, 1955

Sword and Pen
Manfred Weidhorn
Un. New Mexico, 1974

The Man who Flew Churchill
Bruce West, McGraw Hill, 1975

Action This Day
John Wheeler-Bennett, Macmillan, 1968

Churchill and the Prof
Thomas Wilson, Cassell, 1995

Churchill: Great Nobel Prizes
Michael Wolff, Heron Press, 1970

Bibliography - Winston Churchill
Frederick Woods, St Pauls, 1979

Artillery of Words
Frederick Woods, Cooper, 1992

Churchill: War Correspondent
Frederick Woods, Brassey's, 1992

Churchill and Beaverbrook
Kenneth Young
Eyre & Spottiswoode, 1966

Index

*Note: Main entries are indicated in **bold**.*